THE RUSSIAN BALTIC FLEET

THE RUSSIAN BALTIC FLEET
in the Time of War and Revolution 1914-1918

★ ★ ★

The Recollections of
Admiral S N Timirev

Seaforth
PUBLISHING

First published in Great Britain in 2020 by
Seaforth Publishing,
A division of Pen & Sword Books Ltd,
47 Church Street,
Barnsley S70 2AS

www.seaforthpublishing.com

First published in Russian by the American Society for
Russian Naval History New York, 1961
British Library Cataloguing in Publication Data
A catalogue record for this book is available from the British Library
ISBN 978 1 5267 7702 7 (HARDBACK)
ISBN 978 1 5267 7703 4 (EPUB)
ISBN 978 1 5267 7704 1 (KINDLE)

Pen & Sword Books Limited incorporates the imprints of Atlas, Archaeology, Aviation, Discovery, Family History, Fiction, History, Maritime, Military, Military Classics, Politics, Select, Transport, True Crime, Air World, Frontline Publishing, Leo Cooper, Remember When, Seaforth Publishing, The Praetorian Press, Wharncliffe Local History, Wharncliffe Transport, Wharncliffe True Crime and White Owl

Typeset by Mac Style
Printed and bound in Great Britain by TJ International Ltd, Padstow

Contents

Foreword

THE MEMOIR OF SERGEI TIMIREV (1875–1932) of his service as a commanding officer in the Russian Baltic Fleet during the First World War and the Russian revolution of 1917 was written in the early 1920s while he was commanding commercial ships in Chinese exile. Decades later, the manuscript was rescued from oblivion and published in 1961 in its original Russian by a society of Russian naval officers in New York who were a part of the Russian diaspora scattered by the revolution across the world. As an historical document, Timirev's personal account of the war in the Baltic and the revolution in the fleet is distinguishable from the recollections of other senior Russian naval officers by being a coherent narrative written within a few years of the events it describes. In contrast, the recollections of other admirals, such as Kedrov and Pilkin, were fragmentary articles published in various émigré journals through the 1920s and 1930s and the more substantial memoirs of Admirals Bubnov and Dudorov were composed decades after the war. For several decades after its publication Timirev's account thus provided a primary insight for historians into the events and personalities of this time of war and revolution.

While the February Revolution was a largely spontaneous upheaval of the Russian population against a corrupt and badly led tsarist government in the midst of a losing war, it was especially violent in the Baltic Fleet, with its top officers murdered, such as the commander-in-chief Admiral Adrian Nepenin and the commandant of the Kronstadt training base, Admiral Robert Viren (both Finnish names), and many other officers arrested or driven away. In fact, a radical sailor memoirist depicted these events as 'October in February', that is that the more violent 'Bolshevik Revolution' later that year had already occurred in the fleet in February. Timirev survived this turmoil and by the end of 1917 had reached the rank of rear admiral in command of a cruiser squadron, but by that time the fleet had to all practical purposes disappeared as a fighting unit: many officers had deserted and revolutionary sailors had gone over to the Bolshevik Red Guards and then later to the Red Army. This was the final convulsion through which imperial Russia passed after successive 'democratic' provisional governments were overthrown by the more radical socialist revolution and the crucible of civil war tested the Russian people to the limit.

In this chaotic situation, Timirev followed his natural instincts to support law and order and traditional rule, assisting especially the cause of a fellow naval officer, Admiral Alexander Kolchak, a leader of 'White' anti-Bolshevik forces in Siberia, that proved ultimately to be a lost cause. Timirev's exit from Russia by way of Siberia into China, along with many other refugees from the Bolshevik Revolution, represents but a part of the exodus from the turmoil of revolution in post-First World War Europe.

Stephen Ellis, educated in Australia and at Duke University in the United States, has now performed a second rescue effort in this translation of the 1961 original publication that brings the Timirev story to a much wider audience of students of the revolution in the English-speaking world. He brings to it his wide reading in world and naval history, sound knowledge of Russian, experience in academic teaching and archival administration, and especially his personal dedication to the generally less well-known upheaval of a navy in war and revolution.

Norman E Saul
Professor Emeritus, Center for Russian,
East European & Eurasian Studies
University of Kansas,
author of *Sailors in Revolt: The Russian Baltic Fleet in 1917*
(Lawrence: The Regent's Press of Kansas, 1978)

Translator's Preface

My aim in translating these memoirs is to bring an important and authoritative historical source to those interested in Russian or naval history who are unable to access it in the original Russian.

Their author, Rear Admiral Timirev, was well placed to make observations on the character of many of the significant commanding officers and also many of the operations of the Baltic Fleet from the beginning of the war in 1914 up to his discharge from the fleet in 1918. He had trained with many of the key figures as a young man and shared battle experience with them in the Russo-Japanese War of 1904–05 and the siege of Port Arthur. He had spent a year in Japan as a prisoner of war with a number of them. His subsequent career in the Navy had brought him into contact with new recruits as well as with many serving officers. As the executive officer on the Imperial yacht *Shtandart* for some years, he had come into contact with senior members of the Navy establishment and of the Government, including the Imperial Household. His memoirs also exhibit an unusual degree of self-awareness.

The memoirs, written in Shanghai in 1922, remained unknown to scholars for several decades afterwards. However, since their publication in New York in 1961, in the absence of access to authoritative archives, many historians in the West have used these memoirs as an important source for the study of the role of the Navy in the Russian revolution, particularly as it unfolded in the north. They have been used also as a source in multiple studies of the naval war in the Baltic. Following the dissolution of the Soviet Union they have been re-published in Russia and have now been used by scholars there also as an authoritative source on the history both of the revolution and of the Russian Navy in the First World War.

The renewed interest within Russia in this period has given rise to many popular as well as scholarly interpretations. Foremost among the popular interpretations has been the 2008 film, and subsequent television series, directed by Andrei Kravchuk titled *The Admiral*, which focused on the intimate relationship between Timirev's wife Anna and his colleague Admiral A V Kolchak. This interpretation has seriously misrepresented the character of the author of these memoirs, Rear Admiral Sergei Nikolaevich Timirev. This tragic period in the history of Russia inevitably presents many choices to those wishing to interpret it in a creative and evocative way. One may question whether those choices should ever include slandering the character of a decent, honourable man who was loyal to his family and faithful to his duty towards his country. I trust that through this translation readers will be able to make up their own minds about such matters.

I have added notes and commentary on issues that may not be familiar to the English reader, including clarifying some of the contemporary phrases that Timirev uses. The few footnotes in the original publication have been indicated here as an author's note. All text in bold type is so in the original publication. Further information about the text and its context is provided in the commentary.

I thank Rear Admiral James Goldrick AO CSC RAN, Adjunct Professor, School of Humanities and Social Sciences, University of New South Wales (Australian Defence Force Academy), Canberra, for comments and advice about naval terms and customs and the naval history of the First World War. I also thank Associate Professor Kevin Windle, Emeritus Fellow, School of Literature, Languages and Linguistics at the Australian National University, for solving some translation puzzles that challenged me more than usually. I am grateful to Emeritus Professor Norman E Saul of the University of Kansas for encouraging my original proposal to translate the memoirs and for the foreword to this translation.

Stephen Ellis, Canberra, 2020

1961 Biography

'NOTES OF A NAVAL OFFICER' – the memoirs of one of the most distinguished naval officers of the pre-revolutionary period, Rear Admiral Sergei Nikolaevich Timirev – were written in 1922 in Shanghai. As the relative who had received them from the author had not considered it then opportune to publish, the notes lay hidden for a long time and were transferred to a naval organisation[1] only in 1958.

The reader will find in this historical document interesting previously unpublished details of actions of the Baltic Fleet during the First World War, viewed so to speak from the inside, with substantial and impartial characterisations of the leading personalities in them, and a depiction of the disintegration of the fleet, beginning from the very first days of the February revolution.

Few people remain alive who knew Sergei Nikolaevich intimately, and still fewer of his generation who knew him from school days. All of them hold fond memories of him. Beginning from his time as a naval cadet, he unfailingly attracted affection, respect and authority among his classmates and he aroused the same feelings later in his superiors and subordinates. Crystal-clear, uncompromising honour and nobility in thought and deed were his distinguishing qualities. Along with assiduity and punctuality, conducted with great tact, he was imbued with goodwill and heartfelt generosity and this, it may be, more than all the rest, drew to him the hearts of the common people, the sailors, who remained true to him even during the days of revolutionary conflagration and beastliness ...

Son of a naval officer,[2] S N Timirev entered the Naval College (then School) and graduated midshipman in 1889,[3] third in his year. In 1896 he was appointed junior navigation officer on the then recently built cruiser *Rossiia*, in which, over the course of two years, he sailed the Mediterranean Sea and the Pacific Ocean. On his return from this cruise he was enrolled in the Naval Guards,[4] in which he served until 1911. At the beginning of the Russo-Japanese War the would-be senior navigation officer on the battleship *Imperator Aleksandr III*, then fitting out, had good luck and was among three officers from the crew posted to Port Arthur. (His lot seemed lucky because the posting to Port Arthur where he served with distinction in the battleships *Peresvet* and *Pobeda*, and until the end of the siege in the land forces, took him away from the *Aleksandr III*, which perished at Tsushima[5] with its entire crew.) Severely wounded on Vysoki Hill[6] on the eve of the surrender of the fortress, he refused to give his word that he would take no further part in the war and, until the conclusion of the peace, he remained a prisoner of the Japanese. On his return from being a POW, S N Timirev was appointed assistant to the executive officer on the flagship of the first Naval Cadet Squadron and took an active part in the education of young recruits, the future officers of the restored fleet. It was proposed that he take up the position of executive officer of the same ship when, quite unexpectedly, he was chosen to fill the position of executive officer on the Imperial yacht *Shtandart*, on which he served for four years, after which he was named commander of the training ship *Vernyi*. The war found him in this capacity and he describes his service from 1914 to 1918 in his memoirs. By the following waves of revolution, he was thrown up at Shanghai, where for the last ten years of his life he sailed on ships of the Chinese commercial fleet, the only occasion, he wrote from there, when a Russian admiral commanded Chinese steamers. Sergei Nikolaevich died in 1933.[7]

Author's Foreword

In order to avoid any unwarranted expectations of my modest work, I hasten to say that these present recollections, not representing themselves as a connected, complete and objective depiction of the participation of the Baltic Fleet in the recent war and revolution, verified against documents, in general do not pretend to any substantial historical value and, in the best of circumstances, may serve merely as material for the future serious historian. But even in that case, in my opinion, it follows that it is necessary to use the present recollections with great caution, since in view of the complete absence to hand of any documents whatsoever, many facts and experiences are depicted in them exclusively through the prism of such personal impressions and experiences as have been preserved in the memory of the author.

S Timirev

Sergei N Timirev, Helsinki 1915.

S N Timirev in dress uniform of the Naval Guards.

Anna and Sergei Timirev with their son Vladimir (Odia). In the summer of 1915 the Timirevs shared an island retreat near Helsinki with other naval families, where Anna became a close friend of Sofia Fyodorovna Kolchak, wife of Admiral V A Kolchak.

20ºE
30ºE
60ºN
55ºN
FINLAND
Åland I.
Abo
Helsinki
Stirsudden
Kronstadt
Saint Petersburg
Gogland I.
Lavensari I.
Lium I.
Örö I.
Utö I.
Hanko
Lapvik
CENTRAL
POSITION
Gulf of Finland
Narva Inlet
Nargen I.
Reval
Bogskär I.
Stockholm
Baltic Port
Takkhona
Dagerort
Dago I.
Roggekiul
Moön I.
Kuivast
SEA
Oesel I.
Pernov
Arensburg
Fårö I.
Gulf of Riga
Tserell
Irben Strait
Gotland I.
Cape Domesnes
Östergarn
Windau
Ust-Dvinsk
Shlok
Riga
Öland I.
Libava
BALTIC
Memel
0
kilometres
250
Bornholm I.
Danzig
GERMANY
After an original drawn by Capt 2nd Rank N N Kryzhanovskii
CartoGIS CAP Australian National University 19-345_KP

PART I

Chapter I
At Kronstadt (1914)

The state of the fleet before the war · Declaration of war · Organisation of the support services in Kronstadt · The onset of winter.

THE WAR FOUND ME AS commander of the training ship *Vernyi*, cruising as part of the Squadron of Ships of the Naval College. At this time Captain 1st Rank Kartsov, concurrently Director of the Naval College, commanded the Squadron. The cruise was of a decidedly peaceful character and indeed the general mood in the fleet scarcely a month before the war gave no basis whatsoever to expect the imminence of a global cataclysm – of the war that wiped out Russia and devastated the whole of Europe. Although the first distinct signs of the growing conflict were already appearing towards the end of June, soon after the Sarajevo incident, the general political mood in Europe, of which we serving officers could judge only from the newspapers, gave every reason to believe that the conflict would be smoothed over by diplomatic means. Only on about the 10th of July did the spectre of war hang ominously over Russia, after the open support of Russia in defence of Serbia and the first sharp response on the part of Austria to the Russian position.

At that moment, certainly, neither our army nor our fleet were ready for war: this encapsulated our centuries-long historical quirk. For the second time I became aware of a picture of general confusion and lack of appreciation resulting from our criminal lack of any substantial preparedness (the first time being the Russo-Japanese War). Still the position of the fleet was significantly better than that of the army, since the warships, by the very nature of the service, had to be always in a state of battle readiness. However, it was obvious to anyone that this was far from the same as being battle-ready for engagements with a specific opponent – in this case with Germany. I had no doubt, and indeed I knew as a matter of fact, that an appropriate plan for a war with Germany had been prepared in the Naval General Staff and was known in detail to the then commander of the Baltic Fleet, Admiral Essen[1] and his staff. But what value was this plan when the bases remained unprepared, supplies of materiel were inadequate and, finally, the construction of the main strength of the Baltic Fleet – its dreadnoughts – remained unfinished? Within the Destroyer Division there existed only one serious unit, the *Novik*, and sea-going submarines existed only on paper. Indeed it was no secret, even in the first days of confusion and chaos, that the Baltic Fleet had probably avoided destruction exclusively thanks to the courageous decisiveness of Admiral Essen, who gave orders for the establishment of the enormous mine barrier at the entrance to the Gulf of Finland. This decision was taken on his own initiative, before the official declaration of war (but when its inevitability was already obvious to all). But I will not run ahead of events and will try to set out the facts in the proper sequence as they unfolded before me.

On 10 July my ship, having been recently on a detached cruise, lay at the Baltic Port,[2] fulfilling its educational programme. So far as I recall, about 100 cadets from the middle cohort were sailing with me. Quite unexpectedly I received an order from the Commander of the Detachment to go to Reval[3] on 12 July, where a gathering of the whole fleet had been organised for that day and from where, according to the wartime mobilisation plan, manoeuvres were to begin. It was not difficult to work out that these manoeuvres had been prompted by the threatening situation on the political horizon, for earlier there had been no talk whatsoever of any sort of manoeuvres. One cannot but note the foresight and resourcefulness of Admiral Essen, who took all possible steps to correct a multitude of mistakes and deprive the Germans of any possibility of catching our fleet with their bare hands in the very first days of the war.

Almost the whole of the effective Baltic Fleet gathered at Reval. Only some special squadrons (minelayers, submarines) were absent, as well as ships undergoing repairs at Kronstadt. The mood on all ships, especially the battleships, was warily anxious, but at the same time cheerful and merry. The personnel could not fully comprehend all the difficulties of the impending war but were glad, with a rare unity of spirit, at the thought of fulfilling their primary role – to take part in a war at sea. This cheerfulness of spirit was all the more boosted by the fact that everyone believed in Admiral Essen. I cannot recall any other admiral – perhaps apart from Makarov[4] – who commanded such high esteem among officers and crew as Essen did. To him, and to him alone, the fleet was obligated for the preparation of a whole line of valiant military commanders who had passed through the school of the destroyers.[5] All those ships which had been under his direct leadership (the so-called active fleet) maintained excellent spirit and discipline right to the end of the war, even during the first period of revolution. By his moral cast of mind – a veritable knight without fear or reproach – only he alone could have developed such admirals and commanders as were Kerber,[6] Bakhirev,[7] V K Pilkin,[8] Baron Grevenitz,[9] Nepenin,[10] Bestuzhev-Riumin,[11] Verderevski,[12] Kolchak, Trukhachev,[13] Razvozov,[14] M Berens,[15] Krasheninnikov,[16] Shevelev,[17] Cherkasski,[18] Shchastnyi,[19] Dudorov[20] and many others. The deeds of these people above all reflected distinction on their teacher.

Indeed, may these short lines of mine serve as a humble tribute to the memory of Admiral Essen, one of the best of our admirals and one of the best of Russian people, who sacrificed his whole life to the beloved task – a tribute on the part of the most modest of his former colleagues, who by chance survived the perils of war and revolution, although cast overboard by the Reds from his homeland and his fleet.

For a day or two the flag officers met in conference. After that there was a wartime re-grouping of the squadrons and ships. Two brigades of battleships were created – the first of the still unfinished dreadnoughts (*Petropavlovsk*, *Poltava*, *Sevastopol* and *Gangut*); the second consisted of *Andrei Pervosvannyi*, *Pavel I*, *Slava* and *Tsesarevich*. There were two brigades of cruisers – the first of *Oleg*, *Bogatyr*, *Baian*, *Pallada*, and *Admiral Makarov*. The *Riurik*, which later went into this brigade, remained at the personal disposition of the Fleet Commander. The second cruiser brigade was formed by the *Rossiia*, *Gromoboi*, *Aurora* and *Diana*. The two destroyer divisions were combined into one. Second-rate ships were distributed on defensive service around the various ports. It is possible that some of these dispositions were made somewhat later, but in general they came into effect from the beginning of the war. It is characteristic that many of these re-groupings did not in any way conform to the previously prepared mobilisation plans. This shows once again that bureaucratic preparation for war is often out of kilter with real life.

The character of this organisational work undertaken during these days in the Reval roadstead left no doubt whatever that preparations were going on not for occasional manoeuvres but for real wartime operations, although there had been no official directions for mobilisation yet, and indeed the very possibility of war seemed problematical to some (although not many) of the optimists among the powers that be.

The Squadron of the Naval College had been directed to cease training. The senior year of naval cadets were taken on the strength of various ships – it seems that the majority ended up in ships of the Destroyer Division – while the other cadets were sent to St Petersburg. The warships that had been assigned to the Naval College (*Rossiia*, *Oleg* and *Aurora*) re-joined their brigade in accordance with the new arrangements and the unarmed ships (*Rynda*, *Vernyi* and *Voin*) were sent to Kronstadt.

At Reval I embarked about 100 cadets from other ships, then on about 13 July left for Helsinki[21] where we took about fifty cadets of the Naval Engineering School from various ships and, with this live cargo accommodated with difficulty on the upper deck, headed for Kronstadt. Here I disembarked the Naval Engineering School students, and spent some hours searching for my superiors. The *Aurora*, formerly our flagship, lay in the harbour (Kartsov combined being Chief of the Squadron and the commander of *Aurora*). She had come to Kronstadt with the other cruisers to load ammunition and for the discharge of all unnecessary materials that might cause interference during engagements such as furniture, any timber and so on. I had poked my nose into the *Aurora* but found a new commander there (G I Butakov) and a new admiral (Leskov), who both advised me that they no longer had any relationship whatsoever with the former Squadron of the Naval College. Then I turned to the senior officer in port – to the Chief of Training, Rear Admiral Sapsai,[22] who explained to me that on mobilisation, my ship would certainly come under his direction, but since mobilisation had not been declared, then he did not consider himself entitled to give me any sort of instructions. Having thus been made aware of my own autonomy, I decided to proceed to St Petersburg in order to discharge my live cargo there – the naval cadets. Anchoring opposite the Naval College, I disembarked the students there and tried to find Kartsov, thinking that he might know some news of my future disposition. However, Kartsov did not seem to be in town. Next morning I set out to catch the Chief of the Main Naval Staff, to whom I was undoubtedly subordinate, as were commanders of all ships located at St Petersburg. I tracked him down on the Neva yacht pier where he was accompanying the Minister for the Navy (Grigorovich[23]). The Chief of Staff (Vice Admiral K V Stetsenko[24]) ordered me to go immediately to Kronstadt and place myself at the disposal of Admiral Sapsai. When I attempted to respond, he drew me aside and said in my ear: 'Mobilisation has been declared'.

On returning to Kronstadt on 18 July I again attended on Sapsai. I informed him of the mobilisation, but he responded that the pre-arranged signal had not yet been received. However, after half an hour he sent a staff officer with the news that the signal had been received and as a consequence *Vernyi* transferred to his command and was to enter the harbour. From that moment we began to play at war in Kronstadt but as this was in the deep rear it had a quite comical character, although it was extraordinarily trying for us. *Vernyi*, along with *Voin*, the minelayer *Volga*, *Rynda* and *Dvina* (formerly *Pamyat Azova*, adapted for the Mining Squadron) were obliged to defend the approaches to Kronstadt from the enemy (!) and to carry out patrol and guard ship duties. At first the service was organised in this way: over three days in turn the *Dvina* or the *Rynda* formed the outermost guard ship patrol at 10 miles from Kronstadt. The *Vernyi*, *Voin* and *Volga* similarly over three days constituted the innermost guard ship patrol not far from the meridian of the Stirsudden lighthouse.[25] In the first days of the war a large quantity of defensive mines had been laid in this region by the Army Engineering Corps – these mines would explode on contact once the onshore circuit had been closed.[26]

A very narrow and circuitous channel had been established between the mines through which ships were led by special pilots. The general organisation and oversight of this business was the responsibility of the guard ships. At first there was a lot of work guiding ships since a large number of foreign steamers, which had been stuck in the Gulf of Finland at the moment of the declaration of war, passed inwards and outwards. However, in about a month, all movement ceased and the guard ship duty changed to spending three days hanging around at anchor on the open sea without any sort of activity, which in the often stormy weather was both unpleasant and unsafe.

War was finally declared on 19 July.[27] Very soon they took from me all of the regular officers, leaving only an executive officer (at first Blinov,[28] later Nelidov[29]) and formed the ship's crew from recently mobilised naval officers and ensigns. Then they replaced my crew with older mobilised reservists. The character of the service itself quickly simplified as the *Dvina*, *Rynda* and *Voin* were taken for various purposes to Reval and Helsinki. Things continued in this way until 10 December when finally the sea around Kronstadt became so firmly frozen that our ships were quite unable to proceed to the location of their guard ship duties without extra help. They remained in winter formation within the harbour, being in readiness, however, to take to sea at any moment.

Of this period of the war spent at the rear I have the most sombre recollection: on the one hand there was quite mindless, although demanding, service, on the other the awareness that, over there, at the front, lively interesting work was going on, which we knew about only by rumours and the yarns of officers occasionally passing through from warships in an advanced position – more often than not, the minelayers coming in for a fresh supply of mines. Most bothersome of all was the thought of one's own uselessness, that is, of how the war found me, an experienced fighting officer with a fair sort of past, as commander of a ship and in a place removed from the action. The hope yet remained that as I had already commanded *Vernyi* for about three years, I could normally, in peacetime, have expected to receive some sort of promotion. Already several of my colleagues, junior to me in seniority, had been promoted and put into higher positions – but these lucky ones had been there, at the front, in the line of battle. I still had the anxious hope that the Chief of Staff to the Fleet Commander, Vice Admiral Kerber, would remember me as we had been shipmates during the first voyage of the cruiser *Rossiia* in 1897–99. In the meantime, grudgingly and ashamed to look in the eye of my family and acquaintances, and even more so of my colleagues and old comrades returning from the front and the forward positions, I took advantage of all the privileges of life in the rear and frequently repaired to St Petersburg, where my family lived and my son had recently been born.[30] Frozen in with my ship in Kronstadt, I even tried to transfer to St Petersburg, where my old comrade in the Naval Guards, Major General A K Girs,[31] then commanding the Composite Detachment of the St Petersburg depots, offered me a position as battalion commander. These depots were preparing a special naval detachment to send to the front. Subsequently this detachment was made into a regiment that distinguished itself at the front under the command of Captain 1st Rank G N Mazurov,[32] who had also been in the Naval Guards with me.

However, all these plans were overturned in the last days of December, when, one wonderful night, I received a quite short but truly sweet-sounding telegram with the following content: 'Telegraph if willing occupy position Flag Captain Administrative Section. Kerber.'

Although I had never in my life served on a staff and nourished an ingrained revulsion towards staff work, I immediately grasped that it would be impossible to imagine a better means of getting into the line of battle. The Flag Captain determined all appointments and there could be no doubt at all that after serving for some time in that extraordinarily difficult and troublesome position, I would automatically receive the command of some warship, albeit not one of my own choice. The answer was despatched immediately: 'Thanks – willing', and a week after, on 6 January 1915, I left for Helsinki.

Chapter II

On the Staff of the Active Fleet (First Half of 1915)

My appointment as Flag Captain · Composition of the Staff and the characteristics of the people making it up · Activity of Admiral Essen · Imperial inspection · Life ashore at Helsinki · The spring attack · Concerns over the Gulf of Riga · Death of Admiral Essen · Appointment of Kanin and Grigorov · Battle of the 1st Cruiser Brigade by Gotland.

My companion on the train was Captain 1st Rank Alexander Vasilievich Kolchak, who since the beginning of the war had held the position of Flag Captain of the Operations Section of the very same staff where I was going to take up the responsibility of Flag Captain of the Administrative Section. He had come to St Petersburg on official business and was then returning to his post in Helsinki. I was very interested to meet him, since he, better than anyone, could enlighten me on the general war situation on the naval front and give me indications and explanations as to the character and conditions of my duties.[1]

I had known A V Kolchak since we were schoolboys. He had been a year ahead of me, so in his final year at the Naval College we had both served in the same squad: he as the sergeant major, I as the warrant officer. After that we had repeatedly run into each other while on service. For the first two years after graduation we had been simultaneously in the Pacific Ocean, he on the *Riurik*, I on the *Rossiia* through 1897, 1898 and 1899. At the time of the Russo-Japanese War we had both been at Port Arthur, where, at the end of May 1904, we were due to participate in the sortie of the transport *Angara* (until then a steamer of the Volunteer Fleet *Moskva*, then later *Pechenga*). To a considerable degree the devising of the plan for this operation (to break the blockade and take action against the lines of communication of the Japanese transports in the Yellow Sea and the Pacific Ocean) belonged to A V Kolchak. The steamer had been manned by volunteer officers, among whom were: Bestuzhev-Riumin, P M Plen,[2] the commander Kliupfel,[3] the executive officer Lvov. I was the navigator, my assistant was Ensign S A Cherepanov. Unfortunately, our expedition did not take place, since at the last minute Admiral Vitgeft (commanding the fleet after Makarov), although at first positively disposed towards our plan, countermanded it, fearing the risky nature of the undertaking. During the final period of the siege Kolchak and I served in the onshore forces and often met. On the surrender of the fortress we both happened to be in hospital – A V, if I am not mistaken, with pneumonia. The Japanese evacuated him to Shanghai, from where he was sent to Russia, while fate cast me into Japan as a prisoner of war. Over the following peacetime years we met less frequently, as Kolchak served partly in the Naval General Staff and partly in the Destroyer Division (he commanded the destroyer *Pogranichnik*) and on Admiral Essen's Staff. I, as an officer of the Naval Guards, became executive officer of the Imperial yacht *Shtandart*, which, although being a part of the active fleet, was always on detached cruising. However, notwithstanding this, on the train we met as old friends.

On arrival at Helsinki we went together to the cruiser *Rossiia*, in which Admiral Essen at that time flew his flag and where his staff was accommodated. Communication with the cruiser was very difficult, since, although the roadstead was frozen over, direct communication across the ice had not yet been established. It was necessary to travel partly by cab, partly on foot and partly by ice-breaker.

I trod the deck of the cruiser *Rossiia* with a feeling of particular satisfaction: first – this signified my entry into the line of battle, of which I had dreamt since the beginning of the war, and secondly – for me the very best, the springtime memories of my youth were associated with this cruiser. Eighteen years before I had begun my service as an officer on her, sailing on *Rossiia* for about three years in all. At that time she had been a formidable cruiser, the best in the world (her sister ships of the somewhat improved type, the *Powerful* and the *Terrible*,[4] had not then been completed). We, the young midshipmen, were proud of her and loved her as one might love a living being. Now she was somewhat obsolete, having already finished her front-line service, but the old spirit and traditions, the most important element of the living organism of any ship, still reigned strongly in her. Her former achievements at the time of the Russo-Japanese War and the recent successful raid on the coast of Germany contributed to this in no small way. Kanin and Kolchak had taken the cruiser to the southernmost region of the Baltic Sea where, under their leadership, mines were sown under the very nose of the main base of the German fleet.[5] The commander of *Rossiia* at this time was Captain 1st Rank N L Podgurskii,[6] a famous Port Arthur hero.

Having presented myself to the Chief of Staff Vice Admiral Ludvig Fyodorovich Kerber and then to the Fleet Commander himself, Admiral Nikolai Ottovich von Essen, I began the handover of business from my predecessor, Captain 2nd Rank D P Rudenskii,[7] which took about three days. Rudenskii, still a relatively junior officer, had occupied this position up until the war began and since the Staff had not been put on a war footing had been nominated senior staff officer. Then when many of the functions of the Main Naval and Naval General Staff had transferred to the Staff of the Fleet Commander, all positions had been increased in rank and it had been recognised that Flag Captains should be staff officers who had commanded ships of at least the second rank. Rudenskii was appointed to gain his command experience in one of the destroyers of the second rank.

After the early days of chaos and muddle, unavoidable when entering into any new responsibility, I gradually began to get a handle on this new, for me quite foreign, way of working in the brain of the fleet; the mainspring, from which one way or another depended the achievement of the most momentous task of the war – ensuring the security of the right flank of our seriously stretched army front and the protection of the approaches to our naval bases. Besides these merely passive activities, all manner of operations were worked up in the Staff and brought into effect with the aim of causing the utmost damage to the enemy fleet and their transports. At the same time, in the Staff the usual work went on of leading the battle readiness of the fleet across all specialties, through the organisation of supplies, repairs and so on. Here the related registration and accounting functions were concentrated, and the personnel work for all appointments carried out. The health and naval legal service sections of the fleet operated here as well.

Under what conditions did this responsible work proceed? Was the organisation of the Staff services and work appropriate to the colossal demands that were imperiously presented to the Staff with each pressing moment? It must be recognised – not fully.

For all his virtues, Admiral Essen was above all a man of action and could not endure office work or bureaucracy. Somewhat inappropriately, he identified any sort of staff work with bureaucracy and so tolerated it only as a necessary evil. It was natural that he should choose close subordinates sharing similar views on such matters. If people appeared of another persuasion, then they, in the majority of cases, very quickly became infected with the same spirit. As a result, the work of the Staff, composed of officers imbued with the desire to complete the maximum of output, was carried on without system, in a highly-strung manner, discordantly. In addition, the Staff was too small – similar work carried on ashore in peacetime would have been undertaken by easily ten times the number of workers. It is true that such a system, or better to say lack of system, protected the Staff from bureaucracy or officiousness, but to everything there is a limit and I must say, on the basis of personal experience, that the quality of the work suffered because of all the previously mentioned reasons. Officers, above all overburdened with work, often overstepped into other areas, from which arose arguments and altercations. Personal initiative too frequently dominated and coordination of work was undertaken only on the basis of personal relationships, with higher direction of it virtually absent. There is no argument that the work was lively, but very often it was to no purpose or it remained incomplete.

The Chief of the Staff, L F Kerber, was an educated and talented naval officer, who while excellent at working out plans of operations and combining with this the bravery and courage to bring these operations to fruition, was too highly strung and fiery to secure agreement and to direct the work of the whole Staff. He interested himself closely only in operational matters and the disposition of personnel – that is, in appointments and transfers. His immediate colleague and assistant, Flag Captain of the Operations Section A V Kolchak, who had an amazing capacity to create the most unexpected and always well thought out and at the same time brilliant plans of operation, did not recognise any sort of superior apart from Essen, to whom he always reported directly. On this basis conflicts were always arising between Kolchak and Kerber that, however, caused Essen, respecting and valuing them both, to take on quite unexpectedly the role of peacemaker between his two fiery and unyielding assistants.

So the complicated work of the Staff proceeded in these rather abnormal conditions.

As I have set out above, the Staff was excellently composed in terms of quality. All the staff ranks were in truth the best representatives of the active fleet, each according to his speciality. I will name them so far as I can recall: the senior staff officer of the Operations Section (later assistant to the Flag Captain of the Operations Section) was Lieutenant Commander Prince M B Cherkasskii, who later replaced Kolchak. This outstanding and highly educated naval officer, who had passed the Naval Academy of the General Staff, to some extent compensated for Kolchak's main deficiency, namely, his aversion to sedentary work. Cherkasskii was an excellent office worker and a skilful systematiser. The senior staff officer (later assistant to the Flag Captain) of the Administrative Section was Lieutenant Commander Mikhail Alexandrovich Petrov,[8] who had also passed the War Division of the Nicholas Naval Academy. A better assistant, it turned out, one could not have imagined. He oversaw all ships' crews (the lower ranks) of the fleet and, if not he then certainly I, was always delving into the chaos of appointments, discharges and transfers of tens of thousands of people, with the constant commissioning of new ships, changes in ships' crews, complicated tables of establishment, endless requests and claims about transfers and replacements on the part of the staffs of brigades, divisions, squadrons and even individual ships. He also oversaw the external orderliness of the life of the staff. Next came the other staff: gunnery – Lieutenant Commander Svinin[9] – an officer fanatically devoted to his craft, always in the first place in attending to his service duty. By the nature of his duties he was often travelling and laboured hard over the organisation of gunnery matters on the ships and the naval installations at the shore batteries of the naval front. The staff mines officer was Captain 2nd Rank Baron Mirbakh,[10] the main organiser of preparations for defensive mining operations. The staff navigation officer was Lieutenant Commander A N Spolatbog,[11] on whom lay the complicated and demanding work of organising minesweeping and the related preparation of charts of strategic cleared channels. Subsequently he replaced me in the capacity of Flag Captain and later was commander of the cruiser *Admiral Makarov*. An extraordinarily capable officer, he stuck to the service under the Bolsheviks, was later dismissed and apparently shot.[12] Radio telegraph matters were overseen by staff specialist Lieutenant Commander Ivan Ivanovich Rengarten.[13] He demonstrated invaluable service to the fleet by his invention of the radio direction finder and his subsequent work with it. The staff engineering officer (and subsequently Chief Engineer of the Fleet) was Major General Winter,[14] an excellent administrator and expert on repairs and maintenance.

The housekeeping of the fleet and questions of general supply and victualling, as well as the financial section, were overseen by acting staff Quartermaster Lieutenant Iankovich. This officer was the only one of the whole Staff who was not up to the job. He undoubtedly had corporate management capacities but, as a consequence of the lack of general service experience, was quite incapable of sorting out the complicated problems of financial operations, preparations and supply of the whole fleet.

The attorney of the Staff and chief auditor was Captain Martianov,[15] happily distinguished among his naval jurist colleagues first by his knowledge of naval circumstances (he had earlier been a regular officer) and then by his not having the tendency to take the side of the lower ranks in cases of offences against military discipline (I speak of course of the period before the revolution).

The medical section of the fleet was overseen by staff doctor Active State Councillor[16] Zort, who had spent his entire service afloat and consequently had great experience in the organisation of health arrangements on ships.

Then there were four junior officers on the Staff who frequently changed, so that I only remember Lieutenants Dovkont,[17] Tirbakh[18] and Komelov,[19] all three outstanding young officers.

As is evident from the foregoing list, the composition of the Staff was relatively young, having predominantly graduated in 1901–02 or later, but the majority of these officers had taken part in the Russo-Japanese War, as a result of which they possessed quite a solid grounding in the service as well as substantial battle experience.

Also counted on the Staff with the status of a Flag Captain was Chief of the Signals Intelligence Service, Captain 1st Rank Adrian Ivanovich Nepenin. Up until the war, in fact, this responsibility had been quite separate from the Staff. Nepenin remained constantly in Reval, from where, with rare talent, he led the complicated but at the same time extraordinarily well set up Signals Intelligence Service. The unusual fitness for purpose of this service was totally due to the exceptional administrative and managerial capacities of Nepenin – one of the most outstanding leaders of naval units in the Baltic Fleet in the period of the war with Germany. Nepenin had the rare quality of being able to choose people and to set them to work. In addition, the gift of setting out a reliable picture of the movement of enemy ships, and from that the plans and intentions of the enemy, was developed in him to a high degree. This he achieved by means of the logical accumulation of facts and interpretations, provided to him by the posts of the Signals Intelligence Service, and on the basis of decoding of German radio and the maps produced by the direction finders. His forecasts, sometimes very courageous and apparently based on slim foundations, almost always turned out to be accurate.

His activity during the war in the position of Chief of the Signals Intelligence Service gave to the Staff of the Fleet Commander the possibility of seeing and hearing, while having neither eyes nor ears. Not a single operation began without receiving from him an appropriate and almost always accurate assessment of the specified region. Attacks were mounted on the basis of his reports of the movement of enemy ships and transports – and almost always successfully.

I dwell so extensively on the positive sides of the activities of A I Nepenin because subsequently his shining character was strongly overshadowed by his less than successful command of the fleet, culminating in his tragic death in the first days of the revolution. His misfortune was that, while having undoubted intelligence and outstanding capabilities, he did not possess sufficient experience and knowledge necessary for the command of the fleet. He had never commanded big ships and he was totally ignorant of issues affecting naval and battle techniques.

By the time I took up the position of Flag Captain the character of the war at sea in the Baltic theatre had to a significant degree already been settled. The Germans, having not demonstrated the required decisiveness in the first days of the war, had let slip the more favourable time for them to destroy our fleet relatively easily and to create a substantial threat to the capital of Russia itself – St Petersburg. Admittedly this would not have been managed without sacrifice for part of their fleet would have perished in our minefields, from destroyer attacks and in engagements with our warships. Our fleet, even though perishing in the unequal battle, would have been sufficiently strong enough to inflict serious losses on the enemy. However, by such a manoeuvre the Germans might have immediately, at a single blow, ended the war with Russia, regardless of our successes on the land-war front, since their troops, launched on the region of the Gulf of Finland, would have appeared in the rear of all our battle lines, completely ruining our plan of campaign. However, the Germans had not dared to risk it and the propitious moment was lost.

After the declaration of war by England, their hands appeared to be tied by the threat of attack by the much stronger British fleet. The Germans were obliged to reserve their main strength against the chance of an aggressive attack on the part of England and for the protection of their western seaboard. Their more obsolete ships were allocated to the Baltic, where their defensive responsibilities, evidently, were limited to the protection of coastal bases, wide-ranging reconnaissance, and, mainly, the laying of multiple minefields across the courses of our ships. In addition, from the beginning of the war, they began a submarine war on the widest scale, in which the submarines often played the role of minelayers. The German bombardment of Libau and the surrounding shoreline, the intrusion of individual ships into the Gulf of Finland, finishing with the destruction of the *Magdeburg* and the loss of several destroyers, had a purely demonstrative character. The encounters of our units with German ships in the Baltic Sea (such as the so-called battle of the 1st Cruiser Brigade with the German squadron off Gotland and others) had, without doubt, a purely chance character and in these circumstances the initiative had been entirely on our side. There was no doubt that the military task of the German fleet in the Baltic Sea, apart from its purely defensive functions, came down to collaboration with their army, that is, to the protection of its left flank and assistance during attacks.[20]

When the picture of the true activity of the German fleet in the Baltic theatre had been fully clarified, the work of the Staff, having at the start of the war a feverish, circumstantial character, settled more or less into a normal routine. Ceaseless and rapid work began on the establishment of minefields across the widest regions; extensions to the already established central minefield, then for the defence of the approaches to the entrances into the Åbo-Åland skerries[21] and the Gulf of Riga. A plan was prepared for a battle on the Central Position[22] behind the minefield in the event of the enemy breaking through into the Gulf of Finland, and the defence of the entrance to the Gulf of Riga was organised. Appropriate instructions for action were composed for various circumstances and for the various units, which had been distributed to their winter bases with the setting in of the colder weather. Projects for new coastal defensive regions were developed, staffed, armed, and supplied by the fleet and placed directly subordinate to the Fleet Commander. Priority was given to those positions marked for construction at Åbo-Åland and Moön Sound. The reorganisation of the combatant and non-combatant units was finalised while a special Mine Defence of the Baltic Sea was created, into which went the Squadron of Minelayers, the Division of Minesweeping and part of the Destroyer Division. The rather small pre-war Minesweeping Squadron was upgraded to a division, with two squadrons. Commercial steamers of small tonnage and shallow draft were converted for minesweeping. An aviation arm was established, with the mother ship *Orlitsa*, over which Captain 1st Rank B P Dudorov laboured hard. Finally, right up to the very last opportunity, that is until the Gulf of Finland and part of the Baltic Sea finally froze over completely, individual cruisers and destroyers were sent to sea on reconnaissance. However, the organisation of this reconnaissance was not always successful, for proof of which might serve the loss of the cruiser *Pallada*. While on patrol on 28 September 1914 she was torpedoed by an enemy submarine and quickly sank. Not a single person was saved, as no escorting destroyers were near her.[23]

Thus might be described, in general outline, the activity of the Staff and with it of the whole Baltic Fleet, up to the day of my joining the Staff at the beginning of January 1915.

As I have already indicated, the Staff was accommodated on the old cruiser *Rossiia*, where the Fleet Commander Admiral Essen flew his flag and lived. The training ship *Voin* was also available to the Staff, moored alongside the *Rossiia*. The printing and accounting offices were accommodated there as well as part of the Staff. In spite of this extra space in *Voin*, the overcrowding was terrible, which certainly hindered the work in no small way. The urgent need for some sort of solution was palpable. In many foreign fleets the staff of the higher naval leaders were placed ashore or on special non-combatant ships (yachts), and only for manoeuvres or battle would the admiral transfer his flag to a warship, taking with him the so-called campaign staff.

Under the pressure of circumstances, Admiral Essen decided to implement something similar in our fleet. A suitable Finnish passenger steamer, the *Polaris*, was bought and we set about converting her into the Staff base. Essen himself was not very sympathetic to the idea of creating such a base, quite correctly considering that the admiral and his staff should always be located in the ship on which they would stand into battle, and only the total impossibility of accommodating the whole Staff in a warship forced him to agree to the plan of establishing a special Staff ship. However, at the same time, Essen decided that during the navigable period he, with the campaign Staff (the Chief of Staff, the two Flag Captains, staff officers, the fleet gunnery officer and the fleet navigator) would be accommodated principally in that warship on which he expected to engage in battle in the event of a breakthrough by the Germans on the Central Position. The ship chosen for this was the dreadnought *Sevastopol.*

In the meantime, while waiting on the readiness of the Staff ship, we continued to perch in the *Rossiia*. This winter the following units were gathered in the Helsinki roadstead:

the 1st Brigade of Battleships – by this time all the dreadnoughts had entered service – (Rear Admiral A S Maksimov[24]);
the 2nd Brigade of Battleships (Rear Admiral Nebolsin[25]);
the 2nd Brigade of Cruisers (Rear Admiral Leskov[26]);

the Mine Defence (Vice Admiral Kanin), composed of the Squadron of Minelayers, the Division of Minesweepers (Captain 1st Rank Kitkin[27]) and part of the Destroyer Division.

In addition the Transport Squadron (Captain 1st Rank Skalovskii[28]) was established. The Commander of the Sveaborg port[29] was at that time Captain 1st Rank Teshe.[30]

Wintering over in Reval at the same time were the 1st Brigade of Cruisers (Rear Admiral Bakhirev), the 2nd Minesweeper Squadron (Captain 2nd Rank Kovalevskii[31]), part of the Minelaying Squadron and the main part of the Destroyer Division (Rear Admiral Shtorre[32]).

By the time of my arrival in Helsinki intelligence had been received that the Germans, having found out about the gathering there of almost the entire fleet, had supposedly decided to undertake a series of Zeppelin and aircraft raids over the city with the aim of causing damage to our ships, anchored in quite close order in the inner roadstead, completely iced in. Although a simple arithmetical calculation showed that such an operation was almost impossible, taking into account the distance of the German bases and the general range of operation of aircraft and Zeppelins, all the same, conforming to the proverb 'God helps those who help themselves', all possible precautionary measures were taken.

At the suggestion of the staff officer for communication with the fortress, Captain 2nd Rank Shchetinin,[33] all ships were quickly covered with cheap chalky white paint. Not only the sides but also the upper decks and superstructures were painted and so on, so that seen from above, the ships blended into the surrounding ice, covered with snow. To be sure, their complete disappearance could not be achieved, but in any case, according to reports of our pilots, from a certain height and in the presence of cloud it was very difficult to distinguish individual ships. Even from the shore, in sunny weather, the ships had a quite fairy-tale appearance, for all of them, as if by a magic fairy wand from the Sleeping Beauty, turned into blocks of ice, making a single whole with the surrounding ice sheets shrouding the roadstead.

Also, in the city a full system was put into place for the eventuality of an air raid. At a siren signal, repeated in the various parts of the city, all lights were to be extinguished and the inhabitants were advised to take shelter in basements. Usually, at nightfall, all windows had to be closed with shutters and on the streets the occasional street lamps were covered with blue hoods so that they gave out a weak deathly glow. However, the large and lively city, considering itself partly abroad, submitted to wartime discipline with difficulty. Life continued to bubble over, in the evenings all the cinemas and restaurants were full of an assorted public, who, returning homewards, would light their way with hand-held electric torches, creating a real illumination that would have been quite useful for the orientation of any enemy pilots should they have taken it into their heads to fly over.

However, Helsinki never had to endure the anticipated enemy air raid. One imagines that the Germans decided not to touch the capital of Finland, hoping by this to draw sympathy towards themselves from the Swedish population and the mood of Germanophilia of a significant part of it.

As a curiosity, one ought to mention that in the end only one bomb was dropped from an aircraft onto the city, but this bombing was not the fault of the enemy but of none other than A V Kolchak. The latter, when free from operations, amused himself in aviation matters and often took to the air as a passenger. Thus he came to fly with a pilot testing out a new bomb, which they were to drop onto the testing field outside the city. However, they took a preliminary circle over the city and there, I forget now by whose fault, the bomb broke loose and fell into someone's garden, by its explosion frightening the surrounding population almost to death. Fortunately, there were no casualties. Kolchak was mightily embarrassed, since such carelessness was really quite scandalous – but the story was somehow hushed up.

The forced inactivity in fleet operations, caused by its being iced in, was not to the liking of Admiral Essen. His active, energetic nature demanded constant movement. As a consequence, he did not remain in the relative comfort and peace of the flagship but was always travelling – now to Reval to inspect the construction of the new onshore defences and to meet with Nepenin and Gerasimov, the Commandant of the Fortress, now to Åbo, now to Moön Sound to inspect the construction of the new destroyer base in the harbour at Roggekiul. Usually he took Kolchak and one of the staff officers, most often Tirbakh, with him. He avoided going to St Petersburg, since, evidently, he did not much like the atmosphere there; in cases of need, he would send either Kolchak or me there. The example of Essen was followed by Kolchak, too, whose restless nature was sickened by the quiet Staff life. He used any hint of adventure to leave Helsinki for at least a few days.

In the intervals between his travels Essen gathered his formation commanders and the heads of sections for conferences. Of the admirals, Kanin,[34] in whom Essen had special confidence, was most often present.

Kanin, whose service had been almost wholly in the Black Sea, had not long before the war been named Chief of the Minelaying Squadron. He had completed the minelaying programme particularly well in the first days of the war, in the shortest time achieving the enormous task of establishing the central mine barrier without a single casualty, while having at his disposal quite inadequate means. Over the course of only forty-eight hours 2,200 mines had been laid. He did not differ in outstanding capabilities from those of Kolchak, Kerber, and many other assistants of Essen, but he was incontrovertibly an intelligent person and excellent manager, with great service and technical experience. Besides, he had to a high degree the quality of being able to maintain the very best relationships with the most varied types of people.

A self-restrained, obliging person who undoubtedly had a great store of common sense, Kanin gradually won for himself the position of first adviser to Admiral Essen, even of friend. This situation often brought about conflicts between him and Kerber, who could not reconcile himself with such intrusion into his sphere as Chief of the Staff, naturally the primary adviser to the Fleet Commander. Perhaps Kerber was the only person with whom Kanin did not succeed in getting along, notwithstanding all of his adroitness. Everyone was aware that these two were rivals and that the struggle between them for power, for the dominant influence in the fleet, was inevitable. Even then it was clear that the fiery, unrestrained Kerber was not to prevail over the calm, circumspect Kanin.

One must note that in this struggle Kanin also had a substantial advantage – he was of purely Russian ancestry. At this time in the fleet, under the flag of the dangers of Germanophilia and pro-German espionage, a specific campaign was being waged against all people of German background. This partly touched even the irreproachable Essen. A mass of attacks and absurd accusations were lodged against

Kerber, a person generally not given to minding his language and never hiding his Baltic-German sympathies.[35] In the end he understood the danger of his position and tried to salvage the situation by a measure extraordinarily surprising to all of us, his friends, in view of its irrelevance – with Imperial permission, he changed his name and began to call himself Korvin, but it was already too late.

Over the month or two after arriving at Helsinki I more or less got a handle on my new work. The main difficulty in it consisted not in assiduous routine work, stretching each day from 8 in the morning to 7 in the evening, but from the constant discussions and settlement of the claims of senior officers, trying to secure some sort of transfer or posting of officers or lower ranks. All these leaders exclusively took into account the narrow interests of their own squadrons or ships and did not wish to understand that the Staff was trying to carry out a system of absolute fairness, guided only by the degree of significance of the duties entrusted to the various squadrons and ships. This work was indisputably very difficult, taking into account the general lack of good cadres of officers and of lower-rank specialists, but, hand on heart, one must say everything was done by us to avoid partiality and to carry through staffing according to the rules. My conversations with commanding officers, of whom the majority were senior to me in rank, demanded a constant supply of tact, a certain diplomatic dexterity and, at the same time, authoritative firmness. It is not for me to judge how far I met these requirements but I can only say that this type of work affected my nerves quite adversely. It also helped me significantly that in my previous service I had maintained excellent relationships with many admirals and commanders and further, that on occasion of need I could rely on the support of the Chief of the Staff, who related to me with complete trust and wholly as a colleague.

In January 1915, regardless of the difficult navigation conditions, Essen had made a final attempt to display some activity. An operation was ordered to sow mines from destroyers to the north of Danzig, with the 1st Brigade of Cruisers covering the work of the minelayers. The brigade was composed of the *Riurik*, on which the commander of the operation, Rear Admiral Bakhirev, flew his flag, the *Admiral Makarov*, the *Oleg* and the *Bogatyr*. A specially detached half-division was devoted to laying the mines. Having escaped the ice floes not without difficulty, the squadron headed towards the island of Gotland, where it met stormy weather and a blizzard, during which the *Riurik* grounded on an uncharted bank, thereby receiving some serious damage with which she was fortunately able to deal using her own resources. The destroyers, however, did lay the minefield, after which the whole squadron returned to Reval.* The *Riurik* was soon transferred to Kronstadt, where her repair took several months. The accident with *Riurik* showed Essen the risky nature of such expeditions in wintertime, as a consequence of which he decided to refrain from further activity right through until the opening of the navigable season about the middle of April.

At the end of February or the beginning of March there was an Imperial inspection of the fleet at Helsinki that extended over an entire day and went quite smoothly. The Emperor visited the *Rossiia*, where all the commanding officers were presented to him, then several other battleships and after that he travelled by automobile over the ice along the whole fleet, ecstatically greeted by unending cries of 'Hurrah!' by the future revolutionaries and Bolsheviks – the 'pride and glory of the revolution'[36] who were to shatter the monarchy. On this day I spoke for the last time with the Tsar, who looked aged and tired. At the time of this conversation it never even entered my head what a horrible fate awaited this wonderful, decent person with a crystalline spirit, who sacrificed his whole life in the service of his homeland ...

The entourage of the Tsar included the Flag Captain to His Majesty General Adjutant Admiral K D Nilov[37] and the two Aides-de-camp to the Emperor, Colonel Drenteln and Captain 2nd Rank Sablin.[38] It is interesting to note that to assist in preparing for the inspection, Captain 2nd Rank Alfater[39] from the Staff of the Northern Front, seconded himself to our Staff. The convictions of this officer at that time were so monarchist that it would have not entered anyone's head that in the future this very Alfater would become one of the most conscientious assistants of the Bolsheviks. Essen had wanted to use the Imperial inspection to make Kolchak an admiral, however nothing came of this as a consequence of some sort of friction arising

* Author's note: A brief description of the cruise and accident of the *Riurik*, compiled by former Flag Navigator of the 1st Brigade of Cruisers Captain 2nd Rank N N Kryzhanovskii, responsible for the navigational aspects of this cruise, is provided in Appendix No. 1.

between Essen and the court party that then had great influence on the Tsar.

The relatively quiet conditions of service, thanks to the ceasing of navigation, gave the possibility of personnel taking advantage of some of the conveniences of life ashore. Almost each day the married officers of the Staff were able to go ashore and spend the evening at home, returning on board at 7 in the morning. In the event of necessity, the connection of the Staff by telephone enabled a very quick appearance on the flagship at any time of night.

I should note that the families did not in any way impede the proper conduct of the service. On the contrary, they gave rest and calmness to all to whom had been given the happiness of having a family, and healthy entertainment for the unmarried youth. The service was carried on more smoothly and quickly. I generally consider that the peculiarities of naval service demand the indispensable presence of the family, a comfortable domestic corner. Otherwise, the people required to serve on the fleet are made into soulless callous automatons, gradually losing all the better aspects of human nature. Nothing so makes a person cruel and dries them out than the need to serve and work in an artificially created monastic situation, without the possibility of resting from time to time in normal onshore surroundings, in the company of those close to them.[40]

Similar conditions of life on the fleet and the Staff continued until the spring, the beginning of the ice breaking up. By this time all of the preparatory work for the new fighting campaign had been completed, as also had all required repairs. From the beginning of April all ships gradually began to move to their fighting bases: the 2nd Brigade of Cruisers to the Åbo-Åland region; the 1st Brigade of Cruisers (apart from the *Riurik*) to Lapvik and Lium,[41] the Destroyer Division to Moön Sound and also to Lapvik. The minelayers began their work of sowing mines. The Minesweeping Division commenced clearing secret strategic channels, formed along fantastic zigzags between minefields entirely sown with our defensive mines. And the Germans were beginning to stir, too: their submarines began to appear around Dagerort, around Takkhona, by the entrances to the Åbo-Åland skerries and even by Nargen.[42] The mood on the fleet and the Staff became more uneasy and onshore life almost ceased.

From the beginning of spring also our failures on the land-war front began. The gradual retreat of our troops forced the clearing of the coast almost to the Irben peninsula. The immediate threat to the Gulf of Riga and with it to Moön Sound – itself the key to the entrance to the Gulf of Finland flanking the central mine defences – became the new concern of our fleet. The weakness of the Tserell shore positions, where at that time only 6in or 120mm batteries were located, induced Admiral Essen to take the decision to sow mines in the Irben channel and surrounding regions of the sea. Several lines of defence had also to be placed similarly along the seaward shoreline to the south. It was decided to compensate for the lack of heavy artillery by sending one of the older battleships into the Gulf of Riga by way of Dagerort, as Moön Sound could only be passed by ships with a draft no greater than 15ft. The risk was very great but they were prepared to sacrifice this ship in view of the importance of the objective. The main part of the Destroyer Division was assembled in the Gulf of Riga, with its principal base at Kuivast on the island of Moön, its forward position at Arensburg and rear at Roggekiul. On 12 May Rear Admiral P L Trukhachev, a very capable and experienced officer who had successfully commanded the cruiser *Oleg* at the beginning of the war, was appointed Chief of the Destroyer Division and at the same time Chief of Defence of the Gulf of Riga. Trukhachev was a close friend of Nepenin and Kolchak and had won the complete trust of Admiral Essen. All of his previous service had been in the Naval Guards, but almost exclusively on warships. At the time of the Russo-Japanese War we had been chosen together by lot from the Guards to go to Port Arthur, where he had commanded the destroyer *Bezstrashnyi*, showing himself to be an intrepid commander.

The character of Trukhachev's capabilities in many ways resembled those of Nepenin: nature had endowed him with great common sense, he was very resourceful, quick-witted and commanded a rare wit. He was an indispensable conversationalist in friendly company, very quickly got onto friendly terms with people and at the same time was an excellent fighting officer and a stern, demanding superior, not allowing personal relations to influence service matters. He was without doubt superior to Nepenin in his self-control, experience and knowledge and but for his illness and untimely death one would have expected for him a very brilliant military career.

In connection with the troubling situation in the Gulf of Riga at the beginning of April Admiral Essen decided to transfer his headquarters to Reval – closer to the theatre of fighting operations and to the soul of the Signals Intelligence Service – Nepenin. Essen went to Reval with the Staff in the cruiser *Rossiia*, where the *Krechet* already awaited us – the new Staff base hastily converted from the steamship *Polaris*. Before we succeeded in transferring to the *Krechet*, the Baltic Fleet suffered a most devastating blow – on the 8th of March, in a private hospital ashore, Admiral Essen died.

Long before the final illness, the continuous nervous strain, arising from the heavy responsibility to the Motherland, and unending travel on destroyers in all manner of weather, without even the most elementary conveniences, had undermined Essen's health. However, he would not listen to any reasoning by people close to him and continued to work as usual. Immediately after our transfer to Reval, he had undertaken a trip by automobile to one of the onshore positions while dressed very lightly despite the cold weather and sharp wind. On his return he took to his bed and, admitted the next day to hospital, he died of angina pectoris after five days, notwithstanding the efforts of the doctors – his heart gave out.

The loss to the fleet was irreplaceable: Essen had been unique. Everyone believed in him; the single consciousness, by which Essen led all, welded together the most varied elements of the fleet, held back the internecine frictions (unfortunately too frequent among Russian leaders) and impelled all personnel, from the least sailor up to the admirals, to work not from fear but from a sense of honour. Such popularity of Admiral Essen was not attributable exclusively to his extraordinary fighting talent. Also very significant without doubt was the charming character of his personality, his enormous life and service experience, and his glorious past. He had passed on, and there was no one to replace him. True, a whole constellation of excellent officers of his school remained after him – but among them, in conscience, there was not one who would have been sufficiently prepared for the hard and responsible role of Fleet Commander. From the death of Essen onwards dissipation of authority reigned in the fleet, as neither Kanin, nor Nepenin, nor any of the later Fleet Commanders of the revolutionary period, were in a position to draw together the reins of authority. Individual leaders continuously demonstrated unwarranted independence, often damaging to the general cause.

The whole fleet, as one man, wept for Admiral Essen.

For the time being, in accordance with regulations, command of the fleet was assumed by the Chief of the Staff, Vice Admiral Kerber. Over the course of several days persistent rumours circulated that Kerber would remain in the position of Fleet Commander, but on 10 May a telegram was received from the Stavka[43] (Headquarters of the Supreme Commander) appointing Vice Admiral Kanin as Fleet Commander, at the same time advancing him in seniority in order that he should not be subordinate to Kerber, who had been appointed vice admiral earlier than Kanin. It was said at the time that, although many even within the Stavka had looked on him as the natural successor to Essen, Kerber's German origins and a whole range of allegations against him had played the main role in the choice of Kanin. After Kerber, Kanin was the senior and indeed, perhaps, the more popular admiral in the fleet. One must recognise that Kerber did not enjoy the sympathy of the personnel mainly owing to his sharpness and above all his German ancestry. All the same, I personally considered that Kerber could have replaced Essen better than all others, since he knew all of his plans and with his distinctive energy would have succeeded in carrying them out.

Immediately after Kanin's commencement in his position, an order came from the Stavka for the creation of a Squadron of Battleships (that is, it was announced that the 1st and 2nd Battleship Brigades were to be united) and the nomination of Vice Admiral Kerber to the post of Chief of the Squadron. The head of the 1st Brigade of Battleships, Maksimov, was appointed Chief of Mine Defence. I do not recall by whom the plan for these transfers was worked out – in all probability all of this had been decided at the Stavka, where there was a very well-informed Naval Section (as I recall the head of this section was at this time Rear Admiral Neniukov[44]). It was obvious that Kerber had to be moved, since, firstly he had at one time been senior to Kanin, and secondly, the previous strained relations between Kerber and Kanin did not permit the possibility of their joint service in such close proximity.

The transfer of Maksimov also had its own foundations. Admiral Maksimov, the intrepid commander of the destroyer *Bezshumnyi*, had shown himself decidedly not up to higher responsibilities. A person of great self-opinion and pride, blunt and envious, he had always caused a mass of troubles for the Fleet Commander and was hated by everyone under his command. He was sharp and impatient, very erratic and wanted to change everything according to his own view, which was in the majority of circumstances impractical and often breached the core foundations of naval service. To argue with him or change his mind was quite out of the question, owing to his unbounded obstinacy. His appointment to the Mines Defence, a responsibility created artificially, was in effect understood by him (and correctly enough) to be an honourable retirement, which categorically embittered his easily offended and quite shallow nature, thereby providing fertile soil for his later revolutionary exploits.

By Kanin's choice the commander of the dreadnought *Gangut*, Captain 1st Rank N M Grigorov,[45] was appointed to the post of Chief of the Staff and promoted to rear admiral by the same order. An excellent officer, educated and with substantial experience, Grigorov unfortunately had one major deficiency – he was a terrible slowcoach. Not that he was slow on the uptake – he was without argument a person with a brilliant mind but, thanks to either nature or established habit (in truth, thanks to both together) he was unable to make decisions without having thought through, indeed mulled over, every aspect of every detail. In quiet office-like conditions of work, such a system might well have been desirable, but in feverish battle conditions it represented a real danger. The whole success of affairs usually depended on rapid decisions, and delay in decision-making often became the source of complete failure, not to mention that such tardiness produced a very negative impression on subordinates ('the chief is indecisive – it means that he does not know what to do'). It was particularly difficult to get used to Grigorov after Essen and Kerber, who were distinguished by their capacity to make decisions with lightning rapidity and, in the majority of cases, successfully. Unfortunately, Kanin also did not stand out for his bravery in making decisions, so that with the death of Essen the character of the work of our Staff, and with it the activities of the fleet, changed at once in a fundamental manner. There were many conferences, discussions, mullings-over, and comparatively few actual operations. Some liveliness in the work of the Staff was engendered by Kolchak and Nepenin, who acted now with almost complete independence. Kanin related to them with almost complete trust and respect, as if to higher beings. Grigorov himself, although he tried to contain them within the bounds of the Staff regulations and subordinate to him, was usually too late and very often appeared to be in the position of a hen who has hatched ducklings.[46]

I will not set out here more about Kanin's characteristics, since there has already been mention of him at the appropriate time, and several of his yet to be disclosed traits will be revealed in the course of setting out further events.

At the time of the final days of the command of Admiral Essen, or in the first days of Kanin taking up his duties, there occurred a sad event for our fleet – the loss of the minelayer *Yenisei* to enemy submarine action.[47]

Yenisei was returning to Reval after laying mines somewhere in the region of Dagerort or at the entrance to the Gulf of Finland and had been sunk by the enemy boat not far from the Baltic Port. She had capsized and sunk within a few minutes without being able to launch her boats. Only one officer and nineteen crewmen were saved by fishing boats, which witnessed the end of the *Yenisei* from close by the shore. All other officers and about 200 of the crew perished. Many died while in the water, not able to withstand the extreme cold. The commander, Captain 1st Rank Prokhorov,[48] conducted himself heroically: he remained on the bridge to the very last moment, issuing commands in a calm voice and went to the bottom with his ship.*

By this time we had transferred onto our new staff ship – the mail steamer *Krechet*. Hankering after economy in personnel, the Staff mines officer Captain 2nd Rank Mirbakh was appointed commander of the *Krechet* and Staff Quartermaster Lieutenant Iankovich as executive officer. The conversion of the steamer had consisted only of joining together several passenger cabins to create accommodation for the Fleet Commander, the Chief of the Staff and the Fleet Engineer. In the remaining cabins they placed writing desks and shelves and removed the surplus bunks. The cabins were small, crowded and

* Author's note: An interesting and touching detail was told later by the survivors: when it was clear that the loss of the ship was inevitable, the commander sang the national anthem, which was soon taken up by the crew and fell silent only when the *Yenisei* had already finally sunk below the waters. And this less than two years before the revolution!

muggy. However, all the same, all the Staff and its establishment, not excluding the archives and the printing office, had now been brought together. In addition, a powerful radiotelegraph station was established on the *Krechet* as well as a direct line.

Through this summer, we travelled on the *Krechet* quite often from Reval to Helsinki and back and at both of these ports we had a permanent mooring: at Reval at the end of the shore mole, and in Helsinki by the special wharf alongside the coaling station in the naval port.

Over the first half of summer, all the big ships undertook a course of gunnery, with particular attention being paid to the dreadnoughts. Besides the course of shooting, general manoeuvres were conducted in which all the battleships and part of the cruisers participated. The manoeuvres took place in the region somewhat to the east of Reval and Helsinki and covered all possible combinations of battle in the rear of the central mine barrier in the event of the German fleet breaking through into the Gulf of Finland. At the time of the manoeuvres the admiral with his campaign staff boarded the *Riurik*, which led the manoeuvres at the head of the whole fleet. It is not possible to call the manoeuvres successful: there seemed to be a complete absence of practice in the co-ordinated movements of the whole fleet. Neither Kanin nor Grigorov displayed any talent for fleet command, so the manoeuvres went on without enthusiasm, listlessly and indecisively. Of the separate parts of the fleet, the dreadnoughts manoeuvred the best of all, which one must attribute to the energy and managerial skills of Kerber and the excellent quality of the commanders (Pilkin, Baron Grevenitz, Bestuzhev-Riumin and Kedrov). Every precaution was taken during the manoeuvres against the event of enemy submarines appearing, since we already had verified intelligence of individual instances of these boats breaking through into the rear zone of the Gulf of Finland.

On 18–19 June our big ships began active operations against the enemy in the Baltic Sea. After the occupation of Windau[49] by the Germans on 5 June the threat to the Gulf of Riga became so serious that the Fleet Commander decided to make some sort of substantial demonstration in the rear of the Germans to draw their attention and forces away from the Gulf, in order to win time for the completion of the defensive works at its entrance. It was decided to shell Memel. The full complement of the 1st Brigade of Cruisers was chosen to carry out this operation. At the latitude of the island of Gotland, in misty foggy weather, the brigade quite unexpectedly ran into a German reconnaissance patrol consisting of the cruisers *Roon*, *Bremen*, *Augsburg* and the minelayer *Albatross*. Our ships soon opened fire. After a half-hour battle, during which light damage was received by both the Germans and our ships, the cruisers *Roon*, *Bremen* and *Augsburg* made use of some opportune fog and moved out of range of our fire, leaving to the chances of fate their weaker comrade the *Albatross*, which was completely shot through in short order by the fire of our ships and ran aground near Estergarn.[50] After this the *Riurik* lost the remainder of the cruisers in the fog and going in search of them again encountered the *Roon*, the *Bremen* and the *Augsburg*. As it transpired afterwards, not long before this our cruisers had also met the enemy, but declined battle, considering their forces unequal. The *Riurik* soon opened fire with her main armament on the *Roon*, straddling her with their first salvos. After a fifteen- to twenty-minute battle the *Roon*, evidently having received serious damage,[51] declined further fighting, managing to slip away in the fog to the south. Owing to the fog, the *Riurik* lost the possibility of pursuit. Soon after this our cruisers re-joined and the force set off to the north, since there remained insufficient ammunition either for new battles or for shelling Memel. In any event, one must acknowledge that the demonstration came off, although not quite as had been envisaged in the original plan. It is quite probable that the Germans, disturbed by our activity, had delayed their attack on the Gulf of Riga for some weeks.

Our cruisers were feted as heroes on their return to Reval, and actually there is no doubt that their actions were more than praiseworthy. Even while they might not have achieved complete victory, the fault lay not with our cruisers but with the foggy weather conditions that gave the enemy the opportunity of escaping complete destruction. All our ships had received damage, which, however, did not lose them a single day of battle readiness.

Making use of the temporary quietness on the Riga front after our cruiser engagement, the battleship *Slava* was transferred to the Gulf of Riga. The Irben straits had been swept beforehand, after which the *Slava*, covered by the dreadnoughts *Petropavlovsk* and *Gangut*, successfully completed her trip without meeting the enemy anywhere.

Chapter III

Fighting Activity and Life of the Fleet in the Second Half of 1915

First German attack on the Gulf of Riga · The lessons of this attack and new work for strengthening the defence of the Gulf · Subsequent events in the Gulf of Riga and the participation of Kolchak in them · Appointment of Kolchak to head the Destroyer Division · Actions of the larger ships · Overview of the organisation and activities of separate parts of the fleet.

At the end of July, finally, the Germans gathered in strength and attempted to force the Irben Straits. As already set out above, the entrance to the Gulf of Riga was protected almost exclusively by minefields, since our weak shore batteries could pose a danger only to minelayers and minesweepers. Besides about forty old destroyers, only the *Slava* and a few gunboats in Riga were at the disposal of the Chief of the Naval Defence of the Gulf, so to oppose the enemy's larger ships was in fact impossible. Consequently, any serious obstacle to the intrusion of the German fleet into the Gulf of Riga did not really exist and the consequences of this must have necessarily turned out to be enormous. Commanding the Gulf, the Germans would be free to land troops in the rear of our army's lines of defence and to place our right flank in a desperate position, resting as it did on the coast a little to the north of Windau. Therefore one can imagine the panic that arose in our Staff when, on 26 July, the worrying communication was received from Trukhachev that up to fifty enemy ships had appeared in view of Irben, and following that, that the enemy had begun minesweeping and shelling the region on the inner side of Irben, where the naval strength of the Gulf was concentrated, with the long-range weapons of their big ships. Instructions rained down on Trukhachev: 'Hold on no matter what happens', 'Do not permit minesweeping', 'Re-establish the minefields at night' and so on.

Troops (as I recall, a brigade of naval riflemen), stationed on the islands of Oesel and Moön,[1] were hurriedly brought up to fighting readiness. These troops, however, showed complete confusion, thanks to the failure in command and cowardice of the commander of the Brigade, Captain 1st Rank *F**** and the complete inaction of the commander of the position, Captain 1st Rank *Sh****.[2] Fortunately, the assistance of these troops was not required.

Over the course of several days Trukhachev struggled against the attacking enemy, hindering their minesweeping and re-sowing new minefields at night. But – might trumps right, and soon the enemy's big ships managed to get up to Irben, although suffering no small losses in minelayers and minesweepers sunk by mines or suffering from our artillery fire. From this moment the outcome for the Gulf of Riga was decided. Retreating with his ships, Trukhachev in the end made his way back to the southern part of Moön Sound, leaving only patrols in the Gulf itself. On 4 August, the minesweeping was finished and the enemy fleet entered the Gulf. Intelligence of this event produced a natural despondency both among our commanders and throughout the whole fleet. It was not difficult to understand what consequences this event could have: on the one hand, this might bring with it the destruction of the right flank of our army, the taking of Riga by the enemy and so on; on the other, it would now cost them little to take Moön Sound and all the islands and to lock up our fleet in the Gulf of Finland, behind the Central Mine Barrier, depriving it of the possibility of showing any sort of assistance to our army front.

However, even in the first days after the German breakthrough into the Gulf of Riga, something strange began to become apparent. Apart from the demonstration attack on Pernov* and the attempts to sink a steamer in the entrance to the harbour there, and the sinking by gun fire by three German cruisers of the gunboat *Sivuch*, as it was breaking through by night from Riga to Moön Sound, the Germans showed

* Author's note: This operation, quite insignificant and having a completely demonstrative character, was blown out of all proportion thanks to the fantastical report of the head of the local garrison, Colonel Pavel Vladimirovich Rodzianko (Master of the Horse, brother of the President of the State Duma).

no initiative and did not appear in sight of Moön Sound. Finally, an extensive reconnaissance undertaken over several days after the breakthrough on 8 August discovered **not a single** German warship in the Gulf of Riga. The telegram about this, received in our Staff, produced complete rejoicing.

What, however, had induced the Germans to withdraw? At that time everyone was puzzled, but even now I do not know the true reason for the withdrawal of the German fleet from the Gulf – I have not been able to familiarise myself with German writings on this period of the war, wherein doubtless some reasons would be put forward for this quite strange, not to say inconceivable, behaviour by the enemy. Rumours went around that one of the reasons had been that the Germans at the time of the breakthrough had lost too many ships sunk by our mines. According to another version, they said that the admiral, in breaking through into the Gulf of Riga, had exceeded his orders and for that reason had been sacked from his own fleet (preposterous, but typical of the Germans). But, for whatever reason, the Gulf was clear of Germans and our ships again took up their patrol duties by Irben.[3]

The approaches to Irben were immediately sown with a new mine barrier, which placed a decisive tombstone on the major German naval success, converting it to a defeat and giving us a victory. Trukhachev, although scarcely expecting this, was considered to be the hero of the day: he received the St George Cross according to the regulations and was promoted to rear admiral.

It is worth noting that a singularly shining affair, which wrote a most beautiful page in the history of our naval war with Germany in the Baltic Sea, occurred during the breakthrough of the Germans into the Gulf of Riga. The destroyer *Novik*, under the command of Captain 2nd Rank Mikhail Andreevich Berens, while on reconnaissance in foggy weather, unexpectedly met two large German destroyers of new build and engaged them in a gun battle. Despite the superiority of the enemy in guns (six 100mm guns against four),[4] the *Novik*, by means of agile manoeuvring and accurate fire during seventeen minutes of fighting, totally put out of commission one of the destroyers that, having lost the ability to steer, ran aground while heavily on fire. The second destroyer, also having taken heavy damage, made use of a smokescreen to save herself by fleeing. All the while the *Novik* took hardly any damage and successfully returned to her base. For this brave engagement Berens and the gunnery officer Lieutenant Fedotov both received St George Crosses, of which they were undoubtedly deserving.[5]

Over the period of the German attack, our losses, apart from the gunboat *Sivuch** lost in an unequal engagement with three enemy cruisers, had only included the gunboat *Koreetz*. This gunboat had left Riga at the same time as the *Sivuch*, successfully avoided the enemy ships busy attacking the *Sivuch*, but was reluctant to proceed to Moön Sound, presuming that the entrance had already been blockaded by the enemy. Judging their situation to be hopeless, the commander (Captain 2nd Rank Fediaevskii) decided to run the ship aground and destroy it, to prevent its capture by the enemy. This ill-considered decision, unfortunately, was carried out in shallow waters to the west of the entrance to Pernov inlet. After this the officers and crew made their way on foot to Kuivast. Later on all that could be salvaged was taken from the boat, but it was by then impossible to save the boat itself.

The ease with which the German fleet broke through into the Gulf of Riga demanded more serious attention to the defence of Irben. Most important of all was the widening of the mine barriers, to assist with which the sinking of several groups of barges and steamers laden with rocks was suggested, thus narrowing the channel and creating an obstacle to minesweeping. Then a project was prepared to mount a battery of four 12in guns at Tserell on the Svorb peninsula, with a firing range of 150 cables.[6] The guns had to be taken from batteries in the inner Gulf of Finland. In addition, it was decided to proceed immediately with the deepening to 28ft of the dredged channel between the northern and southern parts of Moön Sound, in order to be able to deploy the big ships into the Gulf of Riga.

By this means an actual, and not imaginary, defence of the Gulf of Riga was created. The projected batteries were to have a range

* Author's note: On the night of the breakthrough of the Germans into the Gulf of Riga, about 4 or 5 August, she went from Riga to Moön Sound and on the way was overtaken by three enemy light cruisers, which sank her by gunfire; from the mass of shells falling on her arose a range of fires from which, according to witnesses, her hull glowed red. The *Sivuch*, to the last moment, replied to the gunfire. Two officers and forty sailors were saved from her by the Germans. The commander of the boat was Captain 2nd Rank Cherkassov. (Pyotr Nilovich Cherkassov, 1882–1915. Naval College 1900. Gunnery Officer battleship *Sevastopol* Port Arthur 1904–05). www.navy.su/persons/25/pn_cherkasov.htm]

of fire exceeding that of the largest guns of the German fleet, that is, theoretically not a single enemy vessel could get through to the minesweeping zone in the approaches to Irben. A plan of defence was prepared to deal with the chance of an enemy breakthrough into the Gulf of Riga wholly within the waters of the Gulf relying on the big ships (*Slava*, *Tsesarevich*, the cruisers), ships of the Destroyer Division and submarines.

We immediately set about the work of bringing all these projects into being. The dredged channel was completed within a few months, so that even before winter, the cruiser *Admiral Makarov* was brought to Kuivast to support the *Slava*. The Germans did not hinder the work, since towards spring the centre of gravity of German attacks shifted to the south-western front and all was quiet in the Riga region.

The later autumn and winter of 1915–16 remain for me a pale memory. So far as I can recall, over this period no outstanding fighting events occurred in the Baltic Sea.

However, the initiative remained in our hands and the long-range reconnaissance and sowing of minefields along German shores undertaken from time to time by our minelayers and larger ships must have caused no small disquiet to our enemy.

In the Gulf of Riga, despite the quiet that had set in on the German side, our ships showed enhanced activity all the time, mainly by shelling the coastal positions of the German troops, which, at the same time as the attack on their front in the Gulf of Riga, moved forward along the shore almost to the hamlet of Shlok.[7] On 12 September the *Slava*, not for the first time while shelling these positions, suffered heavy losses: stray enemy shrapnel burst through the embrasure of the conning tower and exploded there, killing on the spot the ship's commander, Captain 1st Rank Viazemskii.[8] our Fleet Gunnery Officer, Lieutenant Commander Svinin[9] (seconded to Moön Sound to organise the shelling of the coast) and four sailors. Of those in the conning tower, only a single officer of the watch, Lieutenant Baksmut, miraculously survived. Everyone was very sorry about poor Svinin – such a fanatic for the war and his speciality, a deeply honourable and honest person, always giving himself wholeheartedly to whatever business he was pursuing.

After the death of Svinin, Captain 2nd Rank N I Ignatiev[10] was appointed to be Fleet Gunnery Officer. Having served until now in the gunnery section of the Main Shipbuilding Organisation and the Naval General Staff, he was a very capable and experienced gunnery officer, combining in himself extraordinary energy with serious technical knowledge and a rare tact in service matters. A lively and sharp-witted person, free of the slightest bureaucracy, he brought to our staff a fresh, bracing regime, which was quite welcome, since for the past year the brain of the fleet, led by the excessively placid and steady Kanin and Grigorov, had begun to be covered with a fine coating of mould.

On 4 September the Chief of the Destroyer Division, Rear Admiral Trukhachev, was taken ill (he had dislocated his arm, having stumbled and fallen on the gangway). Kolchak was temporarily appointed in his place and remained in this position through to Trukhachev's recovery – until 11 November.

Notwithstanding the temporary nature of his appointment, Kolchak managed to expend his ebullient energy in the most fruitful manner. He had been created for service on destroyers – he was in his element. Kolchak often told his friends that the crown of his ambitions had always been to receive the command of the Destroyer Division. He felt that there he would be in his place and he did not dream of more. His operational plans connected with the Destroyer Division were always unexpected, courageous and risky, but at the same time fortune always favoured him. However, it was not merely blind fortune, but his own brand of foresight, founded on the hunter's acuity of vision and habit of success. His lightning attacks on enemy transports in Swedish waters, attacks on enemy destroyers, the most courageous laying of mines under the noses of the Germans, all might well be compared with valiant cavalry charges or sallies. Finally, for a whole range of victories, which would have been difficult to bring within the scope of any particular regulation, Kolchak was awarded the Order of St George by Imperial rescript, without the involvement of the College of St George. Obviously, it would have been difficult to find an officer more deserving of this distinction.

During the period of his temporary command, Kolchak activated a plan that he had pondered over for a long time, for a landing in force behind the German left flank. Kanin, Nepenin and Grigorov had been against this operation, reasonably considering that, if it gave no substantial results, it could provoke a renewed attempt by the German fleet on the Gulf of Riga. But for Kolchak enforced inactivity was too much against his character and he insisted on his view. However, the leadership subsequently came to reduce the scale of the operation to the minimum and finally it became a modest adventure aimed at clearly demonstrating the possibility of such an operation in much greater strength.

The landing party consisted of two companies of naval riflemen, a squadron of dragoons and a party of sappers under the general command of Captain 2nd Rank P O Shishko,[11] commander of the destroyer *Engineer Mekhanik Dmitriev* The landing was carried out on Cape Domesnes[12] on the night of 8–9 October without any hindrance from the enemy, who displayed an unforgivable lack of vigilance. A platoon took the watch post at the Domesnes lighthouse and only after this there appeared two platoons of *landschturm* (in all about 150 men) who were supposed to be defending the surrounding coastline. Thanks to their complete ignorance of our landing, our troops were able to catch them unawares and after a short battle, as they say, we boxed their ears. The Germans lost one officer and forty-two men killed, with seven men taken prisoner, while our losses were limited to four severely wounded. However, immediately after the engagement, fearing the arrival of reinforcements, our units quickly re-embarked on the ships and successfully returned to Moön Sound. In this way, the adventure came off brilliantly and demonstrated that similar operations were quite possible. This did not, however, shake the obstinacy of the leadership, and such operations were not repeated right up to the end of the war.[13]

After this Kolchak busied himself with sea operations. At the beginning of November, he carried out a successful raid on Windau, where he destroyed the enemy patrol ship near the Spaun bank.

The big ships, that is, the dreadnoughts and the 1st Brigade of Cruisers, were also not idle over this period. In the course of the autumn and winter period, under the command of Kerber, Chief of the Squadron of Battleships, two very courageous operations were conducted in the southern part of the Baltic Sea, with the aim of laying mine barriers across the routes taken by German ships. The dreadnoughts *Petropavlovsk* and *Gangut* took part in the expeditions of 29 October and 22 November in the role of a covering detachment from the south. The 1st Brigade of Cruisers under the command of Admiral Bakhirev laid the mines (in the first expedition – the *Riurik*, *Makarov* and *Baian*; in the second the *Riurik*, *Makarov*, *Baian*, *Bogatyr* and *Oleg*). Both operations went quite successfully.

In December, Admiral Trukhachev experienced the first symptoms of the illness from which he subsequently died (in all probability cancer of the stomach). The conditions of service in the Destroyer Division gave him not the slightest possibility of systematic treatment, so the Fleet Commander decided to transfer him to a quieter post – on 23 December he was appointed Commander of the 1st Brigade of Cruisers. In connection with this appointment a whole range of changes were made in the higher command of the fleet. On the question of Trukhachev's successor there could be no argument: it was too obvious to everyone that this place belonged by right to Kolchak. Kolchak was replaced on the Staff by Captain 2nd Rank Prince M B Cherkasskii, who since the beginning of the war had been assistant to the Flag Captain of the Operations Section.

It was a rare appointment that was welcomed as wholeheartedly by the whole fleet and even in society (to be sure, naval society), as was the assignment of Kolchak to the Destroyer Division. And, one must admit, he fully bore out the high hopes that were held of him. Never had the destroyers worked so intensively and successfully as under him. It remains only to regret that he did not stay long at the head of his beloved child – the Destroyer Division, from which he was torn completely unexpectedly to take up the admittedly higher but undesired post of Commander of the Black Sea Fleet. But I will not run ahead.

The cycle of transfers began with the departure of Vice Admiral Kerber. The exit of this brilliant fighting admiral, who had the misfortune to be a Russian of German extraction, had been decided, admittedly, from the moment Admiral Kanin took up the post of Fleet Commander. Besides, it appears that this change did not happen without the knowledge of Kerber himself, and perhaps even came as a consequence of his personal request. As a matter of fact, his position in the fleet had been very difficult, because of the continual accusations about his Germanophilia and the hopelessness of any thoughts of further promotion, which severely wounded his pride. His departure appeared, to some extent, a way out of his predicament, giving him the possibility of expending his energies in new affairs (he was deputed to manage the overseas orders for the needs of the fleet). He left for London on service just before the revolution, where he remained until his death (it seems he died in 1919).[14]

In place of Kerber, Rear Admiral Bakhirev was nominated commander of the squadron, obviously being promoted to vice admiral at the same time. In all probability he would have preferred to have remained with the cruiser brigade, with which he had been intimately connected from the time of his commanding the cruiser *Riurik*, but unfortunately, they did not stand on ceremony with him. Bakhirev, one of the best fighting leaders of the older generation, was always the model of personal bravery, service honour and industriousness. Thanks to his modesty and lack of career ambition, during the war he had remained relatively in the shadows, which did not however hinder him from gaining great popularity in the fleet; popularity that did not waver even in times of revolution. People only thought of him when it was necessary to save an almost hopeless situation, as happened in Moön Sound in September 1917. Over the course of the whole war Bakhirev was President of the College of the St George Cross and St George Sword.[15]

Throughout these times the Germans continued to prosecute submarine warfare, holding under the threat of their boats not only the outer regions of the sea, but even internal waters, which had seemed sufficiently protected by our mine barriers. The submarines sent by the British Government to help us in view of the lack of preparedness of our own large boats also operated successfully.

These submarines, of which at the end of the war there were seven with us, had excellent crews and had made their way through the Sound,[16] where only one, the eighth, *E-13*, having run onto rocks in the Sound, was destroyed by German destroyers in (Danish) territorial waters. At first the commander of the whole Squadron was Lieutenant Commander Laurence, who was replaced in 1916 by Commander Cromie, subsequently villainously murdered by the Bolsheviks while defending the British Embassy in Petrograd.[17] These submarines damaged and sank several German warships. One of our officers who spoke English was stationed on each boat for communications. The boats were stationed at Reval, the old cruiser *Pamyat Azova*, renamed the *Dvina*, serving as their base.

Our big boats also gradually began to come into service but they either did not work well or their personnel were not of sufficiently high calibre. The latter, I may say, was the more likely. One must say that Admiral Levitskii (apparently, a fellow graduate of Essen) had already been head of the Submarine Service for a long time – an excellent technician but a quite weak and dull administrator. Thanks to his connivance, right up to the war, the Submarine Service had become a clique, that is, people gathered there who sooner pursued their personal interests and thought of their careers, being far from enthusiasts for or devotees of submarine affairs. From the beginning of the war Levitskii had been unable to renew his personnel and all these movers and shakers remained at the head of affairs, jealously guarding their clique from the intrusion of any new fresh elements. Certainly, there were good officers there, but there was no pathway for them. Several such officers perished in the first attacks by our boats. It was usual for our boats not to meet with the enemy, although they patrolled the very same regions where the English operated quite effectively. In the last days of Admiral Essen's command, Levitskii was appointed to oversee the construction of new submarines and Captain 1st Rank Podgurskii was appointed as head of the Submarine Division. One cannot call this appointment successful.

To all appearances Podgurskii was fully qualified for this position. He had been a submarine officer and was well acquainted with the technical side. Besides, his distinguished fighting past gave grounds for thinking that he would succeed in infusing a new spirit into the work of the boats. In fact things did not turn out that way. Weakened by illness as a consequence of the wounds he had suffered on 203 Metre Hill in Port Arthur, Podgurskii was already not in a condition to display his former energy, for which reason he quickly fell under the influence of those same people who, more than any, harmed active affairs. The operational plans of Podgurskii, which were hesitant, and scarcely consistent with the general situation, quickly aroused Nepenin, previously his great friend, against him. It was natural that, with the appointment of Nepenin to be Fleet Commander, Podgurskii was removed from the Submarine Service.

The work of the minesweepers, those who were genuinely modest, condemned to death, half doomed to perish, continued without a break, for not a single passage of a big ship, even from harbour, took place without their help. In addition, it was necessary to maintain clearance of all the strategic channels constantly, as the Germans used every opportunity to contaminate them with mines, both from submarines and, in all probability, from Ingrian–Finnish sailboats.[18]

One must pay justice to the Minesweeping Division that they fulfilled their work well and without a murmur. The commander of the Division, Captain 1st Rank Kitkin,[19] managed to inspire in his crews a true understanding of their wartime duty, and this was not easy if one takes into account the selection of these crews, the insufficiency of appropriate officers and the most onerous and dangerous conditions of work, devoid of any sort of external recognition for heroism. Kitkin did not have great capabilities as a fleet leader, and indeed, did not pretend to such. However, he was without doubt an expert in minesweeping matters and, what is very important – was an excellent and considerate manager. Admittedly, he was a most frequent visitor to our Staff, annoying them with all manner of requests about his crews and their rewards, but also with questions of supply, repairs and increase in the complement of ships. Only Nepenin could compete with him in obstinacy and persistence around various service demands, for which he was also considered to be a veritable tormentor of the Staff. Nepenin, in jest of course, called himself 'the infant Adrian, martyr to the Staff'.

As I have already set out, the Minesweeping Division had two Squadrons. The Division and the 1st Squadron were commanded by Kitkin, the 2nd Squadron, formed anew at the beginning of the war, by Captain 1st Rank Kovalevskii. The 1st Squadron consisted of medium minelayers of the *Tsiklon* type, and of genuine purpose-built sweepers. The 2nd Squadron in 1915 was composed exclusively of converted cargo steamers, requisitioned under martial law from all the ports of the Gulf of Finland.

However, despite the strengthened sweeping effort, at the beginning of autumn in 1915 yet another of our minelayers perished on a mine, and this the most substantial – the *Ladoga*. With the commander of the Squadron on board, (Rear Admiral Rein,[20] appointed to the position after the departure of Kanin) *Ladoga* had been sent to lay a minefield in the Baltic Sea to the south of the Åbo-Åland skerries, where the presence of German cruisers was expected. Having completed her task successfully, the *Ladoga* was returning via the strategic channel and at the very entrance, by the island of Ute, struck a mine. She sank quite slowly over about three hours so that the catastrophe turned out almost without sacrifice: only five sailors died, blown overboard at the time of the explosion. The commander of the *Ladoga* was Captain 1st Rank Krotkov.[21]

Over the course of 1915 serious hydrographical work had been completed on the establishment and sweeping of new strategic channels through the mined skerries: a direct route from Helsinki to the island of Åland,[22] with a whole row of exits to the sea, protected by batteries positioned on the islands. This work demanded participation of all the resources of the Hydrographical Office of the Baltic Sea and the Pilot and Lighthouse Organisation of Finland, and one must acknowledge that it had been executed brilliantly. Thanks to this new channel, all the big ships, including even the dreadnoughts, became able to move freely westwards to the island of Åland, without fear of attack from enemy submarines. Defects detected early in the testing of this channel, limited mainly to the sharpness and narrowness of the turns, which made the movement of big ships very troublesome, were corrected. After this the cruisers were able to travel along it at a speed of 16 knots. The channel was marked with two rows of specially designed spar-buoys with cross-pieces so that it had the appearance of a real corridor. Of course, the Germans found out about the existence of our channel very soon and undertook a series of attempts to sow it with mines in those places where there was access from the sea. However, stations of the Signals Intelligence Service positioned along the channel attentively followed the activities of the German submarines and their attempts were promptly rendered null and void by minesweeping.

The works contemplated even under Essen to establish and build new onshore batteries with significance for the fleet were activated at an accelerated pace. The main attention, apart from the Tserell battery, was directed to the strengthening of the island of Nargen and two major islands off the Finnish coast west of Helsinki. These batteries, which were to be supplied with major long-range artillery (up to 14in), were intended to provide support to the fleet in the event of an enemy breakthrough into the Gulf of Finland and a battle on the Central Position.

At the same time, the formation of our forward fortified positions – Åbo-Åland and Moön Sound – had almost been completed. The first of these, in essence, constituted the forward base of the fleet for operations in the Åbo-Åland skerries and the Gulf of Bothnia. Ships finding themselves in this region temporarily fell under the command of the Chief of the Position. Rear Admiral Richter[23] was appointed as first Chief of the Position and chose the town of Åbo as his residence. As enemy ships, apart from the rare submarine, were not found in the Gulf of Bothnia, this Position played no fighting role for the whole time of the war, not justifying at all the enormous financial expense that had been expended on its establishment.

The Moön Sound Position was of quite another character, since it had under its direction only onshore components – army troops, naval battalions and a series of batteries, positioned on the islands of Moön, Oesel and Dago.[24] Its principal significance lay in barring enemy landings on these islands, as a consequence of which the Position was operationally subordinate to the Chief of the Defence of the Gulf of Riga. After the first unsuccessful attempt of the Germans on the Gulf of Riga, the Chief of the Position, Captain 1st Rank *Sh****.[25] was relieved by the authorities for lack of action and Rear Admiral Sveshnikov[26] was appointed in his place.

In order to complete the overview of the naval formations in 1915, one must discuss the Air Fleet. This fleet, consisting at the start of the war of an insignificant number of pilots and seaplanes, was placed in the Signals Intelligence Service and had its main base in Reval. Its formation and recruitment of personnel had been delegated to one of the closest associates of Nepenin – Captain 2nd Rank Dudorov. This officer, outstanding in all aspects, was the first commander of the seaplane mother-ship – the mail steamer *Orlits* – and thus the first Chief of the Air Division. Under his leadership matters progressed very quickly so that by the end of 1915 the Air Fleet already had sufficient aircraft in good repair and enough well-trained pilots to succeed in maintaining an air patrol service over Moön Sound and the Gulf of Riga. The gallant flights of our seaplanes over the southern shores of the Gulf gave rise to not a few heroes – sailors turned pilots, who well justified the expense demanded for the organisation of that enterprise.

It remains to mention one undertaking of the Signals Intelligence Service that had serious significance for complete intelligence about activities of the enemy fleet. In an uninhabited forest location, on the shore between Baltic Port and Reval, the so-called Special Radio Station was established and excellently furnished. The main aim of its construction was the capture and decoding of all German radio signals. Into that fell all German signals taken by our stations wherever they were. At the head of the radio station was Captain 2nd Rank Przhilenskii,[27] while his closest associate was an official of the Ministry of Foreign Affairs, Fetterlein[28] – a specialist in all sorts of coding. According to the word of officers serving with him, the capacity of this person to crack any sort of code was simply astounding. There was no occasion where he, after several hours of completely solitary work, could not find the key to breaking an unknown code, however new or complex it might be. Several naval officers and officials fluent in the German language and experienced in coding work were assigned to help him. There was a strengthened guard squad to protect the station. The seclusion of the place had been chosen to guarantee the station from German spying and to create ideally quiet conditions for the work. All extracted intelligence was immediately sent by direct line to Nepenin.

Now it is necessary to mention the mood among the crews over this period, which is undoubtedly an important factor in the fighting life of any fleet. As a general rule, it must be considered that the best discipline and spirit was maintained in those parts of the fleet that were more often involved in engagements against the enemy, or had contact with them. The selection of commanders certainly played no less a role. But again, as a general rule, one must note that wherever the danger was constant, the commanders were better chosen. For this reason, without doubt, the Destroyer Division must in all justice be recognised as the first in spirit and mood of the crews over the course of the whole war, not excluding the revolutionary period. In second place was the 1st Brigade of Cruisers. Then followed the specialist squadrons (minelayers, submarines, minesweepers), where morale was supported by the continual danger and responsible work, despite the even more frequent interactions with onshore bases. And finally, in last place were the battleships and the 2nd Brigade of Cruisers. The battleships, particularly the dreadnoughts, had excellent personnel but despite this, the crews were quite hopeless, which one must attribute mainly to their extended periods of inactivity, absence of a fighting heritage and prolonged anchorage in major ports, where intense revolutionary propaganda was conducted, especially in Helsinki. Besides, the dreadnoughts still bore within them traces of industrial lack of discipline, always acquired by ships' crews in periods of construction and prolonged repair.[29] Worst of all was the 2nd Brigade of Cruisers, where, in addition to the reasons cited above for the lack of discipline among the crews, the absence of unit cohesion caused by the Brigade having only been brought together at the beginning of the war played a great role, which was compounded by an unfortunate choice of commanders.

With the end of the navigable season, as usual fighting life died down as the Squadrons and ships were distributed to winter stations according to previous arrangements. On our *Krechet* they set to work on new internal alterations for the creation of more suitable accommodation for the Fleet Commander and the reduction of general overcrowding. For this the whole ship was sent to the Sandvik Factory. The Campaign Staff temporarily transferred to the dreadnought *Sevastopol*, on which the flag of the Fleet Commander had been raised. The commander of the *Sevastopol* at this time was Captain 1st Rank L Ivanov,[30] appointed in place of Bestuzhev-Riumin, who had been taken on the strength of the Naval General Staff owing to illness. Kanin sent for his family and settled onshore in the house of the Port Commander. The quiet life set in.

Chapter IV

Fighting Activity and Life of the Fleet in the First Half of 1916

Mission to General Ruzskii · Purchase of ships from Japan · Opening of the navigation and renewal of fighting activity in the Gulf of Riga · Joint attack of the big ships and the destroyers on the Swedish coast · Preparation of a landing operation in the rear of the Germans · Maritime defence of the coast and Admiral Nepenin · Appointment of Kolchak to the Black Sea.

IN 1916 THE FIGHTING POWER of the Baltic Fleet reached full development. All the ships under construction, the onshore fortifications and establishments and, similarly, the preparation of all possible operational plans, either had been or were being completed. However, one must note that this was little to the credit of the Fleet Commander, Admiral Kanin. The general work of creating the capacity of the fleet was carried on independently of him, automatically – partly by the carrying out and development of old plans already established by Admiral Essen, partly by the initiative of individual commanders. Kanin himself only delayed decisions and the development of various plans, subjecting them to endless discussion and review. Neither his listless work in managing the fleet, lacking the slightest flashes of creativity, nor the absence of any sort of initiative and energy in deciding questions of a purely combat character, could in any way whatsoever engender new popularity for him in the fleet, in particular while the memory of Nikolai Ottovich von Essen remained for everyone. Kanin's undoubtedly worthy qualities – his common sense, service experience, technical knowledge and economic capacity – had sufficed for command of the Squadron of Minesweepers, but were quite inadequate for command of the whole fleet.

At the very best, people considered him a pleasant, affable conversationalist, a welcoming host and a skilful player at Russian whist and bridge, but alone these qualities, so valuable perhaps in peacetime life, could certainly not create the reputation of a good leader of the whole fleet during a time of war.[1] As an intelligent person, Kanin himself felt that his song had been sung, as a consequence of which he began to prepare the ground himself for honourable retirement. He continually complained of indisposition because of overwork and a tendency to apoplexy. His illness, evidently, was not entirely diplomatic – he was often actually ill from dizziness and even had fainting fits.

Relations with his immediate superior, the Commander-in-Chief of the Northern Front, General Ruzskii, to whom he was immediately subordinate in operational matters, and with Navy Minister Grigorovich, with whom he was closely connected on questions of technical armaments and supply, became more and more strained. Ruzskii was dissatisfied with the apparent inactivity of the fleet and the obscurity and brevity of Kanin's reports. Grigorovich also, having at first regarded Kanin with favour, began, evidently, to suspect him of playing a double game. In the end Kanin decided to get ahead of the game and, taking advantage of some minor disorders on the *Gangut* (which undoubtedly had their basis in revolutionary soil of German origin) and, connected with this, the refusal of the crew of the *Riurik* to provide an escort for the arrested sailors, sent a report on these incidents to General Ruzskii, joining with it a letter requesting release from his position on account of his shattered health. This took place, so far as I remember, in February.

The reports to Ruzskii's headquarters in Pskov were usually sent through the Naval General Staff via the ordinary courier. Now, however, in view of the importance of the matter, Kanin decided to send someone from the fleet Staff. At first he intended to send someone of relatively junior rank and only at the last minute, barely two hours before the departure of the train, his choice finally fell upon me. I was at home and already preparing to go to bed when the Chief of the Staff Grigorov urgently summoned me to the Staff by telephone. Arriving on the *Krechet*, I received the following instructions from Kanin himself: to go immediately to Petrograd and personally deliver the letter to the Navy Minister. After that I was to go to Pskov, present myself to

General Ruzskii and again personally deliver to him the letter and the report. I was also to report orally to the Commander-in-Chief about the events on the *Gangut* and the *Riurik*, describing their insignificance and attributing them to German propaganda, and about the measures taken to prevent the repetition of similar incidents; that is, the despatch of all the larger ships from Helsinki and Reval and their distribution to their battle bases, spread across less inhabited places (Lapvik, etc.). With that Kanin, demanding I maintain full confidentiality, informed me that in the letters to Ruzskii and Grigorovich he had asked for their help and petitioned for relief from his position owing to illness. At the end of the conversation, having repeated the extreme secrecy of the commission, Kanin said to me: 'If Ruzskii should ask you about my health, you must support me.' Seeing that the conversation was taking on an intimate character, I allowed myself to respond: 'Well now is the most inopportune time to change the command in chief of the fleet – just before the beginning of the spring fighting operations.' To this Kanin, as I recall, said nothing. After this I went to Grigorov, who, in saying goodbye to me, expressed concern over the untimeliness of Kanin's request.

Perturbed by these developments and the seriousness of the commission, I returned home to gather a few things together and head for the railway station as it was 10 o'clock and the train left at 12. Here an incident took place that I bring up now only because it demonstrates simultaneously the orderliness of municipal arrangements and the patriarchal character of those orders. I should point out that almost all houses in Helsinki locked their street doors at 9 in the evening, and in order to get into your home after this hour you had to have the key to the external door with you. If one had the misfortune not to have the key, entering the house by the normal means was impossible. There were not usually doorbells, and even if there were they would be connected to the doorkeeper, who by that hour would have gone home. Knocking at the double-glazed windows might awaken somebody or other, but no one living in the house. I found myself in exactly that situation as in hurrying out I had forgotten to take the key to the outer door with me. Having raised enough noise to arouse the whole street without having woken anyone inside the house, in the end I ventured about 200m to find a telephone kiosk and from there called home to get my wife to come and open the door for me. In five minutes I was at home.

Having arrived the next morning at Petrograd, I immediately went to Grigorovich. Having read the letter, he asked me whether its contents were known to me. Supposing that it raised Kanin's request to relinquish his post owing to illness, I answered in the affirmative. Then Grigorovich said: 'So then, is there a general wish among you that Gerasimov be appointed in place of Kanin?' Astonished by the unexpectedness of the question (among even the Staff no sort of discussion of the possibility of the appointment of Gerasimov[2] had occurred), I mumbled out something along the lines of: 'Admiral Gerasimov is hardly suitable for this position, since he is deficient in purely naval experience.' Then Grigorovich expressed his opinion that now was not the time to change the Fleet Commander and that he wondered whether the state of Kanin's health would permit him to remain in the position for several months more because the character of the German attacks had not yet been determined. After this he let me go, asking that I revisit him after my return from Ruzskii in order to take a letter to Kanin.

That very evening I left for Pskov, where I arrived the next morning. On Ruzskii's staff, accommodated in the building of the girls' gymnasium by the banks of the river, I found Captain 2nd Rank Altfater – the future Bolshevik admiral[3] and one of the main actors in the Brest-Litovsk treaty, showing himself to be a clear example of a very smart, sociable and quite unprincipled careerist. At that time in his words he was the most extreme monarchist, since so far as was known to me, the way to a most distinguished naval career had been mapped out for him by becoming an aide-de-camp to the Emperor. For any participation in actual combat engagements he always showed an innate aversion.

Altfater had always been amiable with me, I imagine in part because he counted on my assistance in the matter of progressing his ambitious plans: he knew that in my time I had been close to the Imperial Family. Although during the war absolutely nothing remained of this closeness, he evidently acted according to the proverb – 'don't spit in the well', etc. In addition, because of his then duties, it was generally beneficial for Altfater to maintain good relations with the Staff of the Fleet Commander.

He received me with open arms and first and foremost tried to get out of me the purpose of my journey. However, following Kanin's instructions, I immediately advised him that the purposes of my visit were a secret that I could only disclose to the Commander-in-Chief alone. It turned out that Ruzskii had only just recovered from a serious illness (apparently he had had pneumonia) and on the day of my arrival had only just got up from his bed. For the time being he would only receive the Chief of Staff, but they promised to report to him about me. During this time Altfater acquainted me with the position on the front. At midday, I was invited to dine at the common table, presided over by the Chief of Staff, General Bonch-Bruevich (also a future Bolshevik personage), who seated me, as an honoured guest, beside himself. The brevity of the conversation did not allow me to form a complete impression of him. However, from first impressions one felt that this was an intelligent, reserved and insincere person.

At 2 o'clock General Ruzskii received me. He lived in a small house almost opposite the Staff and occupied very modest accommodation. Despite weakness after his illness, he created an excellent impression on me. Lean, of short build, very fit and compact, with piercing, cold eyes and quiet confident manners – he expressed himself clearly, directly and categorically. One felt that to argue with him and get him to change his mind would be difficult. Having read the letter, he asked several questions about the disorder on the *Gangut*, to which he evidently attributed serious significance. Having listened to my explanations, he appeared to be satisfied with them and then asked me: 'Do you think that the state of Admiral Kanin's health will really not permit him to remain in the post of Fleet Commander?' I was ready for this question, and notwithstanding Kanin's request, I decided to act in the interests of the fleet rather than his, particularly when I knew from Grigorovich that Kanin intended Gerasimov to be his successor.

I had known Gerasimov for a long time since at the time of the siege of Port Arthur I had sailed with him in the same ship, the armoured cruiser *Pobeda*, and when towards the end of the siege he had been transferred ashore because of illness, I had taken his place as executive officer. After that I had spent twelve months with him as a prisoner of war in Japan and subsequently had often come across him in the period between the two wars. Like everyone, I considered Gerasimov a very talented and widely educated gunnery specialist, but at the same time, knowing his sharpness, unbalanced character, absence of tact and scant experience of running a fleet, I could certainly not bring myself to consider that he was suitable for the position of Fleet Commander. Come what may, he would have been worse than Kanin. I could not understand what had induced Kanin, an intelligent person, to recommend an admiral with such a reputation in place of himself. It seems more likely that Kanin, in putting forward such a candidate, was in effect pressing for the denial of his request to be relieved of his duties.

Having weighed all this up, I answered Ruzskii thus: 'I think that several weeks of full rest would be enough for the recovery of Admiral Kanin's health sufficiently for him to be able to continue in the position of Fleet Commander.' Ruzskii thought about it and then said: 'Let him rest, but now is not the time for change. I will write a letter to Admiral Kanin, which I ask you to take to him. Once you have the letter you may go back.' Then he dismissed me and Altfater, who had been present but silent during our conversation. In the subsequent discussion with me Altfater grumbled about the weakness and indecisiveness of Kanin, and finished thus: 'What do you think, wouldn't it be better to appoint Nepenin in his place?' Suspecting some sort of underhand trick on his part, I replied evasively. On the return journey I went again to Grigorovich, who also gave me a letter for Kanin. In it, as I later found out, Grigorovich had urged Kanin, as had Ruzskii, to refrain from his intention to leave the fleet at least until the autumn.

Kanin, having read both letters, did not express particular displeasure, indeed on the contrary he even appeared to be glad. This confirmed once and for all that his request for relief had been some sort of double game aimed at strengthening his shaken standing.

Not long before this, or soon after, by order of this same Kanin, I had another very interesting commission – to the Naval General Staff. Actually, for several months this Staff had been working on a plan for purchasing several ships from Japan and sending them to our north to secure the Murmansk coast and the entrance to the White Sea from the enemy. The Japanese eagerly agreed to sell us back our own former ships, captured during the Russo-Japanese War and, certainly, were using the occasion to try to extract as much money as they could. Not wishing to pay enormous sums for ships of quite dubious naval value, the General Staff had wavered and dragged out the negotiations.

We in the fleet were in no two minds about this venture. Clearly, our old ships, stripped by us at Port Arthur almost to complete destruction, then captured by the Japanese and superficially repaired by them not for fighting purposes but more as trophies, would be in such a condition that their full refit would double their cost and extend over years. As a consequence of this, one could say with certainty that use of this means to build a new squadron 'to terrorise the enemy' had such an extraordinarily small chance that it could hardly be hurried to completion by the end of the war. In such circumstances why would it be worth giving the Japanese huge sums of money? In our opinion certainly, it was not worth it. All the more so, as far as was known to us, as there was the possibility of buying quite new ships – the Argentine ones then being built in England.

The General Staff was at first, evidently, of the same opinion, but all was overturned when Captain 1st Rank Bestuzhev-Riumin joined it Not long before this he had gone on sick leave from the dreadnought *Sevastopol*, which he had commanded. An ambitious and energetic person, he was tormented by enforced inactivity at the rear. Occupying a temporary position on the General Staff, he had the opportunity to acquaint himself in detail about the business of the purchase of the ships and seized upon it, led above all, unfortunately, by personal ambition. It was necessary for him to achieve some sort of outstanding position in order to rehabilitate himself for his somewhat slippery departure from the *Sevastopol* and make it to rear admiral. A better opportunity, certainly, could not have been imagined.

He immediately pressured the Chief of the General Staff, Admiral Rusin, and, as a clever and amiable person, soon convinced him of the complete appropriateness and extreme necessity of this purchase. The matter was dealt with so subtly that in the end Rusin was convinced that this was his very own opinion and conviction. The affair was hastened at an increased tempo. The ships were designated: our old *Peresvet*, *Poltava* and *Variag*.[4] All the formalities with the Japanese were completed in lively fashion and the timing for the conduct of the ships to Vladivostok for the final handover was established. Bestuzhev was appointed chief of the new squadron, with promotion to rear admiral.

So next arose the question of manning of the new squadron. Higher up it had been decided that the crewing of one ship (the *Poltava*, renamed *Chesma*) would be drawn from the Black Sea Fleet, the other (*Peresvet*) from the Baltic and the third (*Variag*) from the Naval Guards establishment. To implement this decision, particularly in relation to the complement of officers, was extraordinarily difficult. One must not forget that, with the commissioning of a whole range of new ships, there was a deficiency of qualified officers for all fighting ships of as much as 20 per cent and there was definitely nowhere to draw upon to remedy this deficiency. Further withdrawal of officers from the warships of the Baltic Fleet would have led to the loss of a significant part of their combat capability. Taking this into account, and also accounting for the lack of merit in the Bestuzhev venture, the Fleet Commander had replied to the General Staff request to provide officers to crew the *Peresvet* with a categorical refusal. The Naval Ministry got all worked up and accused us of having a narrow outlook and not understanding the general endeavour, and so on. Bestuzhev himself came to our Staff and, having got nothing out of Kanin, dreamed up another way out: he offered to me the command of the *Peresvet*. The calculation was obvious: it would be difficult to suggest that the former Flag Captain Administration, on whom, in his time, depended all officer appointments, could not find officers for his own ship. However, even without looking into the detail of the matter, I categorically refused, as I did not see anything tempting for myself in the command of the crippled *Peresvet*, the fighting mission of which seemed more than dubious. It would be far more agreeable to me to receive a good ship in the Baltic, for which I already merited entitlement and waited only for the appropriate moment.

Following this, a conference was called on the same question in the Naval General Staff, to which Kanin was invited. However, fearing that as the discussion was to be held on the enemy's ground it might constrain him to give way, Kanin declined to attend on the excuse of some operation or other and sent me in his place, having instructed me not to make any concessions under any circumstances. The meeting took place at the Naval General Staff, where Rusin, Stetsenko (Chief of the Staff) and Bestuzhev participated. The admirals spent a good hour pressing upon me the need to meet them halfway on this important military undertaking, but my role was quite simple: to all of their arguments I was obliged to respond in Kanin's name with a categorical refusal, based on the deficit in our establishments and the hopeless military character of the enterprise. This last argument particularly offended Rusin, who could not contain himself and began to accuse me personally of being against the affair from some sort of consideration he could not understand. This made me boil with rage and I quite sharply replied that my personal opinion had nothing to do with it, as I was saying only what I had been authorised to say by the Fleet Commander, but that, certainly, I agreed with Kanin's opinion that he would give not a single officer to this hopeless venture. The discussion thus finished without a resolution. At the end of the conference I met Bestuzhev in the corridor and, still heated from the unpleasant conversation with Rusin, I rounded on him: 'I don't understand what the hell you want! Surely you've got from your venture all you were after – haven't they promoted you to admiral?'[5] Poor Bestuzhev, not expecting such a rebuke, was terribly offended and could only respond that he had not expected such a negative opinion of him from an old friend.

In the end they gathered the officers somehow, the ships were rearmed and victualled with great difficulty and at colossal expense and they set out on their way, arriving at their position (except for the *Peresvet*, which was sunk by a submarine[6]) after the ball was over, that is, at the very height of the revolution, not long before the Bolsheviks seized power.

To Bestuzhev's credit, one must add that he worked hard to secure supplies for his squadron along the way; in truth one might say that it was only thanks to his extraordinary energy and administrative capability that the greater part of his crippled squadron managed to make it to Murmansk. The insuperable task that he had taken upon himself so wore down Bestuzhev that he again fell ill from his old heart problems, from which he soon died.[7]

In January or February, the refurbishment of our *Krechet* was completed. Excellent accommodation was provided for the Fleet Commander on the upper deck, consisting of a large saloon/office, bedroom and bathroom. The Chief of the Staff moved over to the old accommodation of the Fleet Commander. Similarly, new cabins were built on the upper forward deck for the Flag Captains, by the extension of the space of the old cabin area over the forward hold, refitted to be more habitable accommodation. The cabins were very comfortable, with huge American desks, soft leather armchairs, couches and various cupboards and so on. The bunk with its washstand was made into a separate room by a wooden screen with curtain. My old cabin went to the Staff Navigator. After this refurbishment, the physical conditions of work on the Staff improved significantly.

With the beginning of spring the German offensive on the Northern Front was renewed. Fears about, and the real danger of, an attack on the Gulf of Riga arose again, since the Tserell 12in battery had not yet been completed. However, the German fleet did not show any activity, having evidently decided for the time being not to risk their big ships. As a measure of movement towards Riga, the enemy only put forward shore batteries (of not more than 6in calibre), which disturbed our patrol ships quite a bit. Several times during the development of the Germans' attack along the shore of the Gulf of Riga our big ships (*Slava*, *Makarov* and *Diana*) held up their advance by bombarding them.

German aircraft, in their turn, undertook continuous flights over Moön Sound, their main aim being to inflict damage on our big ships. One of the first of these flights on 13 April was successful. The German pilot succeeded in dropping bombs on *Slava* herself, with two falling on the aft deck, above the wardroom. There was no material damage, but unfortunately five sailors were killed by the explosion.

From the very beginning of the German attacks on Riga, the destroyers, led by Kolchak, increased their activity to the maximum. Shallow-water minefields were set in place along the coast already occupied by the enemy. These mines were sown by specially prepared shallow-draft minelayers, converted from river barges, with the aim of preventing the passage of smaller enemy transports and submarines along the coast. The German attack developed very slowly, which gave Kolchak and his Staff, composed of senior staff officer Lieutenant Fomin, staff navigator Lieutenant Boris Muromtsov,[8] and junior staff officer Midshipman Kholmskii, the opportunity to continue to invent cunning new ways to obstruct the enemy. Aerial reconnaissance and attacks by our seaplanes were similarly undertaken on a wide scale. Along with the work in the Gulf of Riga, in this spring period two quite large expeditions were undertaken in the waters of the Baltic Sea, in which the cruisers of the 1st and 2nd Brigades took place, as well as part of the Destroyer Division. Not long before them, information was received that along the Swedish coast, not far from Cape Landsort, there was a lively traffic of German commercial shipping convoyed by auxiliary cruisers and destroyers. It was decided to liquidate this traffic, for which a squadron was designated under the command of Admiral Trukhachev consisting of the cruisers *Riurik, Oleg* and *Bogatyr*, and three destroyers of the *Novik* class (*Novik, Pobeditel* and *Grom*), under the flag of Admiral Kolchak. Despite the very complicated conditions (proximity to the Swedish coast, darkness of the night, etc.) the expedition on 31 May went well: a convoy of steamers was completely destroyed, including five ships (two of them auxiliary cruisers) sunk. We suffered no loss.

The second expedition had quite a different character, although the objective was the same – the destruction of enemy transports along the Swedish coast. Admiral Kurosh[9] was appointed to lead the sortie, and under his command were two cruisers of his own brigade (*Gromoboi* and *Diana*) and part of the Destroyer Division (the *Novik* division and five coal-fired destroyers) under the command of Captain 1st Rank Vecheslov,[10] chief of the 1st Division. The destroyers, deployed at some distance from the cruisers, ran into a group of eight old enemy destroyers. Vecheslov, for some reason, did not engage them, although he had superiority in guns, but decided to draw them towards the cruisers. To this end, he accelerated to full speed and began to flee towards the cruisers, which were not yet visible to the enemy. The ruse, however, almost ended in catastrophe. The enemy destroyers, approaching the cruisers, fired torpedoes at them, after which, covering themselves with a smokescreen, they fled south. Fortunately the torpedoes went past the cruisers, which, for their part, opened the most energetic fire on the fleeing destroyers. There were no losses on our side – whether there was any damage to the enemy could not be established.

From the beginning of the navigable season and the German attacks, the Fleet Commander transferred to Reval, where in actual fact the whole operational part fell to Nepenin, working in the majority of cases in close contact with Kolchak.

Despite the lack of sympathy from Nepenin (which was discussed earlier), at this exact time, on Kolchak's initiative, planning was set in train within our Staff for a new landing operation in the rear of the German positions on the Gulf of Riga. The expeditionary force was to have been made up of naval infantry, for whom as commander a general from the Army General Staff, Gerua, was appointed, joining us from the Northern Front. Responsibility for the transports moving the troops was given to Captain 1st Rank L Ivanov (commander of the *Sevastopol*), who was appointed head of the Special Squadron of Transports. However, this expedition did not eventuate, owing to the departure of its initiator, Kolchak, and the appointment of Nepenin as Fleet Commander.

It appears that, as early as the autumn of 1915, with the establishment of the naval batteries (consisting of naval artillery and manned by naval ratings) at the Reval Fortress, a new position had been established – Commander of the Maritime Front Fortress. Nepenin had been appointed to this position, leaving the position of Chief of the Signals Intelligence Service. This new position was subordinate to the Fortress Commander and Nepenin, who had the most difficult relationship with Gerasimov, only agreed to occupy it because it brought promotion to rear admiral.[11] However, despite the ongoing friction with Gerasimov, Nepenin succeeded in achieving a great deal in this new position. This amazing fellow demonstrated an inexhaustible capacity for work.

One must note, that with all his efficiency and service exactitude, he was a most welcoming and hospitable host, charming his guests with his courtesy and quick wittedness. I repeatedly dined and spent evenings with him, of which I retain the most pleasant memories. Nepenin himself was no mean cook, so therefore the food to which he entertained us was always some sort of masterpiece. His usual guests, besides me, were Kolchak, Trukhachev, Podgurskii, P M Plen, Verderevskii, Krasheninnikov, and others. Adrian Ivanovich loved to show his guests a rare and especially valued gift – a silver decanter with glasses, made artistically in the form of the Tserell lighthouse. This decanter had been given to Nepenin by the officers of the Destroyer Division after the first German attack on the Gulf of Riga, in thanks for the accurate and always timely information about the movement of German ships supplied by the Signals Intelligence Service, which had materially assisted the Destroyer Division in liquidating this attack. One must add that the first news of the withdrawal of the German fleet from the Gulf of Riga was also provided by that same Signals Intelligence Service. It was natural that Nepenin took pride in this material proof of the flattering evaluation of his activities on the part of the best fighting section of the Baltic Fleet.

The Commandant of the Fortress, Vice Admiral Gerasimov, although subordinate to the Fleet Commander, rarely visited the *Krechet*. The reason for this was in part his wounded pride: to him, the most senior of the admirals of the Baltic Fleet, it was insulting to be subordinated to Kanin, who was younger than he. Besides that, he knew how much influence was carried among us by Nepenin – his personal enemy – and, as an intelligent person, he understood that he could not overcome this influence. Kanin, however, quite often went to see him.

At the beginning of summer discussions again began, coming from the Stavka Supreme Command, about the possibilities of changes in the high command of the fleet. They said that the commander of the Black Sea Fleet, Admiral Ebergard,[12] having shown himself from the very beginning of the war to be too cautious and indecisive, was very much out of favour at Stavka and that they had decided to replace him with a younger and more energetic admiral. About this time the naval section at Stavka was increased and two officers were appointed there to specialise in managing the two seas: the Baltic – Captain 2nd Rank Altfater, and the Black Sea – Captain 2nd Rank Bubnov.[13] So it turned out that these two relatively junior officers formed the Stavka opinion on naval matters, in particular on questions not directly related to operations. Both of them put forward their candidates for appointment to high rank, each for his relevant sea. Altfater had begun to propose Nepenin (one must remember his conversation with me at Pskov) and Bubnov – Kolchak. This raises the question – why did Altfater not settle on Kolchak, a person in any circumstances much more suitable for the position of Fleet Commander than Nepenin? The answer, it seems to me, is due to motives of a personal character. Kolchak, as the more genuine and sincere, had long ago worked out Altfater and did not feel sympathy towards him. In contrast, Nepenin, who was easily flattered, had warm relations with him. Bubnov too agreed to the candidacy of Kolchak, who got on well with him. Of candidates from the Black Sea itself who could have competed with Kolchak for popularity – evidently there were none. In this way began the rumours and discussions of the replacement of Ebergard and of the need for rejuvenation of the higher command.[14]

I am almost certain that Kolchak, until his appointment, knew nothing about it, and did not even imagine the cunningly scandalous intrigues being carried on at Stavka. Scarcely a few months had passed since he had received the appointment of which he had long dreamt, and it would have been natural to expect that they would leave him in peace at least until the closing of the navigation. If any thought of some sort of future service promotion had chanced to enter his head this would surely have concerned only the Baltic Fleet. It would have been far too inappropriate to expect that they would wrench an admiral, however outstanding, at the very height of the war, from a known situation and appoint him to a place quite strange to him, and even more so at a position of high command.

At the beginning of June, there was a sort of celebration with music and dances in the Reval Naval Club, situated in a marvellous historical park. Our small circle (Nepenin, Podgurskii and I) took the occasion to meet together in the Club, having also talked A V Kolchak into going there. He had just returned from the Gulf of Riga for some urgent matter at the Staff, since there was a temporary lull on the Riga Front. We were seated at table and chatting quietly when suddenly Kolchak's Flag lieutenant appeared and handed him a note. Kolchak read it and excused himself, explaining that the Fleet Commander had summoned him urgently. He also added: 'It's strange, seeing that I have just talked everything over with him.' He left for the *Krechet*, saying that he would return if it were not too late (he had to leave at dawn by destroyer for Moön Sound). After his departure, Nepenin soon turned up, having gone somewhere not long before. He informed us that a telegram received by the direct line from Stavka appointed Kolchak Commander of the Black Sea Fleet, with promotion to vice admiral. Kedrov[15] (commander of the *Gangut*) was appointed chief of the Destroyer Division, with promotion to rear admiral. We were all thunderstruck – that was how unexpected such an appointment was for all of us. After some time, Kolchak appeared and without any particular gladness in his voice, but on the contrary, rather gloomily, confirmed the accuracy of Nepenin's communication. Our congratulations to Kolchak, naturally, were more like condolences. In the conversation that followed Kolchak expressed the view that it was particularly difficult and painful for him to leave the Baltic at such a serious and responsible time when attacks were continuing on the Northern Front, all the more so in that his new command seemed to him quite foreign and very difficult in view of his complete unfamiliarity with the fighting conditions in the Black Sea.

In the unexpectedness of the appointment, those at Stavka had hit on a certainty: they knew that Kolchak was not the sort of person who during a time of war would refuse an appointment, however much it might not be his own desire.

The appointment of Kedrov did not call forth particular joy either: he was quite unpopular in the Destroyer Division. A very capable officer and excellent worker, he always strove with rare persistence for one aim: to make a brilliant career. Like all confirmed careerists, he was dry and the sooner ill-disposed in his relations with his own colleagues and subordinates. He possessed a strong will and persistence, but was not talented; his actions lacked creativity and inspiration. Besides that, he was relatively young, and his appointment stuck in the throats of many officers of the Destroyer Division, who were senior to him and more experienced and deserving.

On the following day, Kolchak and Kedrov went to Moön Sound for the handover of the Destroyer Division and briefing on the local situation. So after a few days we honoured Kolchak with a dinner at the Staff and then accompanied him to the railway station. He was going to Petrograd, from where he had to go to Stavka on his way to take up his new service post.

Not only the Destroyer Division but the whole fleet reacted to the departure of Kolchak with undisguised dejection. He had earned great and well deserved popularity and everyone understood that to replace him would be exceedingly difficult.

Chapter V

Fighting Activity and Life of the Fleet in the Second Half of 1916

Appointment to command Baian · *The trip to Moön Sound · Personal impressions · Appointment of Nepenin as Fleet Commander.*

Now I will turn a little to matters affecting me personally. I had been in the role of Flag Captain for a year and a half and was definitely feeling quite exhausted. The position demanded a fresh and fit person, and I, besides the exhaustion, had begun to notice in myself the appearance of dangerous signs of Staff bureaucracy and my own form of impatience. I understood that it was time to go, as otherwise the Staff ooze would finally suck me under. The justification was not hard to find – already many of my fellow graduates, even younger than I, commanded big ships to which I certainly held no less right than they. So, on one occasion, I expressed this to Grigorov (when Tyrkov[1] was appointed to the *Makarov*; Tyrkov, being in the reserve, was considerably junior to me). Grigorov paid full attention to my objection that already many junior to me commanded ships of the first rank. In general, it must be said, I maintained excellent relations with Grigorov. He had sometimes been hard with his punctuality and exactitude, but at the same time he was a reasonable, just and calm person, with whom it was very easy to work. Detecting the offence in my voice, Grigorov told me that in his opinion I had a complete entitlement to choose any vacant ship. 'In relation to which,' he said, 'Veis has been on the *Baian* for three years already – would you like to replace him?' I agreed with gladness, since I had dreamt of commanding one of the ships of the 1st Brigade of Cruisers – in spirit and in discipline the best part of the fleet after the Destroyer Division. Besides, at the head of the brigade was Trukhachev, my old friend, who had already hinted several times that he would be very glad if they appointed me to him. The matter was settled quicker than I had expected. My discussion with Grigorov had occurred at the beginning of July and already by the 20th the order came out appointing me commander of the *Baian* in place of Captain 1st Rank Veis,[2] who was appointed Chief of the Staff of the Mine Defence. He stayed in this position for a very short time and was soon appointed head of the newly formed Guard-ship Division, with promotion to rear admiral.

My new ship seemed to be in exemplary order. I took her over in Reval and immediately after this went on her to Helsinki, where the whole Brigade was temporarily gathering. The complement of officers on the *Baian* was excellent. Those who particularly stood out were the executive officer Captain 2nd Rank Katkov,[3] senior navigation officer Lieutenant Ukhov[4] (from the Destroyer Division) and the shipwright Lieutenant Trofimovskii. The spirit in the ward room and on the ship generally was excellent. After the unrelenting service on the Staff, I relaxed completely. The commander's accommodation was so generous that it was hardly conscionable for one person to occupy it. At my disposal was a huge saloon dining room with balcony, with comfortable furniture, carpets, and so on; with that came a study, sleeping quarters with a marvellous bed, and a washroom with a bath.

In fighting terms *Baian*, like all cruisers of her type, had many deficiencies, but thanks to the peculiar character of the present war, she appeared to be one of the more suitable ships for a range of operations of a local character – naval reconnaissance, shelling the coasts and even taking part in naval engagements. It particularly pleased me that my ship, thanks to these properties, would not be doomed, like other warships were, to the enforced wearing inactivity of the rear harbours, but would be all the time at work in forward positions.

To conn the ship was easy, as on a destroyer: two powerful engines, with well-rated screws, allowed for turning in the narrowest of places. Only on rare occasions, with unfavourable winds, were there any difficulties, as to bring the bow of the ship into the wind it was necessary first to go ahead. I could especially value this ease of conning a ship that was in reality quite large, since I had had a great deal to bear with over the course of three years managing the *Vernyi* with only one weak engine.

In the middle of August, I came for the first time to practise sailing in brigade formation. All our cruisers, under the command of Trukhachev, were sent to the Åbo-Åland skerries for familiarisation with their newly swept and marked strategic channels. Over the course of two weeks we went through all the skerries, going right up to the north-western exit from the Gulf of Bothnia. Despite the extraordinary navigational difficulties that we had to overcome, this voyage left me with an enchanting impression. The beauty of the Åbo-Åland skerries, quite unlike the Finnish ones, could be compared only with the Norwegian fjords. On the return journey we went to Åbo, after which we returned to Helsinki. Soon after this, I do not now remember for what reason, they sent me to Reval. Here my sole relaxation was the almost daily visit of A I Nepenin, who kept me abreast of the events around Riga, where, evidently, an attack was being prepared, and fed me tasty meals. Besides that, I visited Podgurskii several times. The Staff of his Division was accommodated on an old converted ship, *Pyotr Veliki*, which until the war had been in the Gunnery Squadron.

Soon I received a secret directive to be in a state of readiness for a voyage to Moön Sound and the Gulf of Riga, in connection with the German attack on Riga then in preparation. Indeed, soon after I received the order to proceed via Porkallaud[5] to Lapvik. There I found the Brigade of Battleships under the command of Bakhirev. I went to him, seeking further orders, but he replied that nothing was known to him; if indeed he received orders, he would immediately let me know. I decided then to use the free time to visit two of my acquaintances among the dreadnought commanders – Vladislavlev[6] and Zarubaev.[7] As I recall it, the next day, or at any rate very soon after, I received by radio the order to go with minesweepers to Moön Sound where I was to put myself at the disposal of Admiral Kedrov. For the whole trip a division of minesweepers, travelling at a speed of 12 knots, led the *Baian*. I was struck by how inappropriate this arrangement was: in my opinion and that of other commanders, in this channel the main danger came not so much from mines as from submarines that constantly showed themselves in the region. The speed of the minesweepers, even at 12 knots, hampered the ships' movements, creating ideal conditions for a submarine attack. However, strengthened watch on the horizon (with the help of special lookouts) revealed no sign of submarines whatsoever for the whole voyage and *Baian* successfully arrived at Moön Sound, meeting at the entrance still more minesweepers that trawled several mines (the Germans sowed mines at the entrance to Moön Sound almost every day). As we followed these new minesweepers at a speed of 6 knots, we had to survive several anxious moments: from Takhkona[8] they radioed that they had sighted an enemy submarine. The distance was about 15 miles and the whole question was whether or not she would succeed in catching up to us before we got beyond Vormsi to Moön Sound. However, we managed to slip through unharmed: either the sub was late or she had not been able to position herself for an attack. The dredged channel joining the northern part of Moön Sound with the southern was very narrow and twisting. We proceeded with two tugs, which helped the ship to go around the sharp turns.

While still on the way I received a radio signal from Kedrov with orders to go to Riga, not stopping in the roadstead at Kuivast. This direction indicated that something serious was going on around Riga. In fact, the final storming of the Shlok positions was in course, concluding on this day with their fall and the retreat of our troops to Riga itself. All our big ships had been gathered around Ust-Dvinsk[9] and gave strengthened support to the troops of our right flank, which however, could not prevent the fall of Shlok. This order put me in an inextricable situation: I had coal only sufficient to go to Ust-Dvinsk, but for the return journey nothing would remain. I advised Kedrov of this by radio, who in reply ordered me to take on coal urgently at Kuivast and to leave there in time to be at Ust-Dvinsk no later than 6am the following morning. I arrived at Kuivast at about 10pm in the evening and immediately the collier that, in accordance with my orders, I had summoned while on my way, came alongside through the destroyers, commanded by Captain 2nd Rank Selitrennikov.[10] However, I had scarcely begun to coal ship when we received a new signal from Kedrov that the trip had been cancelled – Shlok had been taken and the need for further assistance from the fleet appeared superfluous.

On the following day Kedrov returned and with him all the ships that had taken part in the defence of the right flank of our front.

Kedrov went straight to the north on a destroyer, so I did not get to see him on this occasion.

The big ships at this time in Moön Sound were: *Slava*, under the command of Captain 1st Rank V. V. Kovalevskii[11] (appointed after Viazemskii, killed by shrapnel from an enemy shell during the bombardment of coastal positions); *Admiral Makarov*, commander Captain 1st Rank Nikolai Dimitrievich Tyrkov; and *Diana*, commander Captain 1st Rank Modest Ivanov,[12] later famous for his wager on Bolshevism, earning him the general and wholehearted contempt of all decent personnel in the fleet.

The senior officer was Kovalevskii, to whom I soon presented myself. V Kovalevskii explained in detail to me the position in the Gulf of Riga, the character of the work of the big ships, arrangements for anchoring and so on. The big ships were subordinate to the Chief of the Destroyer Division in operational matters, but the senior of their commanders (in the present case Kovalevskii) exercised the authority of roadstead commodore in relation to these ships, without, however, raising the broad pennant. In the absence of the Chief of the Destroyer Division, the command passed to the senior Division Chief of the Destroyer Division, despite all of them being junior to Kovalevskii. This was justified on the grounds that the Division Chiefs, stationed on their destroyers near the Division base, the transport *Libava*, had to hand all operational information, while the big ships lay 4 miles away from Kuivast.

Kovalevskii suggested I go to the anchorage of the big ships, in a deepened inlet to the north of the island of Shildau, not far from the southern entrance to the channel. This place was considered safer from attack by enemy submarines, which could come from the Gulf of Riga into Moön Sound. Generally the possibility of the passage of German submarines into Moön Sound could be considered sufficiently challenging, since the breadth of the entrance was thickly sown with mines and protected by mined nets, and in addition was always guarded by gunboats and patrolling destroyers.

My two months' anchorage in Moön Sound was not marked by anything significant in a fighting sense. The Germans, having reached Riga, showed no activity of any sort beyond strengthening their new positions. No signs of an attack on Irben were noticed either. So for the time being there was no work for the big ships. There were only some flights of enemy planes – bombers, attempting to attack the big ships. Observed in time, the planes were met with strong firepower from the ships, but, in spite of this, they did not alter course and dropped their bombs on the ships. The fall and explosion of a bomb was sufficiently close to the *Baian* that if the crew had not been withdrawn behind the armour in a timely fashion, we could not have avoided losses. Small splinters were peppered over the whole deck; one substantial fragment penetrated the forecastle well above the waterline. On the bridge, wooden handrails were broken and in many places the canvas awnings holed. The anti-aircraft gunnery appeared to be a quite ineffective means of defence. Usually the firing was late, the shooting was exceptionally nervous and only by blind chance might they actually hit the plane. There remained only the moral impact – the close explosion of the shells, certainly, could not but affect the psychology of the pilots, especially the inexperienced ones. But a pilot who had experience under fire did not fear this gunnery. The guns on the *Baian* also suffered from a particular major deficiency: their angle of elevation was limited to 72 degrees, which required the cessation of firing quite some time before the moment when the plane began to drop its bombs. So the pilots had plenty of time to correct their alignment completely and fulfil their task almost without any hindrance at all.

The feelings of people on a large ship lying immobile (we were at anchor, without steam up), being attacked by enemy bombers, could be compared to the state of mind of a dueller, already having taken his shot and waiting on the shot of his opponent, who was calmly taking aim at him. The horror and awareness of complete helplessness overwhelmed people, and when the dark spot separated from the plane poised overhead, you could imagine that the bomb was flying straight at you. Fortunately, the Germans sent their bombers relatively rarely, more often limiting themselves to flights by harmless reconnaissance planes. One time a Zeppelin graced us with a visit, but thanks to the routine nature of the German practices (on the eve of a raid a whole squadron of reconnaissance planes would circle the anchorage points of the big ships), the air raids were anticipated and quite simple measures were taken: before evening the ships shifted their position by about a mile. Indeed, at night the noise of propellers could be heard and then a string of explosions near to those places where the big ships had lain on the previous day.

With the exception of these diversions, life on the big ships flowed along quite quietly and even boringly, particularly for the commanders, condemned to pass the time in complete isolation. The shore was far away, and even to go there was risky, as the ships were always at two to four hours state of readiness. The sole entertainment was the exchange of dinners with other commanders and the invitation to one's own table of the ship's officers. But having passed through the whole course in the sense of these latter invitations, I ceased such dinners, as I became aware how much they embarrassed the officers. After that there only remained reading, writing letters and aimless walking, like a beast in a cage, around one's enormous accommodation and on the quarterdeck. It seems only once did I succeed in luring a lively person as a guest – the commander of the *Kondratenko*, P. I. Krasheninnikov: for me this was a holiday.

Several days after my arrival in Moön Sound the *Makarov* went to Reval on leave, as she had been in Moön Sound for almost a whole year.

On the mainland coast, not far from the Paternoster lighthouse, the big ships had their own economic base, furnished by the *Slava* and the *Makarov*.

A small parcel of land had been leased (apparently from the property of Baron Buksgevden, permanently living in Berlin), where gardens and stables with both draft and saddle horses were constructed. By means of this base, various purchases of and orders for foodstuffs were made; they even bought live cattle. Something in the character of a modest wardroom was constructed in the small country cottage, where in winter time officers had the opportunity to relax from life on board. Even the families of some officers lived there. From the coast and Kuivast (on the Island of Moön) communication was maintained by special steam launches (tug steamers) and ships' boats. There was little interaction with the ships of the Destroyer Division standing at Kuivast itself, because of the 4-mile distance. The Destroyer Division at that time was not inactive. The securing of Irben, shelling of the coasts and sowing of mines continued with their former intensity, obliging the Germans to remain constantly on the alert.

The general mood of the officers and crews in Moön Sound, not excluding even our inactive ships, was everywhere more cheerful than at the rear. Awareness of the proximity of the enemy, the continuous engagements and operations of the destroyers, the air raids – all this created a special atmosphere of cheerful alertness, infecting even the big ships.

In September, receipt of the news of the appointment of Nepenin as Fleet Commander in place of Kanin, withdrawn to the State Council,[13] created something of a sensation. The Destroyer Division, in general, responded favourably to this appointment. A I Nepenin was popular among the destroyers owing to the assistance that he had constantly provided to the Division through his intelligence services and partly thanks to his friendship with Kolchak.

In this way, the work of Altfater was crowned with complete success, and Nepenin received that which he had so assiduously sought. Indeed, to this there had been no particular obstacle from the time when, as the main and, very likely, the only serious rival to Nepenin, A V Kolchak, had been sidelined.[14]

According to information coming to us, A I Nepenin's first steps were in the area of purely external discipline: with insistence and impatience, worthy of better application, he began to demand immaculate uniforms and saluting, severely punishing guilty officers and sailors alike. Such pedantry in questions that in time of war did not have particular significance, produced from the very beginning an unproductive impression on the personnel, and created for Nepenin not a few enemies among the junior officers and especially among the sailors. Even the older officers felt that a tightening up of truly demoralised personnel ought to begin not with saluting and standing to attention for the speeding automobile of the Commander, but with something deeper.[15]

Soon after his appointment, Nepenin came to Moön Sound, went with Kedrov to the Tserell battery, visited several ships (he did not come to me on the *Baian*) and then went back to the north. His inspection of the most forward position of our fleet first of all produced an excellent impression on personnel.

At the beginning of October, the *Baian* was ordered to return to Helsinki to join the brigade, which was due to go to the Åbo-Åland skerries for gunnery and manoeuvring practice. At this time in the skerries, right up to the island of Åland, a whole range of strategic channels had been swept, so that it was possible in the most western region of these skerries not only to move freely in any direction but even to carry out shooting and joint manoeuvre training.

Chapter VI

Continuation (The End of 1916)

Return to Helsinki · Nepenin's inspection · Voyage to Kronstadt and back · Transfer to winter at Reval.

On arrival in Helsinki I immediately fell in with a rapid succession of opinions and gossip concerning the behaviour of the new Fleet Commander. In general, there was little comforting to be heard. Everyone confirmed what had come to us in Moön Sound. Along with the, in most cases, quite rational military and managerial directions concerning our forward positions, individual parts of the fleet and shore establishments distributed along the whole coast of the Gulf of Finland, superficial ostentatious scrubbing and tightening up was going on everywhere. Adrian Ivanovich himself would go about the town in an automobile with the special aim of catching out inattentive and idle officers and sailors. A special staff officer patrol had been established for the town to oversee saluting. The atmosphere in the Staff itself, on the *Krechet*, was oppressive: the air whistled with almost uninterrupted dressings-down; staff officers were run off their feet trying to satisfy the new satrap. In the opinion of many of the more solid officers, Nepenin, drunk with power, had, as they say, taken the bit between his teeth, as a result of which a whole range of tactless actions had been taken, harmful above all to Nepenin himself. Frankly speaking, I had not expected anything of the sort from Nepenin, considering him to be above all an intelligent person. Until then I had always been a genuine supporter and admirer, and therefore could not help feeling within myself a certain disbelief in these stories, considering them exaggerated on account of personal offence. However, soon, from personal experience, I was forced to acknowledge how much they had been well justified.

I had lain at Helsinki with my cruiser for two or three weeks. They had warned me that Nepenin undertook an inspection of all ships newly arrived in Helsinki, during which he frightfully imitated the petty tyranny of Admiral Birilyov[1] of blessed memory, who, having previously donned white gloves, in the course of an inspection would descend to the machinery and engine room sections. If after a thorough inspection and groping into all the nooks and crannies, there was a mark on the gloves, the engineers would receive charges almost up to high treason and were very often dismissed from the service. I did not much fear this inspection, since my ship was undoubtedly in good order, having just come from Moön Sound, where one paid close attention to maintaining order in all sections at all times. Besides, so they had told me, these inspections were not done unexpectedly, but with a warning on the preceding day, so there would be time to prepare and put on a good show.

However, one fine morning, immediately after 8 am, having seen the smart launch of the Fleet Commander with its flag coming straight for me, I felt somewhat unsettled. There had been no warning of any sort, and my ship was decidedly not ready for inspection: ship's work was going on everywhere, as a consequence of which the crew was dressed in very dirty working clothes, the officers dressed in various garbs. Thanks to the quite short distance between the *Krechet* and the *Baian*, we hardly managed to gather together and parade the crew and officers. I met Nepenin (who I now met for the first time since I had dined in friendly fashion with him prior to my departure for Moön Sound) at the ship's gangway and reported to him, not offering the standard officer's report, since obviously there had not been sufficient time to prepare it. At the same time as greeting me, Nepenin immediately attacked me: 'Why is there no officer's report? Why are the crew not in uniform? Why is the ship not ready for inspection?' To this fusillade of questions, given in a quite sharp tone of voice, without any shadow of former affection and friendliness, I could only manage to respond: 'I did not receive any notice that there would be an inspection.' Nepenin again attacked: 'That's not true, that cannot be. Yesterday I ordered it semaphored to you.' I was somewhat worried by this, since it occurred to me that my signalmen might indeed have missed the semaphore. Nepenin went along the line of officers. I was so stunned and upset by

Nepenin's tone that when presenting the officers to him I missed some of their names. Having greeted the guard and the crew, Nepenin again attacked me: 'Why are the crew scattered all over the deck and not mustered on the quarter-deck as I ordered?' To this I replied that I had not received any such order. Then turning to the crew, Nepenin began to shout: 'The ship is in complete disorder! Filthy, an abomination' and so on in that spirit. I could not contain myself and interrupted Nepenin: 'Your Excellency, if the ship is in disorder, then the guilt for this lies not with the crew, who work excellently, but with me as commander, for which I request you address yourself to me.' Nepenin fell silent, obviously having understood that he had gone too far. After a significant pause, he turned to me and said fairly quietly: 'I cannot conduct an inspection while the ship is not prepared. I will order an investigation into who is responsible for this lack of preparedness.' Then, saying goodbye to no one, he went to the gangway and left.

My state after his departure cannot be described: both the feeling of deep offence from the severe accusation made against the ship and the innocent crew and officers, and the wounded pride of a senior, industrious, serviceman, who had never in all his service life received a single admonition, all this stirred up in my spirit such a storm that I had to retreat hurriedly to the cabin lest I commit some sort of stupidity. There I calmed down somewhat and thought through my situation. Come what may, after such an insult, such a coarse accusation, flung against me in the presence of the officers and crew by the Fleet Commander, I could no longer remain commander. So I decided to demand satisfaction from Nepenin for the insult inflicted, when the possibility presented itself, that is, after the war was over: I could see no other way out. I summoned the executive officer and ordered the launch prepared in order to go to the Brigade Commander, Captain 1st Rank Verderevskii, who, while commander of the cruiser *Bogatyr*, had temporarily replaced the fatally ill Trukhachev, who had been sent to the Caucasus for treatment.

Verderevskii already understood what had happened, as he had seen the Commander's launch pulling away from the *Baian* very quickly. Having come to Verderevskii, I agitatedly reported all that had taken place and in conclusion gave him my submission for relinquishment of my command, basing my request on the fact that after the Fleet

Commander had thrown such insulting accusations reflecting on the honour of the ship and my personal blame, in the presence of the crew and the officers, I could not remain as commander. Verderevskii, a great diplomat and friend of Nepenin, tried to calm me down, explaining it all as a misunderstanding. In the end however, at my insistence, he decided to go to Nepenin, taking my submission. I returned to my ship in the darkest mood.

The Executive Officer, having learned from me that I had put in a submission to relinquish my command, left and returning soon after, informed me that all the officers and petty officers, having learned of my submission about relinquishing command, had also decided to request transfer from the ship, as they considered that the Fleet Commander's accusation was completely undeserved and they wished to show solidarity with me. Not long after that, the boatswain appeared with a similar announcement from all the long servicemen. I asked them all to wait until the return of Verderevskii.

About 2 o'clock in the afternoon the Commander's launch again approached the *Baian*, but this time without the flag. A staff officer arrived, who handed me a letter on the envelope of which was written: 'To Sergei Nikolaevich Timirev from the Commander of the Baltic Fleet'. The intimate form of the address immediately indicated to me that Adrian Ivanovich was back-pedalling. The letter began thus: 'My dearest Sergei Nikolaevich, a most annoying misunderstanding has occurred, for which I offer you my sincere apology. The staff officer made a mess of it, for which I have had him placed under arrest. I hope that you will not reproach me and will forgive me for those sharp expressions which involuntarily burst from me and were completely undeserved both by you and by your ship. I beg you to take back your submission and to consider the incident settled.' Signed: 'Your friend A. Nepenin.'[2]

I read out this letter from 'my friend' (although I did not have his permission to do so), to the officers and the crew, during which I added that, taking into account that it was a time of war, I judged that we might be satisfied with this letter, all would remain in their posts and consider the incident resolved, but for the full rehabilitation of the ship, I would demand a new, most strict, inspection. This I also reported to Verderevskii, who promised to convey it to Nepenin. After a month this inspection took place in the skerries, and Nepenin carried out a serious inspection, penetrating meticulously into all nooks and crannies (the furnaces, the lower decks, the bilge and so on). The inspection, praise be to God, went off brilliantly and Nepenin was obliged to thank crew, officers and me on parade for the immaculate condition of the ship. After that the incident might well have been considered finally resolved.

I have deliberately described this, essentially trivial, episode in detail, as it sufficiently clearly paints Nepenin's unbalanced nature and lack of restraint in the role of Fleet Commander, which quite frequently caused similar mistakes and damaged only himself. As a result of this incident, Nepenin lost a friend and a great admirer, and also created ill-will in relation to himself across the whole of our Brigade.[3]

At the end of October our Brigade, under Verderevskii's command, went to the Åbo-Åland skerries for gunnery practice and manoeuvres. This very useful practical voyage continued for about three weeks. On returning to Helsinki in the middle of November, the *Riurik* (Captain 1st Rank Pyshnov[4]) and the *Baian* were ordered to prepare for the voyage to Kronstadt, for our programmed entry to the dock. It might appear that this trip well behind the lines did not represent any danger and any sort of special preparation for it would be quite unnecessary, but in practice it was not so. Mines laid by the enemy had already been discovered in various places in this region. How they had been laid was very difficult to decide. According to one theory, enemy submarines had from time to time broken through into the very deepest rear of the Gulf of Finland. According to another version (which I personally believed more likely), the mines were sown from Ingrian sailboats, either bought or hired by German agents, of which there were many in Finland, and from native Finns. The rumour about enemy submarines obliged ships to proceed without lights and to take the usual measures of protection. The existence of enemy mines also made it necessary to sweep all the usual routes. As another measure, they had begun to prepare a strategic channel through the skerries to Bjorke, but this work was not completed because of the revolution.

We left Helsinki in the evening as a whole squadron: at the head was the *Andrei Pervosvannyi* wearing the flag of Admiral Nebolsin, then the *Riurik* and last the *Baian*. We went along the usual shipping channel, expecting to reach the southern end of Gogland[5] about midnight. All of the guiding lighthouses were lit. I do not know what minesweeping had been done in the rear areas before our departure from Helsinki. In any case, we had been told that the way was clear of mines. Nevertheless, the most dangerous place, the narrows by the southern end of Gogland, had apparently not been swept, as it would be hard to suppose that the Germans would have been able to sow mines there immediately before our voyage. *Andrei Pervosvannyi*, at the head of the line, got through successfully, but the *Riurik*, following her, ran onto a mine, apparently hitting it directly with her stem, which in essence saved her. The catastrophe happened about midnight quite close to the southern end of Gogland. The natural turmoil created on the cruiser after the explosion prevented her from notifying *Andrei* and *Baian* immediately what had happened. Consequently, the former continued onwards and we, approaching closely towards *Riurik* and manoeuvring at the same time at low speed, in effect swept the whole suspect area with our hull. Finally, it became clear what was up. Fortunately, the *Riurik* had not received life-threatening damage. The water had entered only the foremost compartment, taking in about a thousand tons of water. However, the bulkhead held and the damage was limited to the cruiser being down at the bow by several feet. At the very slowest speed we proceeded to Lavensari Island, where we dropped anchor to examine the extent of the damage. Kronstadt was advised through Gogland of what had happened, with a request to send rescue and tug boats immediately. However, at dawn it became clear that *Riurik* was not taking more water and she could proceed independently. Raising anchor, we proceeded at slow speed to Kronstadt. On the way we met up with a mass of tugs sent from Kronstadt to help the *Riurik*, which in the end formed an impressive escort. On arrival at Kronstadt, *Riurik* immediately went into the Alekseev dry dock. The hole proved to be of colossal size, while its location showed how the cruiser had hit the mine with her stem, and the mine had immediately exploded. Had the mine been somewhat to the side, the damage received would have been much more serious and might even have been fatal for the cruiser. On the day after this catastrophe, the region around Gogland was swept and two more mines were found almost in the channel: it had been my good fortune that I had not run onto them while manoeuvring around the *Riurik*.

After several days, I was also taken into the dock and the regular dock repairs on the underside of the ship commenced. In this final pre-revolutionary period about the end of November 1916, Kronstadt produced on me the impression of a well-ordered and disciplined, if somewhat boring, town. Viren,[6] bearing the impressive title Principal Commander of the Rear – in effect was frustrated by inactivity, as a consequence of which he busied himself with particular fervour in putting things in order generally and tightening up discipline, all the while, unfortunately, using methods quite similar to those of Nepenin. In the first days of the revolution he came to pay cruelly for this when he was subjected to horrific torture and murdered.

According to long-established custom, I was obliged to pay a visit to Viren as the former commander of the first *Baian* – which had been at Port Arthur.[7] Viren was very courteous, but as always when meeting him, I could not refrain from a feeling of ill will, which had arisen long before. The matter arose at Port Arthur, during the surrender of the fortress. By demand of the Japanese, the garrison was led out of the fortress, like cattle, into a particular open field, where roll-call was carried out and from which parties for departure into prisoner of war camps were composed. Viren, being at the time of the surrender the Commander of the Fleet, ordered all naval crew and their officers to be dressed in uniform. In order to understand the short-sightedness of this order, one must understand that in the later period of the siege all medically fit naval crews had been onshore in front-line positions, as a consequence of which they were dressed in a great variety of ways.

When the crew of the armoured cruiser *Pobeda*, where I was the First Officer, marched past Viren (himself dressed up spick and span), he began abusing the sailors, almost all of whom wore sheepskin hats, without which, it must be said, it would have been impossible to withstand the winter in the trenches. I marched at the side of the column, supported by one of the officers. I had only that day, despite the objections of the doctor, discharged myself from the hospital, where I had been since my wounding on the Great Eagle's Nest.[8] I had discharged myself from hospital, not having fully recovered from contusions, with the specific aim of not being separated from my comrades, with whom I had decided to become a prisoner of war.[9] All of my clothing had been burnt off me when I was wounded, so I was clothed any old how: I was dressed in civvies, a greatcoat with a rip right down the back given to me by that fine Captain 1st Rank Sarnavskii,[10] and a soldier's sheepskin hat, which I had bought from some gunner for a rouble. Seeing me, Viren had completely exploded in rage: 'Shame on you! You, the commander of the crew – and how are you dressed? What sort of example are you setting for your subordinates?' A definite murmuring arose among the sailors, through which broke some distinct voices: 'It's you who should be ashamed, not him. Look, he's just out of hospital, wounded.' I could not make any reply owing to my physical weakness. Fortunately for Viren, the crew disappeared around a bend in the road. So this particular incident always stood before my eyes whenever I came to meet with Viren, although twelve years had passed since that time.

During our stay in Kronstadt an incident took place involving me and a particular doctor, which, unfortunately, ended unhappily for the latter. For some reason I experienced a severe problem with my eyes several days prior to our departure. On the advice of our ship's doctor, I went to see the manager of the eye section of the Naval Hospital, Doctor Zhoffrio, of which the latter was well advised beforehand. However, Zhoffrio would not see me, but suggested that I come back in general surgery hours in four days' time. I replied to the medical assistant, who conveyed the doctor's words to me, that by that time my ship would have already put to sea, and I added that I considered such behaviour by the doctor towards the sick in time of war to be inappropriate, about which I would make a report to the authorities. This I indeed did, thinking that the matter would be confined to a reprimand for this officious medico. However, Nepenin saw the matter otherwise: whether he wanted to show me some consideration, or he simply decided to use the opportunity to exercise power, after some time I received from the Staff a notification that the Fleet Commander, on the basis of my report, had ordered the dismissal from the service of Doctor Zhoffrio for inappropriate relations towards the sick during time of war.

Not long before my departure from Kronstadt at the beginning of December a new commander of the Brigade was appointed – Rear

Admiral Vladimir Konstantinovich Pilkin. Verderevskii, who had temporarily commanded the Brigade, received the Submarine Service, in place of Podgurskii, who Nepenin, already long holding a grudge against him, transferred to a less responsible position.* In all probability this appointment had been prepared by Verderevskii himself, although he asserted later that he would have preferred to have remained with the Brigade. It would be difficult to suggest that intelligent, adroit and cunning Verderevskii, finding himself in the best of relations with Nepenin, could not have arranged for himself such an appointment, which was more to his liking.

Vladimir Konstantinovich Pilkin was the most senior of the initial commanders of the dreadnoughts, but he was the last to receive promotion in the service. Such disregard by the higher authorities was above all a consequence of some of his personal qualities, which were not acceptable to the authorities. Pilkin was a person of very strict principles, without a shadow of sycophantism or fawning upon authority, never hesitating to express the whole truth, however distasteful that might be. Possessing a sharp mind and substantial education, he always had a leaning towards criticism and sarcasm, which also did not please the authorities. In addition, Pilkin was a great liberal and in the pre-revolutionary period attracted the reputation of being a red. Owing to the constitution of his nature, he may have been better as a public servant, from whom, however, could be formed an excellent social and political activist. Military service somehow did not suit him. Nevertheless, this did not hinder him from becoming an excellent commander and outstanding admiral. The distinguishing characteristic of his nature was internal rectitude – gentlemanliness in the best sense of the word – which is granted only to selected individuals who have had the opportunity of a good upbringing. Pilkin always kept aloof, not entering into friendships and not being closely connected with any of his colleagues in the service. It seems to me that this came in part from him being quite averse to that pally-ness that, unfortunately, was second nature to sailors, who were prone become best buddies after three tumblers of wine.

* Author's note: to be Chief of Security of the Marine region north of Åbo.

On arrival at Kronstadt, Pilkin raised his flag on the *Baian*. The presence of the admiral on my ship, which did not have special admiral's quarters, embarrassed me considerably. However, Pilkin did everything to ensure that I did not feel this embarrassment. He refused my accommodation, installing himself in the two adjoining free cabins across from my office and washroom. But we used the saloon together, as we did the bathroom and washroom. I had met Pilkin relatively little before this and only now, living with him side by side, could I appreciate how much he was an interesting, broadly educated and considerate person. We had endless discussions, completely losing track of time. His ability to discourse on any theme and always interestingly was staggering. He even infected me so much that it seemed that I had never talked so much in my life as in these months of joint life with Vladimir Konstantinovich Pilkin.

At the beginning of December *Baian*, in company with the *Sevastopol*, went to Helsinki under the general command of Pilkin. The entire route had been swept beforehand and, if I am not mistaken, enemy mines had been found in the region around Lavensari and Seskar. In any case, a new channel was chosen to Gogland, a southern one along the shoreline of the Narva inlet. This time we were escorted by destroyers and part of the way by minesweepers.

Soon after our arrival at Helsinki, the entire Brigade, except for the *Riurik*, which remained in dock at Kronstadt, went to winter station at Reval. Pilkin remained on the *Baian* as, according to him, he found it very pleasant there and consequently the cruiser was moored in the inner harbour, at the main quay itself. Ships turned to winter maintenance work. The commanders of the ships in the Brigade at this time were: on the *Riurik* – A M Pyshnov, on the *Oleg* – A S Polushkin,[11] on the *Makarov* – N D Tyrkov, on the *Bogatyr* – S D Koptev.[12] All the ships were located in the harbour, with the outermost position next to the breakwater left for the *Riurik*.

On my ship substantial alterations to the armament were carried out, which to a significant degree were attributable to the submissions of D N Verderevskii. An excellent gunnery officer and practitioner, Verderevskii, during his tenure as commander of the Brigade, had drawn attention to the fact that it would be easy on the *Baian* to strengthen the guns without diminishing her sailing qualities, and in this way to make her much more suitable for the shelling of German coastal positions, destroyers, minesweepers and so on. His project had been approved by Nepenin and with the onset of winter an additional 8in gun was installed on the upper deck, between the aft bridge and the engine room hatches, and four 6in guns on the upper deck in place of the 75mm weapons already there. The work was substantial, the more so because it was necessary to make additional below-deck strengthening and to adapt and convert the magazines and the ammunition hoists. I was generally very satisfied with how this work, as well as other repairs, were fulfilled by the Russian-Baltic factory.

Chapter VII

The Eve of the Revolution (Beginning of 1917)

Travel on leave · Impressions of Petrograd · First news of the revolutionary disturbances · The beginning of disorder · Danger on the front · My return to Reval.

IN THE MIDDLE OF JANUARY, Pilkin went to Kronstadt in order to bring the *Riurik,* her repairs having now been completed, personally through the ice from there to Reval. The voyage was particularly difficult as they met with very hard hummocked ice. The ice-breakers *Yermak* and *Mikhail Fyodorovich* accompanied the *Riurik.* This winter I decided to make use of the privilege, established apparently by Kanin, whereby all officers of the Active Fleet had the right to a three-week furlough during the winter period of the year when the ships could not put to sea. While I had been Flag Captain I had not considered myself entitled to take this leave, as on departing I would have had to turn over the work to an unprepared person, from which the quality of the work would have suffered severely.

My turn at furlough came up at the beginning of February. Together with my family, who had been based at Reval since the time of my appointment to the *Baian,* I decided to go first to Petrograd, and from there to our village in Novgorod guberniia to visit my mother and brother, who were living there permanently. To travel from Reval to Petrograd by railway turned out, however, to be impossible. All trains passing through Reval had begun their trip from the military front and were so overcrowded with people travelling on service, but mainly with those on leave and various refugees (inhabitants of the immediate front-line regions and deserters), that it was impossible even to think of boarding a train, particularly with a three-year-old child. But we were able to go via Helsinki, to which Nepenin conveyed us – he had come one day to Reval on the ice-breaker *Mikhail Fyodorovich* and I met him by chance ashore. So we accepted his proposal as we could not think of a better way out of our situation, although to be obligated to Nepenin was not very pleasant.

In Petrograd we stayed in our old apartment, in which a friend of my wife now lived, Princess Golitsyn, whose husband, a Nizhegorod dragoon, was at that time also on leave from the front. We had not seen the Golitsyns since the beginning of the war and time passed unnoticed with endless conversations and stories of impressions and experiences of the military life of the husbands and the ordeals of the wives. The Princess, a very intelligent woman who interested herself in politics and followed all that was going on in Russia, was the first to enlighten us about the details of the internal ferment that had crept over all classes of the population, to the very highest. The fabled influence of Rasputin on State fortunes and the ill-judged actions of Shturmer and Protopopov played the main role in these tales and were commented upon from all angles. All of these tales were news to me, since service on board ship and its minor daily interests had not given us the time to be interested in questions of internal politics.[1]

Only now, in Petrograd, having heard the tales of Princess Golitsyn and her acquaintances, and also having talked with friends at the Naval General Staff, did I understand how serious the situation had become. None of the elements of society, even on the far right, remained on the side of the Government, which was demonstrating a complete inability to understand the increasingly ominous developments and was persisting with its typical old bureaucratic measures, making no concessions whatever. The State Duma, to the opinion of which all Russia then attended, was in mood loyalist-revolutionary, if one can express it that way. Something had to be done – it was felt that, if not a revolution, then some sort of coup d'état was inevitable. And things were terrible at the front, where generally the situation at that moment was very difficult, what with the failures, retreats, the lack of munitions and of supplies generally, and so on. In those days, certainly, the extent of the approaching catastrophe never entered anyone's head, but fear of the future, I would suggest, had made itself felt among all servicemen who were in the slightest degree thoughtful.

However, despite this threatening atmosphere making itself felt in Petrograd more than anywhere else, the city continued to live an almost normal life. The lack of supplies was felt only by the lowest, poorest layers of the population, which in the end indeed served as a shock – the spark that ignited the general conflagration. The theatres, restaurants, cabarets and cinemas were open, attracting a mass of people on leave from the front and recovering wounded, and even more, all sorts of speculators, who had lived and continued to live at the expense of the national misfortune – the war. The Military Hotel, the former Astoria, where everything was cheaper and one might meet many acquaintances back from the front, was always packed.

Before the end of my leave, on about 15 February, I went to our village, from which I returned to Petrograd about ten days later.[2]

While still going from the railway station to our apartment, I became aware that something unusual was occurring on the streets. Crowds of soldiers and workers were everywhere, meetings of various sorts, processions with banners. The police were taking no action and very often were completely absent. At home they told me that the people had been aroused by a temporary hitch in the supply of bread, which the leaders of the revolutionary movement had decided to exploit. The situation was such that, if the Government did not take extreme measures, then within several days there would occur an explosion that could lead to God knows what. To clarify the situation, I went to the Naval General Staff, where, from my friend[3] and colleague Romanov,* I heard confirmed what they had told me at home, with the addition that the Government, seeing support nowhere, had completely lost its head and could hardly take any decisive measures, all the more so because the troops of the Petrograd garrison, the sole resource available to the Government, had been completely propagandised and would not act against the revolutionaries.

* (1961 Editor's footnote) Here memory has failed the author – someone else had informed him. Romanov was at this time on a business trip overseas, from which he returned only on 4 March. The author always visited Romanov when in Petrograd, so his mistake is understandable. [This note was possibly added by Romanov himself – he was a close friend of the Timirevs and appears to have maintained contact with them after the war. Through his position in the Naval General Staff he facilitated the intimate correspondence between A V Kolchak and Anna Timereva so it could bypass the censorship.]

Influenced by all of these talks, I decided on 25 February, not waiting on the completion of my leave on the 28th, to return immediately to Reval to be on my own ship, so as to be at my war station during such days. I was not worried about my family, as our apartment was in a quiet region.[4] When I went that very evening to the railway station, the streets were already in the full control of the mob. I succeeded in getting across Nevsky Prospect with extraordinary difficulty. The crowd moved in an uninterrupted stream in both directions and on sighting my automobile (I was travelling in a car from the Naval General Staff) gave forth various uncomplimentary shouts. On the train, as I now remember, I shared a compartment with the engineer-constructor of the Reval port, Colonel Iaron[5] and another naval officer, and I was involuntarily struck by how both of these officers, usually quite circumspect, directly condemned the Government when commenting on the events. Earlier it would have been impossible to have heard such speech in a social situation.

In Reval I found complete calm: here the wave of events had found no expression. That day I made a detailed report about the Petrograd events to Pilkin and Verderevskii, the senior naval commanders of the active fleet in Reval. Acting as cautiously as possible, it was decided to await information from Helsinki.

PART II

Chapter I
The Revolution

General outline · Bloody events in Kronstadt and Helsinki · Reval in the first days of revolution · Worker demonstrations.

As is well known, the Petrograd disturbances, gradually spreading, led to the formation of the Executive Committee of the State Duma, which, in view of the state of complete anarchy reigning in Petrograd, was forced on 28 February to take upon itself the functions of the governing authorities. This committee consisted of the following people: Rodzianko, Kerensky, Chkheidze, Miliukov, Karaulov, Konovalov, Nekrasov, Shidlovskii, Rzhevskii, Shulgin V. Lvov. In those same days the Council (Soviet) of Workers' and Soldiers' Deputies was formed, which in essence was the mainspring of the whole revolutionary movement and the further deepening of the revolution. As a matter of fact, from the very beginning of the revolutionary upheaval, power was in the hands of this Soviet, but its leaders did not consider it convenient for themselves (because of unpreparedness, as they afterwards asserted) to take official power into their hands immediately and agreed on a Coalition into which their own representatives – members of the State Duma – entered.

At the time of all these events the Tsar was at the Stavka in Mogilev. Forewarned of the threatening state of affairs by Rodzianko's telegrams, sent on 26 and 27 February, the Tsar, on the 27th, agreed to the formation of a responsible ministry, and telegrammed accordingly to Petrograd. The next day, 28 February, the Tsar himself set out for Tsarskoe Selo while at the same time the St George battalion, transferred to the command of General Adjutant N I Ivanov, was deployed to Petrograd to re-establish order in the capital. However, while still on his way, the Tsar found out that a new revolutionary power had been established in Petrograd by members of the State Duma, for which reason he decided to go to Pskov, to the Headquarters of the Commander-in-Chief of the Northern Front, General Adjutant Ruzskii, where he counted on obtaining full information about the events and support from the troops at the front. However, his latter hope was not realised as General Ruzskii stood firmly on the side of the revolutionaries and informed the Tsar in decidedly sharp terms that the Monarchy must surrender to the mercy of the victors. Then, having decided to sacrifice himself to save Russia, the Tsar abdicated the throne. On the evening of 2 March the act of abdication was conveyed to the deputies who had travelled from Petrograd (Guchkov and Schulgin). The Tsar abdicated for himself and for the Heir Apparent. On the following day word was received of the abdication of Grand Duke Mikhail Aleksandrovich, to whom the Tsar had in his act given the right of succession to the throne.

On 2 March, on receipt of the news of the abdication of the Tsar and the Heir Apparent, by means of local negotiations between members of the State Duma and the Soviet of Workers' and Soldiers' Deputies, the Provisional Government was formed, which came into its own from this day. Its composition was as follows: President of the Council of Ministers and Minister for Internal Affairs, Prince Lvov; Military and Naval Minister, Guchkov; Foreign Affairs, Miliukov; Trade and Industry, Konovalov; Finance, Tereshchenko; Justice, Kerensky; Agriculture, Shingarev; Transport, Nekrasov; Over-Procurator of the Holy Synod, V Lvov; National Education, Manuilov; and State Auditor, Godnev. From this moment the new governing power, 'invested with the trust of the whole nation', entered upon the projected revolutionary course that led the country directly to the horrors of anarchy and bolshevism.

Having described in general outline the main stages of the great bloodless (as it was then called) Russian revolution, which shattered a great empire and laid the foundations for a new time of troubles, I will now turn to describe those events that accompanied the achievement of the great bloodless revolution in the Baltic Fleet.

Events unfolded in particularly splendid bloom in three main locales – Kronstadt, Helsinki and Reval. By far the most fruitful ground for disorders had been prepared in Kronstadt. This was assisted by, first, its proximity to the revolutionary centre, the large collection of the worker element, propagandised in the spirit of the most extreme of the socialist parties, and the almost complete absence of disciplined forces. Along with that went the unpopularity of the Commander-in-Chief (Viren) and of many rear-echelon officers, with whom it was too tempting to settle accounts.

The events at Kronstadt had no connection at all with the course of the revolutionary movement in Petrograd. The first shock – the news of the overthrow of the old powers – was sufficient and Kronstadt fell into the hands of unruly mobs that, without covering themselves with a fig leaf of revolutionary slogans, set about murder and plunder. Even now it is hard to establish the details of the bloody Kronstadt events, since the greater part of the representatives of authority and order were killed in beastly fashion and the revolutionary activists subsequently hid and hushed up much of what happened. It is known only that almost all of the main superiors who were unable to hide were subjected first to humiliation and torture and then were killed. In this way perished Viren, Butakov (Chief of Staff), Rein (Chief of the Training Destroyer Squadron), Major General N I Storiskii (Commander of the Naval Depot), Captains 1st Rank K U Stepanov, Pekarskii, Povalshin (Commander of the *Aleksandr II*), Basov (Commander of the *Vernyi)*, Sokhachevskii, Lieutenant Commander Ivkov, Budkevich, Mikhail Viskovatov and many others. Those spared by chance were imprisoned. Then began the rule of the mob, the rule of the dregs of society, who by their own slogans were closer to the future Bolsheviks. This power at the beginning recognised no other authority – neither the Provisional Government nor the Soviet of Workers' and Soldiers' Deputies and only much later, not quite a month after the beginning of the revolution, succeeded in finding a way towards an agreement with them. Only then emerged the possibility of establishing the likeness of order in Kronstadt and to begin investigative work.

The following episode might serve as an illustration of affairs in Kronstadt at this time. About three weeks after the revolutionary overthrow, when everything on the fleet in Helsinki had settled down and almost normal work had commenced in the fleet Staff, a delegate from Kronstadt appeared on the *Krechet*. This delegate first and foremost astonished everyone by his appearance: he was dressed in an officer's double-breasted jacket, with admiral's shoulder boards sewn not on the shoulders but on the sleeves, wearing a cocked hat and an officer's sabre. He was terribly upset on finding out that the admirals and officers continued to manage the fleet and the sailors only exercised oversight through their committees. This delegate suggested that the local committee destroy or remove all officers and then take all ships into the hands of the crews, joining with Kronstadt. However, he found no sympathy from among the local committee, whose mood at that time was still quite sensible, and was obliged to return home with nothing for his pains, in a complete frazzle about the counter-revolutionary character of the Helsinki 'comrades'.

Events unfolding in the first days of the revolution in Helsinki, which also brought with them quite a few bloody sacrifices, had quite a different foundation from those at Kronstadt. One must remember that from the very beginning of the war, Helsinki had been the centre of German espionage and revolutionary wrecking aimed at weakening our fleet. Conditions were very suitable for such work: first, the foreign character of the city, with its population speaking a foreign language, in certain of its layers prone to Germanophilia, made the work of our counter-espionage very difficult. Secondly, the prolonged anchorage of our larger ships in Helsinki, with the frequent trips of the crews ashore, gave complete freedom for the circulation of the most extensive revolutionary propaganda among the crews. In this way there was no doubt that, long before the revolution, revolutionary cells had been formed on many of the big ships, only waiting for the signal for an uprising.

So far as I know, in the first days of the revolution Nepenin and his Staff conducted themselves completely correctly in relation to the crews. All news received from Petrograd was immediately conveyed to them. At that time, without doubt, a certain amount of confusion prevailed among the powers that be, which must explain the one admitted mistake: they did not organise discussions with the crews or explain the significance and meaning of events in such a way that could provide a serious counterweight to the German agitation from below. The impression was gained that the authorities were succumbing to the inevitable course of events, but did not sympathise with them. The disturbance of the crews, fed by the agitation driven from ashore, grew stronger with each day. There can be no doubt that the essence of this agitation could be summed up in the view that there could be no revolutionary overthrow without sacrifice, and that the old tsarist minions – all the officers – could not remain in place and that, at the very least, those officers who were objectionable to the crews, who now embodied the nation just come into power, had to be destroyed. In other words, into the mass of the crews was thrown the tempting slogan – 'time to settle personal accounts', to which there could not be any reply.

To the honour of the crews, it must be said, that far from all sympathised with this slogan, so strong remained the habit of order and discipline. The fact that only Admiral Nebolsin and several officers of the small ships were killed **by their own** crews serves as proof of this. The majority of the murders were carried out by some sort of special 'fighting' section (it was established without doubt that sailors from the 2nd Brigade of Cruisers were in it), which operated in the main on the destroyers, passing from one to the other along the shore. On the majority of the big ships, which had to be approached over the ice, these hired and volunteer murderers were not admitted. They say that these murderers had lists of condemned officers, on which mainly figured the best, more capable officers, which once again confirms the participation of the Germans in this dark and bloody affair.

However, up to 3 March on the surface order was still being preserved. On this day the news of the abdication of the Tsar and later, that of Grand Duke Mikhail Aleksandrovich was received. Perhaps this served as the shock from which the internal ferment, already noticeable for several days on the ships and ashore, took on a more organised and violent form. In the evening of this day the first meeting took place onshore, to which the ships' crews went armed. At this meeting it was decided to disarm the officers, which was done over the course of the night. On this very night occurred the first bloody uprisings on the *Andrei* and *Pavel*, during which Admiral Nebolsin and several officers were killed. General slaughter on these ships was averted only thanks to the quick-wittedness and firmness of the valiant commander of the *Andrei*, Captain 1st Rank Georgii Ottovich Gadd.[1] The night was passed on the ships in the utmost anxiety; the ships were in fact under the power of the sailors and the officers felt themselves to be wholly in their hands and without hope of help from anywhere. All through the night ominous red lamps shone from the truck of the mastheads – the signal for the murders, as it later turned out. At dawn the arsenal in the city was plundered and the mass killing of officers on the streets began, which by morning had spread to Skatudden,[2] where a whole raft of officers were killed on the destroyers and the other smaller ships made fast to the shore at Norra-Khamn and Sedra-Khamn.[3] On the big ships, praise God, the good sense of the crews prevailed and calm was not broken.

About midday the killing in the city quietened down, since the attention of the mob had been distracted by news that delegates of the new Provisional Government and the Soviet of Workers' and Soldiers' Deputies were coming from Petrograd. Everyone flooded into Railway Square, where in this way an improvised meeting was organised of several thousand people, armed from head to foot. Many officers were also there, although without arms, which had been taken from them during the night. Of the naval hierarchy, Admiral Maksimov took part in this meeting. This stupid ambitious individual, hating Admiral Nepenin, decided to make use of the present moment for personal ends. On the very morning of this day, with the help of demagogic discussions with sailors of his Staff in the Mines Defence, he achieved the election of himself to the position of Fleet Commander. Not long after this 'election', he went, in an automobile flying red flags, together with his sailors, the electors, to Nepenin on the *Krechet* and, notifying him of his election, demanded that he hand over the command. Nepenin categorically refused to satisfy his demand, responding that only the authority of the Provisional Government could remove him. After this Maksimov went to the Railway Square where, thanks to his red flags and quickly growing reputation as the red admiral, he was met with exultation. He promised to serve the revolution faithfully and truly, but in broken phrases, for Maksimov, despite his purely Russian surname, was of half-Finnish extraction and spoke Russian incorrectly with a strong accent.[4]

Then, in a whole string of speeches, various idle orators in sailor's uniform abused Nepenin. Some officers tried to respond, but their speeches were as a voice crying in the wilderness. In the end part of the mob separated and set off for Skatudden to the *Krechet*, with the aim of forcing Nepenin to come to the Square in order to give an account to the people. Nepenin, recognising the inescapable situation he was in, was forced to agree and set off on foot, accompanied by his flag officer, Lieutenant Commander Tirbakh. Not far from the exit from the port he was killed by a rifle shot, fired by some sailor whose identity could not subsequently be verified. The brutalised mob drove off Tirbakh and took away the admiral's corpse, which was found only after a whole day in the mortuary in a brutally disfigured state.[5] With the killing of Nepenin the cycle of murders in the city and on the ships came to an end.*

At 4 o'clock in the afternoon the train finally arrived with Rodichev (the new Minister for Finnish Affairs), Skobelev and two delegates from the Soviet of Workers' and Soldiers' Deputies in Petrograd. On leaving the railcar, they fell directly into the meeting. Received with exultation, Rodichev immediately made the most of the mood of the crowd, trying to calm it by the force of his fiery oratory. His words took effect and from this moment the excesses ceased.

Maksimov entered into command of the fleet without any authorisation but after several days was confirmed by the Provisional Government, which evidently had decided not to go against the people's election. From this moment began the revolutionary period in the life of the Baltic Fleet, in other words, the disintegration of the fleet began, finishing in less than a year with its complete moral destruction. It is difficult to say what brought about the disintegration more: the unbridled mass of sailors, demanding more and more rights, or the vulgar unjustified demagoguery of the leaders of the revolution and the authorities, of the type of Kerensky, Guchkov, Maksimov and others like them – their name is legion.

I turn now to Reval.

It may seem strange, but Reval, until the war a half-German city, had been almost untouched by German revolutionary propaganda. This may be explained by the fact that the native German population of the city and the region had, since the very first days of the war, been placed under control and, enduring all manner of pressure, had been

* Author's note: In all thirty-eight officers of the fleet were killed. Some estimates of officers murdered exceed 100. the exact number remains disputed: see K B Nazarenko [*Baltiiskii flot v revoliutsii 1917–1918* (*The Baltic Fleet in the revolution 1917–1918*), Iakor, Moscow, 2017, pp.181–183.]

forced to retire into themselves completely. The slightest Germanophile demonstration, not speaking even of espionage or any sort of propaganda, was suppressed in the strictest manner and punished by the Russian authorities, with the full support of the indigenous population of the region, the Estonians, who hated the Germans and regarded them as their oppressors, and so eagerly reported on them and generally assisted the Russians. The Estonians themselves, comprising the largest contingent of workers at the local factories, were undoubtedly very inclined towards revolutionary demonstrations, but by the essence of their nature were not very capable of carrying out any sort of agitation especially among the Russian crews, with whom they would have had difficulty communicating. Besides, the main body of naval personnel in Reval consisted of the 1st Brigade of Cruisers where the spirit and discipline, as I have already pointed out earlier, was very high. The crews of the Submarine Division, consisting entirely of specialists who received good financial rewards, were also little inclined towards any sort of revolutionary excesses. The marines were dispersed among the batteries and generally did not count for much.

Such was the local situation at Reval in the first days of the revolution. One had to consider this situation in general more well-founded in the sense of order than that in Helsinki, but all the same, taking into account the unpreparedness and confusion of the shore authorities, it was quite possible to expect excesses, albeit on the part of Estonian workers. However, in relation to the ships, all turned out well. The reason for this, above all, was the extremely sensible and timely actions of our two senior commanders, Pilkin and Verderevskii. Both of these admirals did not lose a moment, quickly got a grasp of events and were able to take into their own hands the matter of informing the crews of all that was going on and explaining the meaning of events. That both of them loved to talk and were able to do so well, helped them extraordinarily, so that it was completely unthinkable that any sort of half-baked agitator could compete with them.

The days of the bloody events in Helsinki and Kronstadt, 3 and 4 March, were also the most difficult days in Reval. On these days a crowd of thousands of workers from the various suburban factories and plants put on demonstrations through the city. Several times they came to the port and virtually laid siege to the ships lying closest to the town – the *Pyotr Veliki* and the *Baian*, moored side by side at the very beginning of the mole. The workers demanded that the sailors join with them and take part in the demonstrations. Our admirals, seeing that the demonstrations were beginning to take on an unruly character, convinced the sailors for a time to remain on the ships, under the main argument that with the departure of the sailors the ships would be without security and could be looted. This latter consideration, strange as it may seem, particularly influenced the sailors, and not a single person went ashore during these days. With the approach of the demonstrators towards the ships, a guard was posted at the gangway and no one from the crowd was permitted to come onboard.

The situation was risky because the crowd of workers stood on the sea wall literally ten paces from the ship's side and over several hours directed their speeches towards the sailors. Although the mood of the crews was very loyal, it could hardly be otherwise than that these speeches would produce a distinct impression. In these speeches the workers frequently referred to the officers, calling them bourgeois, tsarist lackeys, born with a silver spoon in their mouths, who had for too long sucked on our blood, and that it had now come to their turn for retribution. Several, the more radical-thinking type of worker, of whom very many were not quite sober, directly suggested throwing the officers overboard and taking the ship into their own hands.

The crews were permitted to respond, but they preferred to remain silent and only rarely gave brief replies, such as 'Our officers are not like that so there's no reason to throw them overboard' or 'Go away, stop bothering people, today is a working day for us' and so on. I remained above deck the whole time and one worker selected me as the target of his attacks and called forth general laughter by the following sally: 'Look, your captain is so pot-bellied he has obviously grown fat on the back of your hard work!' One must say that I was not exceptional – the worthy labourer himself happened to be twice as fat as I was.

On the *Pyotr Veliki*, which stood across the mole from us, these demonstrations did not go so well. Some wild shot into the crowd, fired by someone unidentified, almost served as the signal for blood-letting. The workers determined that this was officers firing and wanted to storm the ship to settle matters with all of them. However, thanks to Verderevskii's oratory, everything was smoothed over and the crowd was pacified. Over several hours the crowd gradually began to thin out and, in the end, dispersed completely.

After some days, with the permission of the authorities, demonstrations were organised by the ships themselves, during which the crews, in full order and dressed in uniform, with the flag of St Andrew at the head of each ship, marched with their own bands through all the main streets of the city but accompanied, unfortunately, by the usual red rags, for once the revolution had been recognised as legitimate, one could not but admit its emblem – the red flag. On the Square, where the chapel stood, a requiem was held for the victims of the revolution (make of that what you will!) and speeches were also made there. Among others, Pilkin and Verderevskii spoke.

In these first days of the revolution, the solidarity of the crews with the officers was greatly assisted by the fact that the greater part of the officers (I speak only of Reval) did not feel sorry for the old regime. The absence of excesses and insults, the maintenance of strict discipline and order gave every reason for thinking that the revolution would be limited to the establishment of powers standing closer to the people and answerable to the people, in which one could not see anything untoward. For myself personally it must be said that for the first couple of weeks after the revolution I also was of that opinion, although some sort of feeling whispered to me that one should expect some surprises yet: the transition had been too sharp from the old bridle to various freedoms for which our people were certainly not yet mature enough.

But such a mood of sympathy in relation to the revolution among the officers could certainly not survive long. The first demagogic steps of Guchkov in the area of naval discipline and order clearly showed that abyss towards which the people's power intended to drag us. This authority, consisting initially of serious and business-like people, turned out to be powerless to carry out anything without the orders of the clutch of socialist theoreticians sitting as the Soviet of Workers' and Soldiers' Deputies.

Of our naval leaders, Pilkin sincerely welcomed the revolution (understood as outlined by me above). In my opinion, Verderevskii only feigned acceptance, for by his nature he was too much of a monarchist.

In the city the first days of the revolution did not go as smoothly as on the ships. On the day of the worker demonstrations a mob of scum gathered at the city gaol and demanded the release of those allegedly incarcerated for political reasons, who were immured in a special casemate. The legend of these immured people had gone round the city long before the revolution. Not finding any such people, the mob began to sack the gaol. The Commandant of the Fortress, Vice Admiral Gerasimov, arrived and in quite a pacifying manner, began to exhort the crowd with the most liberal of expressions. Someone in the mob, evidently not hearing his words, whacked him on the head with a stick (or a rock – I really can't remember which) so that he was carried home in a dead faint. Later however, he completely recovered. In substance, the disorders were limited to these.

At first the rumours, and later the official news, of the bloody events at Kronstadt and Helsinki were taken by the crews as they were explained to them by the authorities: that is, as the irresponsible uprising of unruly villains, whose exploits planted a blot on the 'pure' dealings of the revolution. Only in relation to Nepenin did I happen to hear several quite unflattering comments on the part of the crew, who at this time did not hesitate to express their opinions of officers. Apparently the unpopularity of poor Nepenin had had time to form deep roots within the crews.

Chapter II

The Revolutionary Reforms

Initial experiences of revolutionary creativity: establishment of the committees, Order No. 1 · Persecution of the officers · The beginning of the downfall of the fleet: decline in discipline and general order · Elective command.

When the revolutionary tumult of the first days had passed, the new Government set to its creative work. The breaking up of the old order began, very often motivated only by the fact that this had been how it was under the Tsarist regime. In this manner, much that was good and sensible was done away with and replaced with premature novelties, in themselves lacking anything of real life and very often directly damaging. Unfortunately, this logic was applied most of all to military arrangements. First of all the committees of soldiers and sailors were established. The primary aim of their establishment was to transfer to them purely administrative functions – in the main, the complex matter of the victualling of crews, against which, in essence, it would be difficult to find anything to object, as it took from commanders and quartermasters only unnecessary work and responsibility. But quickly, partly without prior authorisation and partly by the directions of various Petrograd Soviets and Committees, the scope of competency of the ships' committees expanded extensively. All interactions by the command with the lower ranks had to proceed through these committees; the distribution of work, all manner of service orders, oversight of order and cleanliness, shore leave and furlough – all went into the hands of the committees. In the end, oversight of discipline and the right to impose penalties and to prosecute were also handed over. It is true that all resolutions of the ships' committees only went into force legally when confirmed by their commanders. But generally this right remained only on paper: in the majority of cases, when the commander for whatever reason did not confirm a decision, it was nevertheless implemented. To the command, that is, the officers, were left only specialist matters: the navigation of the ship and technical issues, in a word, that which demanded specialist knowledge and greater experience than the revolution could give in a few weeks to half-literate sailors.

The operational section, that is all that concerned the preparation and conduct of fighting operations, was similarly taken out of the scope of the committees, but very quickly they began to interfere even in this matter under the excuse of carrying out auditing and having lack of faith in the officers, who, under the cover of operations, might work against the revolution. The famous Order No. 1, composed by the revolutionary Senator Sokolov and confirmed by the demagogue Guchkov, granting the soldiers and sailors a mass of privileges and all civil and political rights, completed the annihilation of the rights of command. In fact, from this moment, that is, two months after the beginning of the revolution, everything necessary to destroy the fighting capacity of the fleet had already been done. For this it had been sufficient merely to fulfil accurately all the new instructions and the positions undertaken by the deepeners of the revolution, who in the best of circumstances were incapable of managing what they had created, and in the worst were working hand in hand with our enemy to weaken the fighting strength of the fleet.

Happily, at first affairs had not been quite so. On many ships (among them, on our brigade) the initial committees had been composed of sensible people, among whom had even been officers (on the *Baian* the President of the Committee was for a long time an officer), for which reason the reforms were introduced very carefully. In this way, on the surface things accorded with the new arrangements, while internally all went on as before, thanks to which discipline and order were preserved. This was helped by the fact that the crews on ships that had sailed and engaged in battles together a lot were very solid and had well-established trust for their officers and commanders. Such was not the case in those ships stationed to the rear, the battleships and the 2nd Brigade of Cruisers. There the crews had not had the opportunity to get to know their officers well, which is why implementation of the reforms went on without any compromises and the decline in order occurred at a far greater pace.

The committees were also given the right to settle all manner of misunderstandings between officers and the lower ranks. This led, on the ships where there had earlier been roughness between officers and crew, to the beginning of a complete Bacchanalia, on a legal basis, of challenges, that is, to the drafting out of officers from the ship, in the majority of instances on the basis of the settling of personal accounts. The reason for expulsion usually came down to one and the same thing: counter-revolution, a lack of sympathy towards the revolution, and so on. The authorities, even the highest, were powerless to combat this phenomenon, as the committees acted within their rights.

In this way the fleet lost within a few weeks a good quarter of its personnel, along with which the majority of those departing were among the best. In the first period of the revolution those who departed in one way or another included Grigorov (replaced as Chief of Staff by Cherkasskii); Bakhirev transferred to a sinecure – in the Mines Defence; Plen (Commander of the *Slava*); Pyshnov (Commander of the *Riurik*); Richter (Chief of the Åbo-Åland position); Liubimov (Commander of the Reval Port); Gerasimov (Commandant of the Reval Fortress); Liubinskii (his Chief of Staff); Kurosh and several tens of junior officers, of whom some were forced to leave or even to flee their ship under the threat of violence from their crews, even without any committee decision. One must recognise that some of these officers had indeed in the past been guilty of severe and coarse dealings with the crews. The following people were promoted from the very beginning of the revolutionary wave: Maksimov, whose personality I have already sufficiently characterised above; Zarubaev (to the post of Chief of the 1st Brigade of Battleships) – in his time a good officer but later pursuing careerism and making himself an ardent defender of the idea of subordination to any, even the Bolshevik, authority; Modest Ivanov (to the post of Chief of the 2nd Brigade of Cruisers) – an unprincipled, envious and malicious careerist, and several junior officers, almost all from the dregs of the fleet. Soon (three months from the beginning of the revolution), the atmosphere on the ships had become so intolerable for officers that it seemed that all would be ready to flee, although two circumstances held them back: for the best – the recognition of their duty to stay at their fighting post so long as the war with Germany had not finished, for the worst – the possibility of an easy career with the help of demagoguery and denunciations.

The old close solidarity of the officers with the crews on several ships in Reval, noted by me in the description of the first days of the revolution, evaporated like mist, giving place to suspicious distrustfulness and, very often, even mutual malice. The whole crew, starting from its most sensible elements and finishing with the most ardent deepeners of the revolution, clearly understood that the officers had been placed in such a difficult situation, insulting to their self-respect, that to expect sympathy towards the revolutionary reforms from them was inconceivable. The crews as a whole could not understand the genuine reason for the submissiveness to the new order of the majority of the best officers – that is, that they (the officers) considered themselves obliged to continue their fighting duty for the Motherland until the end of the war – and so they (the crews) continuously tormented them with suspicions of counter-revolution and so on. Only the recognition that things could not go on without the officers, that not one sailor could manage the complicated technical aspects of the ships, induced the crews to hold back from more coarse insults and direct violence.

Thus, from around about the beginning of May, all the officer corps of our fleet laboured to preserve the necessary fighting capacity of the ships in such unbearable conditions, feeling oneself on a volcano and working all the time under the most difficult burden of not having behind oneself almost any sort of real authority.

As I have already noted, our brigade found itself in relatively fortunate circumstances. For a long time, discipline and order prevailed among us from inertia, thanks to the established trust in the officers and the sensible actions of the committees.

In May the reforms in the fleet were completed with changes to the officers' uniforms. These reforms were carried out, in essence, without proper authorisation, and in a manner most insulting to officers. It began with several instances in Helsinki of shoulder boards being torn off officers ashore. The Fleet Commander, Maksimov, seeing in these hooligan activities the will of the people, like a true demagogue, immediately made concessions: an order was issued to all officers for them to remove their shoulder boards immediately. Certainly, things did not turn out without misunderstandings, since not everyone shared Maksimov's point of view. Among us, at Reval, there had been no excesses of any sort,[1] as a consequence of which the order for the removal of shoulder boards (without their replacement by anything whatever) could not be explained as anything other than yet another attempt to belittle officers. Our admirals, however, talked around those officers not wishing to fulfil this order (I was among their number), to make a concession again, since, in their words, 'this order has already gone out to the crews and to counteract it would without fail lead to excesses, which would result in complete disorganisation on the ships'. It was necessary to agree and to submit. The order about the new uniform (known as the Kerensky, although it had already been implemented under Guchkov), was only issued after about ten days, while we flaunted the uniform of couriers of the Naval Ministry – without shoulder boards and without any sign of rank whatsoever. Our crews reacted to this reform fairly indifferently. However, on the part of the older sailors, a certain unspoken bewilderment was felt – why had the officers so lightly and meekly renounced all of their privileges?

April, May and June were months when all manner of delegations and tourists (one cannot call them anything else) visited Reval: various famous people of the likes of Kerensky, the mother of the Russian revolution, Breshko-Breshkovskaia and others. These delegations were of the most varied tendency: there was the likes of the famous 'Batkin'[2] from the Black Sea, whose arrival one could only welcome, but the majority were the damaging deepeners, of the likes of the Kronstadters, with Raskolnikov at their head. Raskolnikov, later a very famous fanatic for Bolshevism, was then only beginning his revolutionary career and still stood for the continuation of the war, as the struggle of democracy against imperialism. Still quite a junior officer (a midshipman of the latest expedited graduation), he adhered to the revolution like a blind puppy, endowed, however, with unlimited ambition. His role in the fleet was extraordinarily damaging, since, repeating, like one obsessed, on every appropriate and inappropriate occasion, all the most extreme Bolshevist slogans, he impressed the crews as a real officer.

However, all these delegations, even those of the very best tendency, only had a disturbing effect on the life of the ships. The crews were agitated and constantly distracted from their immediate duties. Of the officers I need hardly speak: each such delegation caused them a mass of disquiet and worries. Firstly, by force of circumstances, we were obliged to debate with the delegates, who were all very often experienced windbags, while our brother officers, unfortunately, were completely unprepared for haranguing at meetings, and very often seemed in a laughable position that, to be sure, the opposing side exploited.

As commanding officer it fell to me personally to reply more often than others. For a certain time I maintained a system of ignoring purely political questions on the basis that 'we are naval people, and must do our fighting duties and not get entangled in politics', but later, when all politics particularly affected military people, especially in the fleet, such an excuse began to sound anachronistic and it became necessary to extricate oneself through other means. Subsequently, after the departure of the delegations, the sailors would turn to us, the officers, for the most varied of explanations, both political and purely military. In this one had to talk about the substance of the matter, which sometimes created insuperable difficulties.

The tourists also annoyed us considerably. The very first of them, members of the State Duma, officially sent by the new Government to explain to the crews the essential aims of the revolution and for the implementation of the necessary calming of the military masses, were more useful. These were in the main sensible people and not inclined towards deepening work. For the first two months of the revolution the State Duma was still popular among our crews and these delegates were heard with full attention. But with the radicalisation of the Government things became worse and worse. The last of such tourists during our time moored at Reval was 'himself' – Kerensky, at that time still Minister of Justice but already noted as playing first fiddle within the Government, by then wholly within the hands of the Soviet of Workers' and Soldiers' Deputies. Kerensky came to Reval (as I recall about the beginning of June), together with the famous grandma of the revolution, Breshko-Breshkovskaia. The latter having been left to meet with various town revolutionary committees, Kerensky decided to visit the ships.

I was warned of his visit not by the authorities but by some sort of onshore committee, which in recent times had romped around in huge numbers. Orders were given for a ceremonial reception for him, that is, the mounting of a guard and parading of the crew and so on. One must say that this was at the apogee of Kerensky's popularity when many even from right-wing sections of the public were enraptured with him, hysterical ladies and gentlemen of all persuasions adored him, as high-school girls adore their teachers and even the school porters. However, all of my preparations were without avail, since the old revolutionary Kerensky, wishing to avoid all ceremonial which could damage him in the eyes of the comrades, came to the ship in a cab with the top raised and was noticed by the officer of the watch only when he was already on the gangway. I rushed on deck and found Kerensky already on the mid-deck chatting with groups of sailors who happened to be there. I introduced myself and invited him to my cabin while we gathered the crew on the mess deck as it was raining. Kerensky followed me very reluctantly, repeating all the while: 'Certainly, only please not on parade, gather them just in a group like this.'

His wishes were fulfilled. Going into the midst of the crowd, among which I was present with my officers, Kerensky began a typical meeting speech with some hysterical cries, like a woman having a fit. At first everything went without significance: he spoke of the victory of the proletariat, of the need for collaborative work, of securing the front, of the need to continue the war to the complete defeat of world imperialism, personified by Germany, and so on. But he concluded in such a confronting way that there was no other course but for me and my officers to leave. Speaking of the officers, at first he advised taking care of them, as in his words, 'nothing will succeed in our complicated business without the officers'. But then he added: 'If you notice that your officers are not sympathetic towards the revolution and hanker after the old regime – sort things out with them without mercy!' You can imagine what an effect must have been produced by such advice from such a popular national leader, thrown into the heads of the sailor masses, inflamed and clouded by all manner of revolutionary rubbish! After this visit, in my eyes Kerensky once and for all lost any sort of fascination. Such a speech could not have been given by a government official (even one of revolutionary tendency, such as we until that moment had thought Kerensky to be) but only by a demagogue of the lowest school, lost in revolutionary thickets and reaping cheap laurels from success in packed meetings.

All the while as in Petrograd so in the regions, the work of devising various new reforms in the fleet by the various newly established committees continued at an increased tempo. It had scarcely begun but the unbridled imagination of various actors knew no restraint, which certainly very much aided the ease of bringing into being all these reforms that tended towards one end, the complete discrediting of the officers. Next in the queue came the question of elected command. Fortunately, this measure, which would have brought any concept of officer to nought, met with sufficient opposition even from among the sailors that it was not officially implemented. But informally it had already been adopted in many ships and even squadrons, in particular in those circumstances where it had been necessary to remove objectionable officers. And indeed what could be said against it, when the appointment of the very Commander of the Fleet, Maksimov, had in essence, been the confirmation of such an election. In practice, from this time onwards (from the month of July), any sort of responsible appointment on a ship, however significant or not, was made like this: at first enquiries were made as to whether the crew had anything against a candidate for appointment, and only then was the appointment made.

Chapter III

The Fighting Work of the Fleet after the Revolution

Battle readiness of the ships · Changes in the higher command of the fleet · The beginning of the German attack · The voyage of the Baian *to Moön Sound · The situation in the Gulf of Riga · The sailors' meetings · Lebedev's visit to the ship · The Kornilov attempt · Appointment of Razvozov as Commander of the Fleet.*

DESPITE ALL THESE REVOLUTIONARY obstacles, which had created almost unbearable conditions for the correct flow of service life, the ships had completed repairs, although with some delays, and had been brought to a relatively battle-ready state by the beginning of June. In our brigade, where internal order had been somewhat maintained, even all of the training and live-fire gunnery exercises had been carried out. This was particularly important for my ship, where over the winter, as I have already noted earlier, major work on strengthening the armament had been undertaken. One must yet note that in the matter of the maintenance of order in our brigade and more generally in Reval, the fact that the enemy front was comparatively very close played no small part and it was secret to no one that the Germans, sooner or later, must make use of the revolutionary demoralisation that had begun among our troops and in the fleet to mount an attack. Then Reval would very quickly come under direct threat.

From the very beginning of the revolution major changes occurred in the senior command of the fleet. I have already noted the departure of Grigorov, Kurosh, Gerasimov, Liubimov, the transfer of Bakhirev and the appointment of Zarubaev and Modest Ivanov (on the basis of elective authority). In addition, in place of the murdered Nebolsin, Patton was appointed Commander of the 2nd Brigade of Battleships,

Colonel Iaron as Commander of the Reval Port, and Major General Skvortsov as Commander of the Sveaborg Port in place of Major General Protopopov, murdered in the first days of the revolution. The Chief of the Destroyer Division, Kedrov, was appointed Assistant Naval Minister, so Razvozov received the Destroyer Division. Of all of these appointments it was possible to welcome only that of Razvozov – an outstanding officer with an excellent fighting record. One can only regret that this appointment occurred too late, when the revolutionary decline, which was beyond the power of the most talented leader to stop, had already begun. However, to the credit of Razvozov it must be said that he did everything in his power to delay and alleviate this process of demoralisation, thanks to which the Destroyer Division, to the very end of the war, to the Battle of Moön Sound, preserved its conbat capability in almost full measure. It helped Razvozov a lot that he had the gift of the gab, and in rhetorical disputations with various confirmed gasbags he almost always came out the victor.

Over the two months after the revolution Maksimov, overdoing it with the most desperate demagoguery and having shown no talent at all for leading the fleet, lost all authority not only in the eyes of Guchkov, but even among the comrades, who openly said that they had no need of a fool. Maksimov was recalled to Petrograd and in his place Verderevskii was appointed, distinguished by his skilful actions in the early days of the revolution and attracting the noted sympathy of the comrades by his ability to participate in meetings. Vladislavlev was appointed Chief of the Submarine Division, I do not know for what reason. He had never been a submariner and had generally not distinguished himself in recent times. One must conclude that a revolutionary qualification played some role in his appointment: Vladislavlev[1] was able to get along with and converse with the crews.

At the beginning of May, when life on the ships and in the city had, on the surface at least, begun to return to normal, my family arrived from Petrograd. Although the revolution had removed all the old order from the city, without replacing it with anything new, apart from countless committees (the Administration and the Government Commissar, in essence, had no authority), nevertheless some sort of order was maintained still by inertia, so that daily life went along relatively quietly: the shops were open, goods were sufficient and one did not yet hear of robberies or assaults. But the general mood was anxious, all were waiting for something to happen and were naturally in a nervous state. I was able to go ashore almost every day, but not for long, as on the ships in essence the ferment had not ceased and each hour might bring some sort of unexpected surprise. And the awareness that many eyes followed my every step, even ashore, spoiled any pleasure in time spent at home.

We were all under the yoke of disintegration and punishing conditions of life on the ships, the end of which could not be foreseen. There was no doubt whatever that our enemy vigilantly followed the course of the 'Great Russian Revolution', in the preparation of which he had taken not the least part, having ensured the arrival of the apostles of Bolshevism, Lenin and Co., in the sealed railway carriage. In the first months, however, he had not shown any sort of activity on the front. Evidently, the indubitable lifting of the spirits of the troops that accompanied the first days of the revolution had held him back somewhat. The Germans could reasonably wait things out, little doubting the inevitable final demoralisation of our troops. In this way, it was only in the month of June, when they had apparently received accurate intelligence about the growing influence of the committees and of the widespread decline in discipline, that they began active operations along the whole front.

Fearing for the fate of Reval and the capture of the approaches to Petrograd, the Commander-in-Chief of the Northern Front (General Cheremisov) requested the Fleet Commander to take all necessary measures to prevent the entry of enemy forces into the Gulf of Riga. It was clear that so long as the Gulf of Riga remained in our hands, the Germans could not begin an offensive along the edge of the Gulf of Finland. The general strategic situation in the Gulf of Riga was at that time more favourable for us. The 12in Tserell battery had, finally, been completed; the Destroyer Division and the big ships, moored at Kuivast, were in battle readiness and, comparatively, less affected by revolutionary decline. For these reasons, Fleet Commander Verderevskii, in reply to the request of the Commander-in-Chief, decided at least to strengthen the unit of big ships moored in Moön Sound by dispatching the *Baian*, whose armament had been specially strengthened for engagement with shore batteries, transports and minesweepers. The following battleships were stationed in Moön Sound at that time: *Slava*, *Tsesarevich* (renamed *Grazhdanin*[2]), and the cruiser *Admiral Makarov*. With the arrival of the *Baian*, the *Admiral Makarov* had to go on leave to Reval, but with the proviso that she was to remain in full readiness to return to Moön Sound at the first alarm. In addition, the battleship *Pavel* and the cruiser *Diana* stood as a reserve at Lapvik, ready to go to Moön Sound at the first demand.

On about 20 June Verderevskii came to Reval and personally visited me on my ship, directing me to proceed to Moön Sound within twenty-four hours, where I was to place myself at the disposal of the Chief of the Destroyer Division, Razvozov.

I went to the forward position with none of the joyful feelings of a year ago: revolutionary ruin had already so much undermined the organism of our fleet, strong up until then, that there could not be full trust even in one's own ship. Besides which it was clear that further revolutionary events, spontaneously erupting, would still bring many surprises capable of completely destroying our battle capability. However, one must note that in the first days after our departure from Reval the crew pulled themselves together significantly and any convening of meetings was temporarily halted. The sailors, especially the older ones, clearly understood that in the current military situation their personal good fortune wholly depended on the commanders and the officers who, for their part, could only work successfully in the presence of strict discipline. For the first time I gave attention to a phenomenon that I had not noticed before: all the sailors with whom I conversed on the voyage looked me in the eye with a particular expression of fawning humility. The explanation for this could only be that the issue of self-interest had dawned on them, which earlier would not have entered the head of anyone in the crew thanks to the existence of a generally healthy discipline. Now, deprived of this cohesion, and conscious that the officer corps had been undeservedly humiliated, the sailors trembled, feeling themselves wholly in the hands of these very officers.

The voyage from Lapvik to Moön Sound was undertaken according to the new system, without minesweepers, at 20 knots. Only convoying destroyers were with us, the forward pair of which followed a zigzag course. Such a method was certainly more rational, as the great speed gave a better guarantee from submarines, which on this voyage it was much more appropriate to fear than chance minefields.

At Moön Sound I anchored at Kuivast. Having visited Razvozov, flying his flag on the mail steamer *Libava*, and received the appropriate information about the situation at the front, I moved to the inlet to the north of Shildau, where *Slava*, *Grazhdanin* and *Makarov* stood. I visited all three of the ships and acquainted myself with their condition. Unfortunately, with the exception of *Makarov*, the impression was scarcely comforting. Everywhere the crews were young, by this time from the post-revolutionary call-up. On the *Makarov* (commander Captain 1st Rank Spolatbog) discipline could still be felt, preserved thanks to the old fighting mettle present in all ships of the 1st Brigade of Cruisers. On the *Grazhdanin* and especially the *Slava* (commanders Rudenskii and Antonov[3]), power wholly belonged to the committees, in whose hands the commander and the officers were mere pawns.

On the ships of the Destroyer Division, according to Razvozov, order and discipline were still maintained thanks to their constant active service, but it took only a week 'on relief' for the demoralisation of the crews to begin. This was assisted, in the main, by various visiting agitators and intercourse with the crews of the *Grazhdanin* and the *Slava* and the newly commissioned destroyers of the *Novik* type (in this the *Pobeditel* was particularly distinguished). Speaking frankly, I had counted on getting some relief at Moön Sound from the revolutionary chaos that we had experienced in Reval, but I was bitterly disappointed. There, in Reval, the crews had attended meetings mainly onshore, and, besides, there was always the possibility, even if only for a few hours each day, to escape from the unbearable shipboard atmosphere by being at home among one's closest people. Here we felt ourselves on the ships to be literally in the power of the comrades, who had very quickly become convinced that the battle situation in Moön Sound was for the time being not terrifying and who arranged meetings almost every day out of idleness.

I made an attempt to occupy the crew through lectures on general educational subjects. The officers eagerly rose to the occasion and took on the role of teachers of grammar, history, geography and mathematics. I took on the explanation to the crew of the varying events on our front and the Western Front. However, at the first lecture by an officer only two people came, and to the second – **not a single one**. So there for you is that thirst for knowledge of which so much had been spoken at the meetings! At the same time, the meetings at which various visiting gasbags expatiated on stereotypical revolutionary themes, the sense of which was unintelligible for nine-tenths of the crews, were attended by **all** of them. According to the older sailors with whom I often chatted, the reason for such an 'interest' in these meetings and the complete absenteeism from the officer lectures was completely understandable: anyone who so much as dared not to attend the meeting would immediately be accused of counter-revolution and, in the best of circumstances, subjected to a boycott on the part of the left-wing committeemen who were gathering power into their hands everywhere. And on the contrary, many wishing to go to the officer lectures feared to do so, fearing the same accusation of counter-revolution, since the understanding of 'officer' and 'counter-revolutionary' was at this time already becoming synonymous.

My lectures, or more simply brief summaries of the situation on the fronts, had great success, as the class-conscious comrades were all great cowards and were rather afraid of a German attack. Very often they themselves approached me with a request to explain to them one or other event at the front, concerned about the consequences for themselves. In such circumstances the crew gathered to the last man, not fearing any accusation of counter-revolution, for after all, the initiative for the gathering belonged to the comrades themselves. Recognising this, later I completely gave up calling them together myself and always awaited the call from their side.

In this way, languishing in enforced inactivity and bearing the whole time the upsets of events at the front and the progressive fermentation among the crews, we passed the whole of July. Various delegations and individual agitators came even here, but noticeably more rarely than in Reval. All these gentlemen were rather afraid of the proximity to the front and preferred to pursue their nefarious activities in the rear, in complete safety. The most outstanding event of this month was the visit to Moön Sound of the new Manager of the agitation section of the Naval Ministry, the personal friend of Kerensky – Lebedev.

As with many of Kerensky's closest collaborators, this gentleman had quite substantial qualifications as a revolutionary. In 1905 he had been serving as an officer in one of the foot regiments and took an active part in SR[4] revolutionary propaganda among the troops. After the suppression of the revolution he fled abroad, saving himself from being shot, and finally based himself in France, where he took upon himself the conduct of revolutionary agitation on any of our warships arriving at French ports. Thus, by his own account, he successfully agitated through 1906 and 1907 on ships of the Naval Cadet Squadron, which lay for quite a long time at Cherbourg and Toulon (at that time I was sailing on the *Tsesarevich*). From the beginning of the German war, however, Lebedev threw aside his revolutionary activity and as a former officer of the Russian Army joined the French forces as a volunteer. Evidently, he managed to distinguish himself, as by the time of the revolution he was again an officer and had a decoration for military merit. The revolution opened entry to Russia for him, where he was received with open arms by Kerensky and other party comrades. Not a stupid fellow, reasonably well educated and an experienced public speaker, he was used by Kerensky as a party agitator at the front in support of continuing the war.

After the unsuccessful attack on the south-western front in the month of June, Kerensky transferred him to serve in the fleet, where at that time Bolshevik undermining had begun to take on threatening proportions. In the role of Manager of the Naval Ministry, Lebedev was supposed to visit all the units of the Baltic Fleet, to clarify the mood of the crews and try to encourage them to maintain order and discipline with the aims of containing German imperialism and strengthening a united revolutionary front. By this time this task was already very difficult and the results, according to Lebedev himself, had been scarcely comforting.

The northern shore, that is, the fleet stationed in the ports of the Finnish coast, attended to his speeches closely. The crews there stood decidedly on the side of the Soviet of Workers' and Soldiers' Deputies and recognised only matters issuing from this Soviet. Any sort of government agitator, even though they might be left SRs, were accorded no trust and considered almost counter-revolutionaries. At Åbo, where the centre of our fleet Bolshevism was formed (the

2nd Brigade of Cruisers lay there with the trusty servant of the Bolsheviks, Modest Ivanov, at its head), they almost killed the poor old revolutionary activist Lebedev merely because he touched upon continuing the war to its end. Most comical of all was that Lebedev, telling me about his Åbo misadventures, quite completely forgot about SR slogans and complained, like a regular officer of the old regime, about the dominance of the committees and the decline in discipline.

The southern shores, that is Reval and Moön Sound, were more comforting for Lebedev. Here they listened to him attentively and seemed to agree with everything. He was quite crestfallen when I assured him that by now nothing could stop the decline (even less so mere words) and very soon things with us would be as they were at Åbo.

Lebedev's visit to the ship had a rather comical character. Razvozov had received a telegram from the War and Navy Minister Kerensky about the official visit to the fleet by the Manager of the Naval Ministry, Lebedev, without any indication of his rank. Unable to work out who this Lebedev was, he gave orders for him to be received with all the pomp and ceremony that could still be permitted by revolutionary rules. Lebedev first went to Razvozov on the *Libau* and then proceeded to the most senior ship, to me on the *Baian*.* The crew had been paraded on deck and I waited at the gangway with my report. None of us then had any idea who this Lebedev was, but in any case, judging from the high service position, everyone expected to meet a mature and solid person. You can imagine our amazement when at the gangway up jumped (literally jumped, not came) a manifestly awkward, short, swarthy fellow of thirty years old, dressed in the very frayed uniform of a French officer. No kind of report was given by me, as Lebedev, like Kerensky on his visit to the *Baian*, had hardly greeted me than he hurriedly requested that the ship's crew be mustered at the stern. The crew, gathered on the quarterdeck, looked on this operetta minister with mistrust. However Lebedev, finding himself in a crowd, felt himself to be in his own sphere, so I had hardly looked around before

* Author's note: Up to this time the revolution had significantly enjuvenated the composition of the command: at Moön Sound – I was the most senior of the commanders and the Chiefs of Division. Even Razvozov was junior to me in service, although now he was my superior, thanks to his position as Chief of Division.

he had scrambled up on the capstan loudly declaiming: 'Comrades! The revolution awaits your sacrifice' and so on. The picture was quite comical, as even the crew, with a certain amount of dissatisfaction, assessed it to be: 'What sort of minister is this? More like some masquerading agitator', the sailors said to me later. Excluding this operetta-revolutionary window-dressing, it must be said that Lebedev's speech in substance was very sensible. He spoke all the time of the war, of the need to continue it to the end, of support for order and discipline, of relating carefully towards officers, about the fulfilment of all operational directions and so on. Despite the initial frivolous impression, the crew listened attentively, not infrequently encouraging the orator with calls of 'That's right'.

After the departure of Lebedev and right down to the Kornilov affair,[5] comparative quiet again reigned on the front and in the mood of the crews. However, exactly about this time one could note a significant change in the attitude of the crew of the *Baian*. Up until this time the ship's committee, led by sensible people from among the older sailors, had still enjoyed recognised authority and in the majority of cases restrained and suppressed irresponsibility and the hooligan attempts of a small group of sailors – Bolsheviks (who however, did not yet declare themselves Bolsheviks – so much had this clique been at that time unpopular among the crew). But towards the end of July several of our sailors returned from Petrograd after having been sent there for a month and a half to undertake a course at the 'university of the revolution'. The full course at this university extended over only six weeks, as, obviously, no learning of any sort in the genuine sense of that term was undertaken there. In reality, these gentlemen, sent up to learn, in order to avoid combat, were instilled at the university with the most extreme Bolshevik slogans. In addition, they were imbued with complete mistrust of the commanding personnel, who, in the words of the leaders of these courses, declaimed for the continuation of the war to the end only the better to destroy in battle the best revolutionary workers.

From the very moment of their arrival on the ship, these sailors won great popularity among the crew and began their demoralising work almost without hindrance. The solid older members of the committee who tried to protest were soon accused of counter-revolution and removed from their positions. New elections were arranged in which not a single officer was chosen, while the university graduates all became members of the committee. The loudest shouter of them, an unintelligent and semi-literate diving petty officer, was chosen as president of the committee. This quite immature sailor had great ambition and hated all who were superior to him. He supported his authority by all the time stirring up the crew against the commander, the officers and generally all in authority, using every triviality to make various absurd accusations. The crew submitted to him, although among them were people much more intelligent and sensible than he, since they feared his vindictiveness and the connections he had made in Petrograd.

I attempted to deal with him on a business-like basis but nothing came of it, as he avoided any face-to-face discussions with me and preferred meeting with all the crew assembled. To compete with him there was not possible: whatever rubbish he proclaimed, from fear the crew was always on his side or, in any case, they could not decide to support me openly. He was unable to destroy shipboard order completely only because of the closeness to the front. The most class-conscious comrades, with their president at the head, felt panic-stricken terror before the Germans and this held them back from direct accusations and insults addressed to me and the officers, since they knew that in battle they could not do without us.

At the end of August the Kornilov epic was played out by that provocateur Kerensky. This had been the last energetic attempt on the part of sensible state-minded revolutionary activists to prevent power from falling in a steep decline into the arms of anarchy and Bolshevism. This attempt, which was sympathised with by the best, still disciplined, parts of the Army, had every chance of success. It was brought to nothing by the treachery of Kerensky: feeling that power was slipping from his hands, he went over to the side of the Soviet of Workers' and Soldiers' Deputies, which was against any sort of forceful repression of the Bolsheviks, then a still comparatively weak party. As a result, Kornilov and his collaborators were proclaimed enemies of the revolution and state criminals. Kerensky also assumed dictatorial powers, in words at least. The possibility of any sort of regular work ceased completely, creating excellent conditions for the full flowering of Bolshevism.

The failure of the Kornilov affair had a very serious impact on the position of officers in general, and particularly in the fleet. The crews, knowing the fabled popularity of Kornilov among officers, not without foundation, considered all officers sympathetic to Kornilov – Kornilovtsi to use their expression. From this arose the wholesale persecution of officers one and all. Earlier the governing authorities had to some degree defended officers. Now, after the liquidation of the Kornilov affair, the Soviet of Workers' and Soldiers' Deputies had already finally taken all power into its hands, as Kerensky and the new composition of the government appeared to be merely an obedient weapon in the hands of the Soviet, in the best of circumstances acting as its executive organ.

The seizure of power by the Soviet was immediately felt by us locally. Until the Kornilov affair the Soviet very rarely issued any sort of directions directly, independently of the Government. Now this became quite frequent. The crews quickly figured out in whose hands the real power lay and began to show genuine trust only to those directions that came from or had been sanctioned by the Soviet or some sort of Central Committee connected with the Soviet.

Desiring to be done with the Kornilov issue all the sooner, the Soviet, in a whole flood of official announcements, sent to us by radio (to the great satisfaction of the Germans) and by direct line, tried by all means to blacken the participants in this venture, painting them as enemies of the people, counter-revolutionaries and usurpers of power and so on. In the end, a direction was received from this same Soviet that failed to lead to widespread excesses against officers only because the officers had already had some revolutionary experience and were able to smooth things over when necessary and, in extremes, make concessions that were often against their conscience. One must not accuse all of such weakness; actually, while some of them acted thus out of fear for their lives, it must be noted that only the desire to maintain order on the ships, which was still necessary for the struggle with the enemy, induced very many of them to compromise with their consciences.

The ships' committees sought to clarify whether the officers sympathised with the new Government, working in full contact with the Soviet of Workers' and Soldiers' Deputies and where appropriate, to secure from the officers signed confirmation of this. Clearly, such a direction created an extremely oppressive and tense atmosphere in the fleet. Fortunately, on many ships the crews themselves understood in how difficult a position such penetration into the soul of officers, quite contrary to any sort of understanding of freedom of conscience, placed them. So the demand was limited to general directions on the theme of the necessity for subordination to the new power. But on some ships, where Bolshevism had already sent down deep roots, the demand was implemented with full severity, which, naturally, brought with it excesses. Thus, on the *Petropavlovsk* several junior officers refused to give their signatures, at which, without any sort of court proceedings, they were shot on the shore at Norra-Hamn, in full view of the passing public.[6] On several other ships the matter was limited to the discharge of 'unsympathetic' officers.

On my cruiser the matter turned out thus: after the receipt of the direction, the crew, through some old sailors, came to me in a private capacity with the question – how would I and the officers respond to such a demand and requirement to sign. I replied that such a demand would appear to be an unnecessary insult for officers who had up to this time conducted themselves with complete loyalty and had honourably fulfilled their service and battle duties, despite unbelievably difficult conditions. So far as the signature was concerned, then neither I nor my officers would give it under any circumstances, as no power could force our conscience.

After a day or two the crew gathered in a general meeting on the mess deck, to which I and the officers were invited. The crew stood in a crowd around the table where the members of the committee were seated; alongside the table chairs had been prepared for me and the officers. The secretary of the committee read the text of the direction, after which the president of the committee, in fairly proper form, suggested that I reply to the question: Did I subordinate myself to the existing Provisional Government? To such a question, of course, one might have answered affirmatively without the slightest straining at interpretation. But so antagonistic was it for me refer to the Provisional Government, to which I related, obviously, with a complete lack of sympathy, that I thought of another way out. I answered: 'I am a soldier, stationed in a fighting post, and therefore I subordinate myself immediately to that person from whom I receive battle instructions, that is, in the present circumstances, to the Fleet Commander. The question of subordination to one or the other Government I leave to the decision of the Fleet Commander himself, in whom I have unqualified trust and who, being placed closer to the governing powers, might the more easily work out to whom one must be subordinate.' Strangely enough, my more or less evasive answer completely satisfied the listeners and I left the gathering in complete silence. As it turned out, all of my officers, without the slightest prior agreement, followed my example, only they stated that they were subordinate to me as their commander, and so on. The incident was dealt with without any sort of reference to signatures.

After the Kornilov affair, Kerensky became Prime Minister and took on the functions of Supreme Commander. Not long before the Kornilov affair, major changes were made in the higher command of the fleet: Verderevskii, who had been summoned to Petrograd to explain why he had not fulfilled the directions of the Government to send ships to the Neva for defence of the Government during the first Bolshevik attempt at the beginning of July, had at first been arrested and then, liberated by demand of TsentroBalt – the Commitee at Fleet Headquarters – was appointed Naval Minister. Razvozov was chosen as Fleet Commander in his place. This was the last appointment to a high command in the Baltic Sea that was welcomed equally by both the officers and the comrades. As with the appointment of Razvozov to the Destroyer Division, one could only regret that this outstanding officer had been promoted to a high post when in fact the situation in the fleet was already hopeless. In the position of Fleet Commander Razvozov came not to lead the fleet, but to play the purely political role of intermediary and connecting link between government organs, all manner of committees, as well as officers and crews. Each day the situation changed and became more and more complicated. The committees, in particular TsentroBalt, gathered into their hands more and more power, so that the work of the Fleet Commander became truly a labour of Sisyphus. However, the major and undoubted merit of Razvozov was that he, from the first days of taking up his position, decisively and skilfully stood in defence of the officers of the fleet and generally supported all sensible elements, in no way succumbing to demagoguery, in which his predecessor Verderevskii had not been without sin. In this area Razvozov achieved much. Officers ought to remember with deep gratitude the selfless activities of Razvozov, risking his life every moment in pursuit of the possible lightening of the service conditions of unfairly treated officers in these last, most dark, days of the existence of our battle Fleet.

Iu K Stark[7] was appointed to replace Razvozov in the Destroyer Division (with the agreement of the crews, obviously). Up to this time he had been commander of one of the divisions of destroyers of the *Novik* type. Here was a quiet and sensible officer, able to smooth things over with the crews. Having served for so long in the Destroyer Division, he understood the situation at Moön Sound excellently and continued the work of his predecessor with complete success.

Chapter IV

The Final Events at Moön Sound

The fall of Riga · Appointment of Bakhirev · Plan of defence for the Gulf of Riga · The morale issue · Surrender of the Tserell position · The battle at Kuivast · Retreat of our fleet to Vormsi · Retreat from Moön Sound[1]

At the end of August the German offensive on the Northern Front culminated in the fall of Riga, the defence of which had been distinguished by being much less steadfast than it had earlier been. From that moment (22 August) German ships – minesweepers, destroyers and big ships – frequently began to come within sight of Tserell, which created some alarm in our staffs and plunged the comrades literally into panic. But every cloud has a silver lining. From the moment of the first appearance of the enemy fleet within sight of our shores, the sailors noticeably braced themselves and began to occupy themselves less with revolutionary rubbish. Moreover, the interest in explanatory lectures of a military character significantly increased.

In view of the importance of the events taking place in the Gulf of Riga, Vice Admiral Bakhirev (Chief of the Destroyer Division) was appointed Chief of the Defence of Moön Sound, with all of the naval forces in Moön Sound, as well as the shore garrison and batteries located on the islands, subordinated to him. Bakhirev came to Moön Sound and established himself for the time being on the *Libava*, hoisting his flag on one of the destroyers.

A detailed plan for the defence of the Gulf of Riga was worked out under Bakhirev's leadership. The battleships *Slava* and *Grazhdanin* were assigned to support the Tserell position, which consisted of the main battery of four 12in guns (commandant Captain 2nd Rank

Kniupfer[2]) and the two 6in batteries. It must be said that this support was purely moral, as the range of the Tserell batteries was 150 cables (27.8km) while the guns of the *Grazhdanin* could only reach 105 cables (19.5km) and those of the *Slava* even less. In the event of a breakthrough of part of the German fleet into the Gulf of Riga, the plan developed was for a fighting retreat in which all of the big ships would take part – *Slava*, *Grazhdanin*, *Baian*, *Makarov* and *Aurora*.

The first engagement had to be in the northern part of the Gulf of Riga around the Irben strait itself. Our ships were intended to manoeuvre in a specially swept area (the manoeuvring pocket), then, as the German fleet came to attack through areas mined by us, it would be attacked by our destroyers. In the event of this engagement being unsuccessful the final part of the retreat would be to the southern section of Moön Sound where, behind the defence of the shore batteries and of our minefields, which blocked the entrance to the channel, our fleet would make its final attempt to repel the enemy.

The whole plan only made sense in the indispensable context of the most energetic operation of our 12in Tserell battery, which outranged the German dreadnoughts by a whole 20 cables (3.7km). It might be expected that, even in the event that the Tserell battery were put out of action by the gunfire of the German fleet, the enemy in doing so would suffer such losses that very few of his ships would get through into the Gulf of Riga and that our forces there would be able to deal with them without particular effort. However, certainly, in the event that the Tserell battery for some reason or other did not come into action or even operated without the required energy, then the whole plan for the defence of the Gulf of Riga would lose its very meaning. The Tserell battery was manned by sailors from the Naval Guards, formerly under the command of an officer of the Guards, Kniupfer, an experienced gunnery officer who had previously commanded the destroyer *Voiskovoi*. In their day, according to Kniupfer, these sailors had been keen to defend their position, and one must say, they had fulfilled their duty brilliantly. But times had changed. In the Tserell batteries, thanks to their isolation, discipline had been maintained but to vouch for the crew completely was certainly impossible, which unfortunately was quite clearly confirmed at the very beginning of the attack on the Gulf of Riga.

At the same time all possible measures were taken to prevent a landing of enemy forces on the seaward shores of the islands. In general, the coasts of the islands of Oesel and Dago on the Baltic Sea side were not much good for landings. However, on the island of Oesel there was Tagelacht bay, where a landing was quite possible. Besides, this bay had the still further advantage for the enemy in that, isolated on the north-western part of the island of Oesel, it gave him the possibility of landing troops and without particular difficulty cutting off the western part of Oesel from the main base at Kuivast along with the town of Arensburg and the Tserell batteries.

All of this had indeed been taken into account by Bakhirev and his predecessors. In the prominent places forming the entrance to this bay two batteries had been constructed, each with four 6in guns. In addition a considerable part of the garrison of the island (around two regiments) as well as a field battery were concentrated in the region of the possible landings. The approaches to the bay had been carefully mined. It seemed that, in such conditions, the possibility of a landing, if not completely removed, had been made difficult to the utmost degree. However, while all of this might have been adequate in normal times, now all those particular misgivings appeared again: would morale stand up to the challenge, having been undermined to the core by revolutionary decay? Further events, unfortunately, showed that these apprehensions were completely justified.

Poor Bakhirev, constantly running into this incalculable morale issue during operational conferences and well aware of the general decline in the ships, became quite crestfallen. He did not hide from us, the senior commanders, his anxieties about the outcome of the attack and consoled himself and us only with the fact that we were doing all that was in our power.

He had chosen the *Baian* as flagship in the event of naval operations, first as the more mobile ship and second, as having preserved more than the others a fighting trim and established discipline. Possibly the fact that Bakhirev had known me for a long time also played some role in this choice, since the commanders of the other ships were almost unknown to him.

Through the course of September enemy ships came within sight of our shores more and more often. Enemy aerial reconnaissance flights also became more frequent. Even a Zeppelin appeared at a range of several miles, out of the range of our guns, clearly observing and noting down the disposition and number of our ships and shore batteries, and then departing. All of this spoke of the proximity and inevitability of decisive engagements.

Finally, the catastrophe befell. On 29 September a strong enemy fleet appeared in sight of Tagelacht bay along with minesweepers, which set to work under the cover of the main forces, deployed beyond the range of our artillery. One of the 6in batteries, guarding the entrance to the bay, opened fire on the minesweepers, thereby disclosing its position. The enemy big ships, in turn, opened fire on this battery and soon compelled it to fall silent. The other battery did not open fire in order not to disclose its location, but then, when the shelling of the shore by the heavy guns of the enemy ships began, its gun crews fled (the morale issue!). Subsequently the enemy deposited its landing party without any hindrance, as the garrison of the island retreated in disorder, having shown no opposition whatsoever.

Reports of the most panicked nature flowed into the staff: that the enemy had landed with enormous forces and was attacking both Moön and Arensburg. In actual fact the Germans had landed no more than a battalion and in the first days did not attack anywhere, considering their position to be very precarious. The fleet covering the landing soon departed, leaving two or three cruisers, one of which ran aground near Soelo Sound. There was a fresh westerly wind and these cruisers, unable to persist in the quite exposed location under the threat of our torpedo attack, had to leave. After that the landing appeared to be without any support, with no direct communications to their base, without provisions, without communications, and in normal times it would have been destroyed by our garrison without difficulty. But everything favoured the Germans: the weather remained calm and foggy, while the morale issue did not allow our troops to attack and destroy the enemy landing forces. Our larger destroyers, the *Noviks*, and gunboats approached Soelo Sound several times and fired on the grounded enemy cruiser, which returned their fire. After a day or so she broke free and left for the open sea.

After several days, having assessed our troops' incapacity for offensive actions, the German landing party began to move towards the causeway joining the islands of Oesel and Moön. Our shore batteries located on Moön and the destroyers and gunboats from the north held up this attack with energetic fire. But again everything was spoilt by the morale issue. To secure freedom of action of our ships along the north-eastern coast of Oesel and northern Moön, it was necessary to bar the enemy's entry into the inner waters of Moön Sound by mining the straits of Soelo Sound through which, despite the narrowness and twisting character of its channel, the largest destroyers could proceed. One of the shallow-draft minelayers, *Pripiat*, was directed to carry out this work on the first night of the landing. However, the crew of this minelayer, who had previously worked without reproach, suddenly went into meeting mode and refused to undertake the operation.

Within a day or two the Germans had penetrated the Sound and from this moment began a series of destroyer engagements in the shallow waters of Kassar Basin stretching between Soelo Sound and Moön Sound. The tactics of the Germans were very simple: six to eight of their destroyers, passing through the straits, would come within sight of our squadron standing at Kuivast. On reaching the maximum range of our heaviest guns, they would turn back on their course and retreat, followed by our larger destroyers of the *Novik* type and gunboats. A long-range engagement would ensue, causing very little damage to either side, but, when our destroyers, pressing the chase, approached Kassar Basin, they would be met by the fire of the heavy guns of an enemy cruiser stationed on the other side of the strait. In these engagements we lost the destroyer *Grom*.

The German destroyers, apparently, also bore no small losses. However, the main aim of the enemy was achieved. The greater part of our destroyer forces were drawn away from the enemy landing operations and from patrol duties in the Gulf of Riga, where the enemy had at that time already begun the minesweeping work on the seaward end of the Irben Straits beyond the range of our batteries.

All of these events, having a somewhat chaotic character, strengthened even more the anxious state of mind of the leaders of our fighting operations in Moön Sound – Bakhirev and Stark. By Bakhirev's order the cruisers *Aurora* and *Admiral Makarov* came to Moön Sound to form a northern reserve. On the island of Moön, the shock battalion was deployed as reinforcement, along with landing parties from ships that, as the more reliable element, were specially charged with defending the causeway joining the island of Oesel with Moön.

On 1 October, having received the news of the panic-stricken mood of the garrison of the Tserell batteries, Bakhirev boarded the *Baian* and went to the Svorbe peninsula, counting on his personal involvement and the presence of a big ship to bolster the demoralised spirit of the gun crew. But while still on the way a radio signal was received from Tserell about the firm steadiness of the garrison, which was said to be prepared to struggle against the enemy to the last drop of blood. About 15 miles from Svorbe the cruiser reversed course and by nightfall was at anchor in her old place at Kuivast. However, the very next day, at the very first appearance of enemy ships on the horizon, the gun crews at Tserell, forgetting all their promises, adamantly refused to obey their commanders. They convened a meeting and passed a resolution on the impossibility of further struggle with the enemy, basing their decision on the isolation of the Svorbe peninsula from the main base. As a result of this premature decision, dictated by the panicked state of mind of the class-conscious comrades, the batteries were partially blown up and abandoned by their crews.

Having received a telephone message about this decision and the subsequent events, Bakhirev immediately sent the *Grazhdanin* to Svorbe. He calculated that the arrival of a big ship with 12in guns would breathe courage into the garrison and induce it to continue to defend Irben and the Gulf of Riga. In the event that the situation was hopeless, *Grazhdanin* had orders to destroy the batteries with her guns, remove the garrison and then return to Kuivast. On the morning of 3 October, *Grazhdanin* returned and reported that they had found part of the batteries already blown up and the garrison so demoralised that there could be no thought of bringing the batteries back into action. She had bombarded the batteries with her own guns and taken off part of the garrison. The rest, together with several officers (Captain 2nd Rank Kniupfer and Eiler[3]), remained at the batteries and later fell into German hands as prisoners of war.

In this way the morale issue, or better to say, the decay of morale as a consequence of revolutionary wrecking, ruined the whole scheme for the defence of the Gulf of Riga, on the creation of which had been expended almost superhuman energy, a mass of materiel and of money. The Tserell battery, on which so much hope had been laid, and which had not yet been threatened by any immediate danger, was given up without a single shot fired. With its fall, virtually nothing at all prevented the enemy from occupying the Gulf and destroying our naval forces trapped in the southern part of Moön Sound.

Notwithstanding the hopelessness of the situation, Bakhirev decided to defend the entrance to Moön Sound to the very last, including the loss of all of the big ships. The necessity of such a decision inevitably flowed from the strategic position of Moön Sound: with its fall, all means for turning the right flank of our troops and for occupying the coast of the Gulf of Finland right up to Reval itself would be open to the enemy.

As early as 3 October our patrolling destroyers in the Gulf of Riga discovered the presence of enemy minesweepers and big ships, advancing on a course towards the entrance to Moön Sound. On the same day, over the course of several hours, an enemy Zeppelin cruised in sight of Kuivast but beyond the range of our anti-aircraft guns. Its intentions were all too evident – it was observing the disposition of our ships, batteries and troops.

At dawn on 4 October our patrol destroyers, located to the south of the entrance to Moön Sound, reported that they had sighted a large fleet of minesweepers, transports, destroyers and big ships. At 8 o'clock Admiral Bakhirev boarded the *Baian* and hoisted his flag. With him came his staff, which consisted of only one officer – Captain 2nd Rank B V Muromtsov. By this time the enemy forces, with minesweepers ahead, had already approached to a distance of about 200 cables (37km) from Kuivast. Our big ships, moored between Kuivast and the island of Shildau, had had steam up since early morning and were in complete battle readiness with anchors at short stay.

Recognising the inevitability of a battle and not wishing to subject the defenceless transports and lesser auxiliary ships to that danger, Bakhirev ordered the departure of all these ships to the north by the dredged channel, in accordance with the previously arranged plan. At the very height of the implementation of this order, that is, when the whole roadstead to the very start of the channel was full of a moving line of ships, enemy bomber planes attacked the area where the ships were located. The raid was carried out from three different directions by three separate squadrons, each with no fewer than four planes. Our artillery was somewhat tardy, as all attention had been drawn towards the approaching enemy fleet, as a consequence of which the attacking planes were able to carry out their task almost unhindered. In the course of no more than five minutes they virtually plastered the roadstead and the shore region around Kuivast with bombs.

The scene was extraordinarily impressive. The watery expanse around the ships virtually boiled with exploding bombs; tall columns of water, mixed with thick black smoke, incessant noise and the crack of shell bursts, small shards whistling in all directions – all this gave the impression of some sort of hell. The impression, however, was not consistent with the results. No damage whatsoever was inflicted on the ships, if one does not count the falling of several smaller splinters. Onshore their actions were somewhat more successful: one of the bombs, falling among the camps, killed several soldiers, civilians and horses, creating complete panic.

All the while the enemy forces were getting closer and closer. Our situation was particularly difficult as a consequence of us being without any capacity at all to oppose their victorious progress. Our artillery was out-ranged, and attacks by destroyers and submarines (of which we had only one[4]) were impossible as the region where the enemy was located had been thickly mined by us and had a mass of shallows and submerged rocks. The closer the enemy came it was finally possible to establish the approximate composition of his attacking forces. The lookout officer (Midshipman Golitsyn), stationed on the foretop of my ship, discerned three cruisers or ships of the dreadnought class and five cruisers of a smaller type, not counting the smaller ships. In this way a genuine picture of the battle was becoming clear. Before we would be able to begin firing on the enemy minesweepers (at a range of 105 cables (19.5km)) the enemy dreadnoughts, following immediately behind, would be able to open fire on our ships with broadsides of their 12in guns, since the range of their guns exceeded ours by fifteen to twenty cables.

The joylessness of such perspectives, dooming our ships inevitably to perish, could not in any way help to bolster our courage. I was on the bridge with Bakhirev the whole time and we exchanged small talk in order to distract ourselves somewhat from anxious thoughts. Occasionally from the foretop Golitsyn reported to us the explosion of a mine against an enemy minesweeper or destroyer. Of this we immediately informed the crew, who from the very moment of the appearance of the enemy on the horizon had remembered the old-regime discipline and looked Bakhirev and me in the eye with a guilty countenance.

About 11 o'clock in the morning the distance to the enemy minesweepers had reduced to 110 cables (20.4km). Bakhirev gave the order to make the pre-arranged signal 'buki'[5] to the *Slava* and *Grazhdanin*, ordering them to move to their battle position, which was located behind our minefield 3 miles to the south of the Kuivast parallel. At this moment the greater part of the non-combatant ships and the destroyers that were not linked to the big ships were already located in the channel or to the north of it, on the way to Rogokiul. Simultaneously with the signal, *Baian* weighed anchor and hoisted the day-shape for 'stopped'.[6] According to the previously arranged plan, it had been intended that, on the signal 'buki', *Slava* and *Grazhdanin* would proceed at full speed to the fighting position; *Baian*, following them, had to station herself somewhat to the rear, at a distance of one and a half cables from the position. It must be noted that the role of *Baian* was purely moral, as the range of her guns was ten to twelve cables shorter than those of the battleships.

Several agonising minutes passed after the signal was given; *Slava* and *Grazhdanin* weighed anchor and hoisted the day-shapes for 'half-ahead', but ... did not move. Not the slightest bow wave was visible at their prows. Could it really be the morale issue again? Terrible moment! But the enemy continued to approach and from minute to minute it could be expected that he would open fire with his 12in turrets. It was clear to us that then no forces whatsoever would be able to draw the ships into position. Bakhirev came up to me and through gritted teeth exclaimed: 'They don't want to go! What can we do?' It occurred to me that if we went forward then the ships would follow us – partly from the practice of conforming to the movements of the admiral and partly from a feeling of shame that they were being shown the way by a weaker ship. I proposed this to Bakhirev. And so we did. We dropped the day-shapes and went to full speed ahead, turning towards the position. The ruse worked – the big ships similarly dropped their day-shapes and the water seethed under their bows. For Bakhirev and me a weight was lifted from our hearts.

However, the indecisiveness of the big ships had delayed us by about ten minutes so that, when *Baian* came up to the position, the German dreadnoughts had already opened fire, at first falling significantly short. We lingered for a little at the position, waiting for the *Slava* and *Grazhdanin* to close with us. At this time the enemy's third salvo landed right beside us with a slight overshoot. In order to leave the field of fire, we went to full speed and, circling around our battleships, came to a stop about three cables behind them. At the same time *Slava* and *Grazhdanin*, forming a front not quite up to the position, opened fire with their 12in guns on the enemy minesweepers and destroyers, which were by now at a range of about 100 cables (18.5km). So far as could be seen from our foretop, their shells were well placed: disorder was noted among the minesweepers and some were put out of action. After several minutes, however, the enemy dreadnoughts found the range of our battleships, which owing to the lack of space for manoeuvring were forced to remain almost in one spot, and the German shells began to fall directly on them. Finally one of the salvoes landed directly between the funnels of the *Grazhdanin*, causing a fire that, however, was quickly extinguished. To the credit of *Grazhdanin* it must be said that during this time she did not cease fire and continued to maintain her station, wherever possible changing her position. Soon after this there occurred the hit on the *Slava* which, immediately after this, noticeably listing and down at the bow, turned to the north and made off in the direction of Kuivast. She did not reply to our signals or semaphores.[7]

At this moment the enemy fire had so increased that the waters around *Grazhdanin* virtually boiled with exploding shells as she continued shooting. Recognising the absurdity of the idea of continuing the battle in the prevailing conditions, that is, with the availability of only an inferior damaged ship against three dreadnoughts, Bakhirev hoisted the signal '*Grazhdanin* to proceed to the channel' and with that also signalled to *Slava*: 'Allow *Grazhdanin* to pass ahead'. The latter signal was prompted by the realisation that the *Slava*, evidently damaged below the waterline and seriously down at the bow, might easily run aground in any attempt to pass through the channel, which would completely block it, making the passage of other ships impossible. *Grazdanin*, whose actions in the battle had been beyond reproach (her commander was at that time Captain 1st Rank Rudenskii) immediately acknowledged the signal and turned towards the north, keeping on shooting all the while. Apparently at this time there was another hit on her. The *Slava*, however, already near the island of Shildau and out of the field of fire, did not reply to the signal and continued to go towards the entrance of the dredged channel.

Wishing to deflect the enemy fire from the damaged *Grazhdanin* while she had not yet passed out of its range, Bakhirev suggested to me that we remain on station. The distance to the enemy had by this time reduced to 90–95 cables (16–17km), so that the *Baian* could open fire with her 8in guns. It was all too obvious that the position of the *Baian*, drawing to herself the whole of the enemy fire, was desperate: against our **three** 8in guns (of which the midship mounting could not act, as the gun crew was completely without protection) were ranged **thirty** 12in guns of the enemy.[8] The only thing I could think of as a way of hindering the enemy gun fire was to change our position continuously in the most unexpected directions. Fortunately for us, the engines responded without fault and the large cruiser leapt about like a fish, completely denying the enemy a hit. For the entire fifteen minutes of our remaining on station **not a single** shell hit us, although since the departure of the *Grazhdanin* the enemy had turned the **whole** of his fire onto the cruiser. But, despite this, I will never forget those fifteen minutes: the knowledge that the slightest inaccuracy in the engines or in the actions of the steering gear could have made us into a simple bull's-eye, and that a **single** chance hit would have been enough to send the cruiser to the bottom, did little to help maintain the required cool headedness. Only the steadfast support of that experienced hero, M K Bakhirev, supported me. With complete outward calm, he paced about the bridge, not interfering in my directions at all and, with only a sympathetic smile, watched my madman's play with the engine-room telegraph.

Finally, the *Grazhdanin* disappeared behind the island of Shildau and Bakhirev ordered me at the top of his voice 'Get out of here'! Now came the most dangerous moment: the channel to the north very soon narrowed and we had immediately to maintain a steady course, which gave the enemy the most straightforward opportunity for a hit. I ordered full speed ahead at the shortest notice, which was fulfilled promptly: I reckon that in no more than five minutes we were doing 20 knots. The enemy increased their rate of fire and finally were successful: a 12in shell hit the cruiser forward. It passed under the bridge itself, broke through the upper deck on the starboard side of the forward turret and exploded on the armoured deck of the cable locker. In several places shrapnel penetrated the armoured deck and the outer hull below the waterline. In the compartment where the shell exploded there was a lot of flammable material: hemp ropes, mats, tarpaulins and so on. A fierce fire broke out. It was necessary to flood the neighbouring 8in and 6in ammunition magazines. Through the underwater damage and thanks to the flooding of the magazines, we took on more than 1,000 tons of water, as a result of which the *Baian* was down at the bow by about 4ft. However, it must be considered that the cruiser came off very cheaply as the bulkheads held, which eliminated the danger of the cruiser sinking, and, since the engine room and the boilers appeared to be completely unaffected, we continued on our previous course, not reducing speed, although steering the cruiser had become extraordinarily difficult. The fire that had broken out could not be extinguished for a considerable time and thick black smoke penetrating through the shell holes and the battened-down hatches billowed directly over the bridge. All of us on the bridge were choked by this smoke and it was difficult to see anything ahead of the bows. Someone had the idea of bringing gas masks to us on the bridge and then things went along somewhat better.

To our relief, immediately after the hit on us, the enemy ceased firing and began to withdraw. In all likelihood they had decided that by then all our big ships had been decisively put out of action. But for whatever reason, thanks to this we had the possibility of assessing our damage in relatively calm conditions, without stopping engines, and then to concern ourselves about the other ships. Passing beyond Shildau, we were able to discern the general situation for ourselves. All the transports were already in the dredged channel. The *Grazhdanin*, which had not noticeably suffered serious damage, was positioned with stopped engines in the so-called strategic pocket before the entrance to the channel, waiting for the transports, crowded near the earlier part of the channel, to move somewhat further up.

The *Slava* appeared to be grounded to the right of the pocket on a bank marked by spar-buoys; she had a substantial list. As became clear later on, the cause of her grounding had been the complete confusion in the direction of the ship, in which, in the most criminal manner, members of the ship's committee had interfered. Unfortunately it must be stated that when we passed very close by the *Slava*, only committeemen were visible above deck – no officers were observed. Individual cries broke out: 'Send destroyers to take off the crew!', 'Save the crew!' Bakhirev immediately sent a destroyer to her with orders first to ascertain the seriousness of her situation and, in the event of the impossibility of refloating her immediately, to take off the crew and blow up the ship. Meanwhile, considering the damage to the *Baian* to be serious as the fire had not yet been extinguished, Bakhirev ordered the *Grazhdanin* to follow after the *Baian* and not proceed ahead of her, until the *Slava*'s situation had been clarified. Some destroyers and minesweepers had remained in the southern part of Moön Sound to carry out patrol duties and to support communications with the northern part of the island of Moön, where our land troops and the naval shock battalion under command of Captain 2nd Rank Shishko still remained.

With the greatest difficulty I was able to get into the channel, where usually, in normal times, we would have been accompanied by a tug boat. Now we were obliged to enter under our own steam with the forward trim down by 4ft, which considerably changed the handling characteristics of the ship. However, all turned out well and after two hours we were at anchor in the northern part of the channel where it widened, where the *Aurora* awaited us. It must be noted that in handling the ship during the battle and the subsequent passage through the channel my senior navigator, Lieutenant Commander Ukhov, was indispensable to me. This outstanding fighting officer possessed all the qualities of an excellent pilot and never wavered in the most critical minutes.

After an hour the *Grazhdanin* came up and reported that it would be impossible to refloat the *Slava* without lightening her with the assistance of a crane, as a consequence of which they had had to blow her up, having previously removed the crew. After this all ships headed towards Vormsi. One of our transports was scuttled in the southern part of the channel, completely blocking the passage. In this way, albeit for only several days, the entrance of the enemy's big ships into the northern part of Moön Sound was barred. The cruiser *Admiral Makarov* and a chain of patrol destroyers were stationed as a barrier to attacks on our fleet by enemy destroyers, which could freely pass to the north beside the channel from the Kassar Basin side. A similar patrol was sent north from Vormsi.

Now I must backtrack a little in order to tell of one very distinctive episode that took place on my ship during the battle. I did not address it in its place, so as not to break the continuity of the narrative.

As I have already mentioned throughout, the crew of the *Baian* at the time of the battle behaved themselves without reproach, calling to mind the best of old-regime times by their work and discipline. But ... even with us things did not go without a but. The president of the Ship's Committee, whom I had not seen since the beginning of the engagement, had no specific duties while the ship was at battle stations as he was the diving petty officer. Having figured out, in his opinion, the safest place in the ship – the compartment in the bow under the turret – he convened there some sort of meeting. Besides him, there were in all five people present from among members of the committee, quite simply those who were like-minded. All of these people, under stand-to conditions, were counted as stood down, which is why their absence would not have been immediately noticed. According to the account of the crew, who related to this meeting quite negatively, the object of discussion had been the 'criminal' behaviour of Bakhirev and me, engaging in battle with an overwhelmingly superior opponent deliberately in order to carry out the execution, through enemy gunfire, of several hundred of the most class-conscious comrades – the deepeners of the revolution. There then occurred something truly in the nature of a miracle: an enemy shell landed directly in the clutch of meeting-goers, fatally wounding or killing **all without exception**. The president of the committee had both his legs torn off above the knee. All the wounded died over the next twenty-four hours. Was this not fate? This event caused the strongest, most stunning impression on the crew, who said with one voice that 'God had found out the guilty'. When, immediately on arrival at Vormsi, the fatally wounded president of the committee was borne onto a launch to be sent in to Rogekiul, he hysterically cried out 'Bakhirev and Timirev are traitors! Turncoats! Blood-suckers!'. The crew, gathered at the gangway, were at first silent but then could contain themselves no longer and cries rang out: 'Shut up, you yourself are guilty! God has punished you for this affair!' and so on.

This incident I have narrated, itself a trivial thing, had for me the most unexpected consequences. The mass of the crew, tending towards superstition perhaps more than ever, despite its revolutionary emancipation, felt towards me and my officers a sort of particularly heartfelt, if one might express it so, trust that, despite all the following events, was not broken right to the very end, to the moment of my demonstrative departure from the brigade.

I return now to the description of events.

Bakhirev understood perfectly well that the comparatively successful withdrawal of all naval forces from the Gulf of Riga to the north of Moön Sound after the battle by no means signified the final conclusion of the operation. Towards the evening of 4 October, when all our ships had gathered at Vormsi, the following situation of the enemy was apparent. With the conclusion of the battle, all the big enemy ships had gone off to the south; the minesweepers, without even the slightest hindrance from our side, had come right up to the entrance to Moön Sound, after which, under the cover of several destroyers, transports with troops had approached Kuivast. That evening these troops, having landed and taken the island of Moön, joined up with the Oesel group of the enemy landing forces, having met scarcely any opposition. Our troops on Moön retreated at the first appearance of the enemy, some crossing over in fishing boats to the mainland and some being taken off and deposited at Rogekiul by our minesweepers and destroyers, which had been left by Bakhirev at the northern end of Moön after the departure of the big ships. The only shore-based unit to show any fortitude had been the Naval Shock Battalion of Captain 2nd Rank Shishko. It refused to evacuate and, having sustained several unequal engagements with the enemy, part of it had been destroyed and part taken prisoner along with its wounded commander. If our fleet had remained in Moön Sound, then undoubtedly the most likely further action of the Germans would have been as follows: having formed a covering detachment to the north with the help of minefields and submarines, they would have begun to attack along the dredged channel, clearing it of the sunken transport. So our ships, partly put out of action and partly with exhausted ammunition reserves, would have been trapped and in one way or another destroyed.

Conscious in full measure of the uselessness and extreme danger of our ships remaining any longer in Moön Sound, Bakhirev, however, did not judge it possible to take any decision whatsoever without direction from the Fleet Commander. In response to the query about this sent to him, along with a brief report of events, an imperative direction was received for the immediate clearing of Moön Sound and the transfer of the fighting ships to Lapvik. The batteries were to be blown up and the crews and signals intelligence posts removed. The Moön Sound rear base – Roggekiul – was to be evacuated and blown up. The transports and smaller ships were to go via the Nukke–Vorms channel[9] to Reval. Working out the details of these orders was left to be overseen by Bakhirev himself.

Bakhirev gathered all the commanders of the big ships and the commanders from the destroyer divisions together on the *Baian* to discuss this directive. Rear Admiral Stark, the Chief of the Destroyer Division, also attended. The main question for discussion was the timing of the withdrawal of the big ships and the smaller craft to the northern shore. Everyone understood that it was desirable to carry this out as soon as possible, while the Germans had not yet succeeded in sending their submarines to the northern exit from Moön Sound and had not established a special minefield. The majority of the commanders were in favour of leaving that day, in darkness, so as to make any attacks by enemy submarines more difficult. But this proposal had its weak point: we had only a single pair of minesweepers and the division of better minesweepers summoned from Lapvik could only arrive the next day. In addition, it was well known that the Germans had systematically sown mines north of Vormsi and the latest sweeping of this region had taken place about two weeks earlier.

To proceed with only one pair of minesweepers was effectively the same as going without any, as with the first mine discovered these two would be put out of action. So it could be said with considerable certainty that during a slow passage to the sea without sweeping, several ships would be damaged and possibly would perish. Taking this into account, I (speaking last as the most senior of those present, not counting Bakhirev), expressed the opinion that to leave that day was nothing other than unwarranted folly, and that it was necessary to defer the departure for twenty-four hours. In the morning the large minesweepers would arrive and within the day could sweep and render safe the exit channel. To that I added that, taking into account the tardiness and indecisiveness of action on the part of the enemy, it was difficult to expect that he would succeed in organising anything within that twenty-four hours. I considered myself obliged to speak particularly definitely, since as the most senior among the commanders it would fall to me to command the squadron: Bakhirev himself proposed to remain at Moön Sound with several destroyers until the evacuation of the islands and Rogekiul had been completed. Bakhirev vacillated for some time but then agreed with my opinion.

To our good fortune, the following day was heavily overcast, becoming at times foggy, which prevented the Germans from observing our activities. The minesweepers despatched from Lapvik were able to set to their sweeping work on the exit channel without any hindrance. Over the course of the day the evacuations of the islands and of Roggekiul were almost completed so that Bakhirev decided to come with us, remaining in the *Baian*. I was very pleased at this, since in this way the extra responsibility was taken from me, besides which it was very pleasant for me to pass several more hours still with M K Bakhirev, with whom I had become particularly close over the preceding two frantic days. Mikhail Koronatovich himself also, evidently, felt comfortable in my ship, since he preferred to stay in her rather than transfer to another undamaged one.

In order to be able to pass through the navigationally more difficult part of the route before nightfall, the ships weighed anchor an hour before sunset and proceeded to the exit in line-ahead column, with *Baian* in the lead. After her went: *Admiral Makarov*, *Aurora*, *Grazhdanin*, *Amur*, all the gunboats and several large transports whose draft would not permit them to go via the Nukke–Vorms channel. The destroyers were stationed on both sides of the big ships. Abeam the Vormsi lighthouse the ships were met by the minesweepers, who led the armada to the exit to the open gulf along a course not usually taken by ships, as on such a course there was less chance of meeting enemy mines or submarines. At the very beginning of the movement, in about half an hour the minesweepers had swept up seven mines: how good would it have been for us had we left the previous day with only one pair of minesweepers!

The remainder of the passage was completely without incident. The enemy submarines patrolling around Dagerort missed us. By dawn all the ships had entered the Lapvik roadstead, where the 1st Brigade of Cruisers awaited us. Immediately on anchoring, Bakhirev bade me and the crew farewell in a heartfelt manner, transferred to a destroyer, while we came under the command of our direct superior, Admiral Pilkin, who had already come aboard while Bakhirev was with us. Pilkin, having received from Bakhirev a very flattering report of the cruiser's battle actions, congratulated the officers and crew and ordered us to proceed immediately to Helsinki in order to begin the work of repairing the damage.[10]

During the cruiser's passage through the roadstead, the *Sevastopol*, the brigade of dreadnoughts anchored there, and the 2nd Brigade, all gave us an ovation. But the character of this ovation was so unbridled in revolutionary spirit that our sailors, unaccustomed to anything of the sort, were quite stunned and did not respond in any way. It began with all the ships blossoming with signal flags. The first we could decipher seemed to be pure rabble-rousing balderdash such as: 'The revolutionary proletariat welcomes the valiant struggle for freedom' and so on, all in a similar spirit. Obviously, all these signals had been raised by the crews, without orders from officers. Indeed what significance could the officers have in ships where, obviously, all was stained with the blood of their tortured and murdered colleagues and where the murderers still lived side by side and continued to play a leading role, quite unpunished? The rails, turrets and bridges of the ships were covered with people who by their dress and unruly appearance bore little resemblance to sailors. The band on the flagship (*Petropavlovsk*) played the Marseillaise and various revolutionary rubbish, during which the playing was very clumsy: evidently the conscious lack of discipline had touched even the musicians. In between items the crews called out 'hurrah'. Our crew, crowded on the forecastle and amidships, were astonished and appeared scandalised by such a reception. In the literal sense they were speechless. One must add to this that our sailors had always openly condemned the murders committed in the *Petropavlovsk*, *Andrei* and *Pavel* and, in all truth, looked upon these ships with a feeling of some loathing and even terror.

Towards evening we arrived at Helsinki and anchored in an almost empty harbour. We were the first to report here the details of the Moön Sound battle, which had sown some natural anxiety among the wives of officers who had been at Moön Sound. From the very next day, in the most energetic manner, the repair of the damage received in the battle began.

Chapter V

The Bolsheviks in Power (October and November 1917)

Arrival at Helsinki · Promotion to admiral and appointment as Head of Brigade · Relations with the crews · The beginning of decline on the Baian *· Assembly of the whole brigade in Helsinki and visitation of the ships · The Bolshevik coup in Petrograd · The reaction of the higher command of the Naval Department to the coup · Captain 1st Rank E A Berens · Reaction to the coup in the Baltic Fleet · The beginnings of Bolshevik interference in the business of the fleet · The decree on the reform of authority in the fleet.*

On the day after our arrival at Helsinki the repair of the battle damage began in the most energetic manner.

For most people it was obvious that with the fall of Moön Sound the role of the fleet in defending the right flank of our Army was over. It had been difficult to imagine that the Germans would thrust through into the Gulf of Finland with their big ships, risking losing them on our minefields and taking some losses in battle with our dreadnoughts, when on their left flank they had quite a free hand, in an extreme case even so far as Reval itself. Besides that, their advance along the whole front had met with the weakest opposition. However, with the aim of preserving some semblance of a shred of fighting spirit, and with that of discipline, Razvozov and his Staff decided to exaggerate in every way the idea of a possible German attack on the Gulf of Finland. Thanks to this the big ships remained at their battle positions in full battle readiness and my cruiser was ordered to complete repairs in the shortest possible period, in order again to be able to take up her position in the line of battle (according to the new battle dispositions, the 1st Brigade of Cruisers was to take on the role of a reconnaissance vanguard).

I went to Petrograd from Helsinki for a single day. I had not been there since the time of the revolution and the abomination of desolation that reigned in the city produced an oppressive impression on me. The mood in society was anxious: no one trusted anyone or anything and everyone lived for the current day. In our Ministry and the General Staff the dominance of the commissars had already begun but still the majority of the officers remained in their positions (in their number: Verderevskii, Dudorov, Kukel,[1] Kapnist,[2] Berens, Dunin-Barkovskii,[3] Romanov). Outwardly some sort of order was being maintained, even the old couriers and watchmen were in their places, although bearing themselves far from as of old: each of these gentlemen by his words and manner strove to demonstrate that they, and not the officers, were now the bosses.

Several days after my return to Helsinki the Chief of the Brigade of Cruisers, Pilkin, came there, but was obliged to go ashore at once because of illness. His old pulmonary indisposition had intensified and threatened to develop into full-blown tuberculosis. He advised me confidentially that the question of his retirement on grounds of ill-health had already been decided (the doctors were sending him to a sanatorium) and that I was to be appointed in his place. In fact, about 15 October I received a telegram from Verderevskii, then Minister for the Navy, in which he congratulated me on promotion to rear admiral for distinction in operations against the enemy. Almost at the same time a telegram came from Fleet Commander Razvozov with the proposition that I immediately take up the command of the 1st Brigade of Cruisers, in accordance with the order already issued about my appointment (Razvozov was apparently at this time at Reval).

In ordinary times such a promotion, not through favouritism, not through seniority, but for distinction in battle at the nomination of such a leader as Bakhirev, and equally the appointment to command our very best fighting Brigade, would have overwhelmed me with natural feelings of pride and would have represented the complete satisfaction of my ambition in the service (which was, speaking frankly, quite poorly developed in me). But now, having observed the general progressive decline and being unable to foresee it ending, and also being aware that my power as a commander was reducing to nothing with each passing day, the promotion, and in particular the appointment, evoked far from feelings in me. To speak realistically, my responsibility had increased, new, increasingly complicated relations with the comrades had been created, and the pre-eminence of my new position bestowed almost nothing positive of any sort.

Immediately after my promotion and appointment I experienced several exceptionally pleasant moments that gave me great personal satisfaction. These were particularly valued in that time of endurance, when almost nothing still remained of the old respect towards officers. From my arrival from Moön Sound I had usually passed the night ashore, so on the day after receiving news of my promotion and appointment, I went on board ship, mustered the crew and, informing them of the content of the orders, said a few words to the effect that I considered the present rewards accounted to my credit as flowing not from my own service but from the irreproachable conduct of the officers and the crew of the cruiser, managing in such trying times to preserve both discipline and an excellent fighting spirit.

In response to my speech, which I had delivered in far from flowing terms owing to my emotional state, however much it had come from the heart, the delegate chosen from the crew (the gunnery petty officer) with my permission delivered a thorough, well-ordered veritable dithyramb about my valour in which he particularly emphasised that through my actions I had saved our ship from almost inevitable doom and with the ship, the crew. After this speech the crew, behaving overall with complete discipline and correctness and all correctly dressed in uniform, as in the old regime, without exception wished to shake my hand. On the completion of this somewhat tiresome procedure came a most unpleasant moment: the crew expressed the desire to toss me in the air ... However, even this turned out quite well: they tossed me very carefully and did not subject me to any sort of maiming.[4] As a finale, from somewhere an armchair appeared in which they sat me and, accompanied by the customary old-regime cries of 'hurrah', they carried me around the whole ship, not missing out the engine room and the stokers' hold. Then, at midday, with the usual ceremony, my newly awarded admiral's flag was hoisted.

It must be noted with regret, however, that this day, which might have been called a day of complete triumph of the old healthy fighting spirit of the ship over the corrupting influence of Bolshevik propaganda, was never again repeated. On the contrary, the noxious influence of the atmosphere onshore at Helsinki, saturated with distrust and hatred towards officers, began to tell extraordinarily quickly. This was assisted no little by the rapid progressive decline in discipline and the legal and well deserved rest and relaxation, that is, translated into ordinary language – the complete absence of any sort of work whatever and the constant coming and going ashore of a good three-quarters of the crew, where, assuredly, various deepeners did not slumber.

At the same time, by order of similar deepeners in Petrograd, measures were taken by which the ships lost that part of their crews who were most reliable and steady in terms of their convictions. The two most senior years of call-up, retained for service in the war, were retired to the reserve. The younger ones remaining after this were already deciding not to take an open stand against the Bolshevik leanings of their leaders and at best shrank into the background. On the streets I would quite often meet my own sailors, of whom I knew the very best side. Notwithstanding my recent popularity, these people tried to slip past me unnoticed. For them it was obviously better to pass me by without saluting, even though saluting had been preserved in the revolutionary regulations not as an obligatory measure but as a freely expressed greeting. On the other hand they feared that the conscious comrades would interpret such an act as counter-revolutionary. Frequently, in order to remove these people from difficulty, I greeted them first, addressing them by name, which caused them great embarrassment.

At the particular time of my appointment as Chief of the Brigade, no ship of the Brigade other than the *Baian* was at Helsinki. All the cruisers were at Lium or Lapvik. In the telegram Razvozov had suggested to me that I raise my flag on the *Baian* and remain at Helsinki. This slightly obscure direction is explained by the fact that Razvozov was not quite sure that my appointment, made without the authority of the comrades, would go through smoothly and might meet with protests from their side. For although Razvozov did not recognise the elective authority that had been implemented autonomously in several ships and even brigades (the 2nd Brigade of Cruisers and the battleships), all the same, in the interest of the service, he had to take into account the opinions of the crews in making higher appointments and so far as possible to sound out the ground in this direction. In this way, leaving me temporarily distant from the brigade entrusted to me, with only the cruiser whose crew related to me with definite good feelings, Razvozov wished to allow time for agitation about my unexpected appointment to dissipate.

However, things went smoother than might have been expected. Around about a week after my appointment I received an official rescript from the 'Brigade Committee' (the existence of which I first found out from this paper itself) that informed me that as a result of the election conducted by all crews of the brigade for the post of Chief of the Brigade, I had been chosen by a huge majority of votes. At the end of this curious paper, was written: 'Informed of this election, the Brigade Committee proposes that you, Mr. Admiral, fully enter into the responsibilities of this position in its strategic and political (*sic*!) character.'

In this way Razvozov's fears were dispersed and one way or another my appointment appeared to have been sanctioned by the comrades. When after several weeks the whole of my brigade gathered in the Helsinki roadstead (apart from the *Riurik*, which had been sent directly to Reval) I took up the actual command of the brigade without any sort of misunderstanding, making the rounds of all the ships according to my office. Things did not go off, however, without revolutionary curiosities: on doing the rounds of the ships, I would gather the crew and make a speech, previously carefully thought through, befitting the occasion. Obviously it did not touch on any political matter but described the existing military situation (that is, the danger of a breakthrough of the German fleet into the Gulf of Finland) and the pressing necessity to keep the ships in order and in full fighting readiness, not allowing themselves to be distracted by anything irrelevant. In general, the crews related to this speech very sympathetically, which was expressed by them replying to me clumsily: 'We'll try, Mister Admiral.'

On the *Bogatyr*, where I dined in the wardroom, the commander (Captain 1st Rank Politovskii[5]) informed me that one of the sailors, a confirmed Bolshevik, definitely wanted to talk with me. I expressed agreement, after which a sailor with a very affable manner appeared, and, beginning with a robust: 'Your good health, Mister Admiral,' immediately recommended himself as from my home country – a peasant from one of the villages located quite close to my family estate. He said that he had not been home for seven years and was quite behind the news from there. After that he posed to me a whole raft of questions about various landowners and other people known to both of us. Having satisfied his curiosity as far as I could and interested by the well-wishing tone of his inquiries, which so little fitted with his Bolshevism, I put the question to him: 'Is it true you are a Bolshevik?' He replied in the affirmative. Then I began to question him about his property situation, from which it emerged that he was a relatively significant land owner, holding about 50 desiatinas.[6] After this I said to him: 'But then, won't you be sad to give up your land, since under the "just" redistribution you would be left with no more than several desiatinas?' He immediately erupted: 'Give up? Under what article? No, no, this can't be so: the land will be taken from the big landholders and merchants and given to us, but they will take nothing from the peasants. Well, I won't be giving it up!' No reasoning of any sort would help, as he remained of his own opinion. I reckon that nine-tenths, if not all, the peasant-Bolsheviks, reasoned thus, and indeed do so to this time.

On 26 October the ultimate coup of the Bolsheviks took place in Petrograd, after which power finally passed into the hands of Lenin and Trotsky. The putrid, fussing about on all sides Kerenshchina regime passed over its place almost without struggle to the reign of impudent ruthless adventurists, thanks to the personal narrow aims of those deciding to perform their wondrous experiment on the living organism of Russia, weakened by war and the peculiarities of the revolution. In complete concord with the laws of historical consequences, the final act of revolutionary deepening was set in train, plunging Russia to the very depths and expunging her from the list of cultured nations for many years.

In a fundamental manner the Bolshevik slogans contradicted all sensible long-established understanding about the organisation of authority, as a consequence of which there were major changes immediately and automatically in the composition of the higher management of all establishments. All the business-like and sensible elements remaining still in their place, not having lost completely an understanding of personal honour and service orderliness, felt that to remain in authority any longer in the intolerable conditions now created would be a crime against the Motherland and against one's own conscience. So from the higher administrative staff of the Naval Ministry departed Verderevskii (Minister), who, claiming illness, avoided arrest; Graf Kapnist (Chief of the Naval General Staff) and Kukel (Assistant Naval Minister), who openly stated his unwillingness to subordinate himself to the new authorities, for which he was arrested. Dudorov, the other Assistant Naval Minister, already appointed to the position of Naval attaché in Japan, made his way through Siberia to his post. The best officers of the Naval General Staff and the Headquarters Staff had already left. There remained only about twenty people who would have served under any sort of regime, even be it of Hottentots. The Head of the Navy Department turned out in fact to be that purser's clerk from one of the dreadnoughts, a certain Dybenko, and the leader of the brain of the fleet – the General Staff – was Midshipman Raskolnikov, to whom I have referred earlier.

Captain 1st Rank Yevgenii Andreevich Berens,[7] the assistant to the previous incumbent Kapnist, officially remained at the head of the General Staff. Up until the Bolsheviks came to power this no longer young but very capable officer (before the war he had been the Naval attaché in Germany and from 1915 to 1917 in Rome), had not caused anyone to doubt his internal stability. His remaining in the service of the Bolsheviks, freely decided, struck us all, his former colleagues and friends, as a major riddle. In conscience I can say that of the naval officers of higher rank, completely stainless in a moral sense, he was the sole one agreeing to serve the Bolsheviks faithfully and truly. What was this about?

Subsequently, before my departure for the Far East in the spring of 1918, I had several occasions to talk heart to heart with him. He told me that he had remained in service to the Bolsheviks in the humiliating and difficult role of implementer of the most absurd commands of the leaders of Bolshevism and the clutch of illiterate sailors comprising the Supreme Naval Collegium with the sole aim of carrying on secret work to support and re-establish a necessary, certainly non-Bolshevik, new order. To my response that had he not taken upon himself an unsustainable and physically unrealisable task, and would not his activities lead quite simply to the strengthening of Soviet authority, he answered that he had already himself begun to realise that in the existing conditions of constant surveillance over him, such work was extraordinarily difficult and almost unbearable. But now it was already too late; all the same, there was no way back for him and he would stay at his post to the end. I little doubt that the mission taken on by him was basically, perhaps, well intentioned, and could have led in the best of circumstances to showing some degree of moral support for that mass of unfortunate lower-rank naval officers whom hunger and family circumstances obliged to work for the Bolsheviks. As with all the others remaining to save their own skin, he had to swim with the tide, that is, to say otherwise, Berens and his like would not cause Bolshevism to evolve, but Bolshevism would drag them along with it, making use of them forcefully for its own purposes.

So far as is known to us, all of the more or less honourable and energetic opponents of Bolshevism who had entered into service with the Bolsheviks to pursue a secret struggle against them have already long ago been shot or have fled abroad. Those who, like Berens, remained and still live to the present continuing to be accounted in power, have inevitably had to waive their fine slogans and have turned into rank-and-file workers of Bolshevism either under the lash or for a crust of stale bread. For Berens as justification there might yet serve the fact that as a convinced Germanophile and supporter of German culture he hoped that the Bolsheviks, having completed the peace with the Germans, would have fallen under their beneficial influence, by which their own internal evolution would be accelerated in high degree and so they might leave the scene, having not succeeded in causing significant harm to the country. Having realised his mistake, in all probability, he decided to pursue a temporising policy, all the more so because for him there was no other way out. By that time, at the very beginning of the existence of the communist experiment, to flee abroad for such as he, so close to the persons of Lenin and Trotsky, was obviously impossible.

Possibly I have spent too long over the personality of Berens and the motives behind his decision to serve under the Bolsheviks. But I was drawn to this firstly by the extraordinary nature of his figure, and, secondly, by that burning interest that evoked, and evokes particularly now, among thinking honourable officers, the question of what was the more proper course: to remain with the Bolsheviks trying, like Berens, by secret work to prepare the way for a reactionary evolution, or, realising the futility and even harm of such work, to struggle openly with the Bolsheviks, as did Kolchak, Denikin, and many others who staked their lives and condemned themselves, in the event of failure, to the dragged-out life of the émigré? For me personally the question was always quite clear, as it is now: never could secret, crooked, Jesuitical means give rise to good or generally appropriate results in any sort of affair. A building constructed in such a manner sooner or later would collapse, like a house of cards. If the direct route of honourable struggle is not possible, then better to stand aside and commit oneself to exile than to take part **voluntarily** in the ruin of the Motherland, wrapping oneself in Jesuitical logic and sophisms.

In the first period after the Bolshevik enthronement, among people worthy of respect there had been no difference of opinion in deciding this question: everyone considered that to work for the Bolsheviks was impossible. The force of direct impressions and personal, very severe, life experiences connected with bringing the Bolshevik paradise on earth into being promoted this view to a significant degree. Nowadays, when the sharpness of sensations have long gone, weak, although honourable, refugee hearts are beginning to entertain doubts, so they propose: Might it not have been better to remain in the Soviet? The weariness of émigré life, the natural yearning for one's homeland and the insolent lying Bolshevik propaganda about the 'Soviet paradise' conducted by their agents abroad, although occasionally sweet-sounding, fostered the development of such thoughts to a high degree, leading directly to the 'changing signposts' movement.[8]

Unfortunately, all those leaning towards appeasement forget or do not wish to think about the fact that any sort of thoughtful emigrant wishing to return to their homeland at present, that is, any irreconcilable opponent of Bolshevism, above all has to contend with the need to choose between three alternatives: either make a break with all the past, wholeheartedly bow down before the Bolsheviks, taking thereafter the path of active collaboration with them to the glory of the International but certainly not for the Motherland; or else, recognising from the first steps the impossibility of such a repudiation, commit oneself to a miserable humiliating vegetative life under the yoke of the Bolshevik regime, in the manner of the majority of the intelligentsia who remain in Russia, carrying out senseless, unconscionable work under the lash, for the sake of a crust of bread.

There is yet a third pathway – underground work aimed at the overthrow of the Soviet regime. But in my opinion, in the light of the ideal organisation of secret surveillance in Soviet Russia, such work, for which the majority of our intelligentsia are quite inept, would be quite unfruitful. So what is the better path in such conditions – go to Soviet Russia or vegetate abroad, awaiting a natural death or the expiry of Soviet power? It seems to me that there can be no two opinions. I consider that for a person of steady and honourable awareness, to go to Russia now, while Soviet power still exists – this is to condemn oneself to suicide, physical or moral, depending on the circumstances.

However, I have sharply deviated from the thread of my story, diverted by so painful a theme for all Russian émigrés. I will have reason yet to return to this question, but for now I will carry forward the further description of events.

During the first days of the Bolshevik overthrow no excesses nor any sort of substantial change in the Baltic Fleet occurred. This can be explained by the fact that in recent times military events had significantly withdrawn the fleet from participation in internal politics, as a consequence of which interest in the struggle for power at the centre had greatly diminished. All operational orders and instructions came directly from the Supreme Commander of the Northern Front, General Cheremisov, to whom our fleet was subordinate; the connection with Petrograd was purely formal. Along with that, the Bolsheviks, having seized power, felt themselves in the initial days still to be in a precarious position and were far from confident in the crews of the active fleet being in support of them, as a consequence of which they did not hurry with the implementation of their new arrangements in the fleet. It is also possible that, aware from experience that the intelligentsia did not wish to go along with them, they were afraid that acting with undue haste might alienate the command structure in the fleet, in a similar way to what had happened in the central establishments in Petrograd. The fleet might then have lost the last trace of fighting capacity and there would have been nothing to stop the Germans from taking Reval and advancing on Petrograd. Whatever the cause, we were only made conversant with events, but no particular instructions were received.

On the second day after the overthrow, Razvozov gathered the available admirals and tried to get an understanding of the present situation. It was decided, without officially recognising Bolshevik authority, that all would remain for the time being at their posts and continue their military work, awaiting further developments. The principal motive for the retention of the commanders and officers at their posts was the awareness that the war with the Germans was still continuing and it was fully possible there would be further fighting engagements. At the same time, as final authority had not yet been taken from us leaders and the ships had not yet lost their fighting capacities, so we considered it our military duty to remain at our posts, to continue our fighting obligations towards the Motherland to the end, so far as possible ignoring those who had usurped government authority. However, political events continued to unfold and very quickly, within about ten days, it was already clear that such an arrangement could not last long.

The first indication of this was the direction, issued not through the Fleet Commander and his Staff, but directly through the committees, of the immediate despatch from the ships of fifty to one hundred 'volunteers' to the internal front around Petrograd for the defence of the Bolshevik powers from the troops supposedly advancing from the front. The crews, who were in some confusion from the moment of the coup (I consider that at most three-quarters of the general number of sailors were not sympathetic towards the Bolsheviks, but were deathly afraid of them), fulfilled this order without question, informing the commanders only *post factum*. So by the evening the volunteers had already been sent by train and I, the Brigade Commander, found out about this only in the morning, when I came aboard ship. Moreover, my orderly was among the sailors dispatched from the *Baian*, a very fine fellow and certainly not a Bolshevik. It was reported to me with some embarrassment that the lot had fallen on him, so apparently volunteers had generally not been forthcoming. I raced off to Razvozov but he only spread his hands helplessly and said that he was powerless to do anything. All the orders had bypassed him and he had only been able to gain an assurance that all these people would be immediately returned to the ships when the need had passed. Razvozov, however, telegraphed a protest to Petrograd, but received the reply (apparently signed by Dybenko) that this direction was not an operational one but in the sphere of internal politics and therefore in general did not concern the admirals and commanders.

Soon after this came a crash of real thunder. The decree of the People's Commissars about the complete reorganisation of the higher management of the fleet was received. At the head of the hierarchy was placed a collegial establishment, which was to be composed on the same basis as the committees, that is, it would not have a single officer in its composition. This establishment, which was named as previously the Central Committee (in the Baltic Fleet – TsentroBalt) would exercise the full powers previously belonging to the Fleet Commander. Within the composition of this committee was established a special section – the War Section, at the head of which was one of the members of the committee, also a sailor, called the President of the Section. To assist the President, one of the senior officers of the fleet was appointed after being selected by TsentroBalt, who was called the Manager of the Section and, in essence, continued to fulfil all the previous functions of the Fleet Commander, but under the immediate control and instructions of the sailor-President, and in more serious circumstances, of TsentroBalt itself. The former Staff of the Fleet Commander went wholly into the War Section but with the difference only that a member of TsentroBalt – a sailor – was placed at the head of each separate part of it.

The decree addressed the reorganisation of only the higher levels of fleet management, that is, the responsibilities of the Fleet Commander and his Staff. However, implementing it suggested the development of a template for similar reconstruction of all similar subordinate parts of the fleet, that is, the separate brigades, divisions and shore establishments. However, the Bolsheviks did not hasten with bringing this into being, so that up to the time of my own departure from Helsinki at the beginning of January 1918 my brigade continued to exist on the old basis. It was clear that with the implementation of the new order the role of officer commanders had changed unquestionably into carrying out the orders and instructions of the sailors placed at the head of the various establishments. To protest or argue with the latter would have been senseless, since in such a case there would immediately arise an accusation of counter-revolution and any free-thinking officer would in the best of circumstances be arrested. The continuation of any sort of military work had been rendered senseless, as first of all it demanded a single line of command, which in reality this decree had brought to naught.

Chapter VI
The Death Throes of the Fleet

Razvozov's struggle with TsentroBalt and the Naval Collegium · The visit of Modest Ivanov · The arrest of Razvozov · His departure from the position of Fleet Commander · The gathering of the Admirals with Bakhirev · Schism among them · The officer meeting at the Naval Club · Ruzhek in the service of the Bolsheviks · Giving notice of retirement from office · Transfer with the Brigade to Reval · The situation in Reval · Leaving the Brigade and moving to Helsinki · Departure for Petrograd and discharge from service.

Immediately on receiving the decree on about 15 November, Razvozov gathered together the division heads to discuss the situation created by it. As it turned out, this was to be the last gathering in which the sailor members of TsentroBalt did not participate. All participants in this gathering unanimously agreed that the implementation of such a decree was fatal for the fleet, depriving it of the possibility not only of continuing military work but also of maintaining any sort of further good order. Then it was decided to endow Razvozov with all possible means to resist the implementation of the decree and insist on the preservation of the former arrangements. In the meantime, until the actual implementation of the new order, all, together with Razvozov, were to remain at their posts. This meeting was not attended by Bakhirev, who had earlier, as soon as the decree became known, announced that he would leave. Learning of the decisions of the meeting, he agreed not to leave his post so long as Razvozov remained in authority.

On the subsequent demand from TsentroBalt for the immediate implementation of the new arrangements, Razvozov replied that he could not agree to their implementation before it had been reviewed by a special commission in which representatives of the Staff – officers – were to participate, about which he had telegraphed to Petrograd. In the event that TsentroBalt were to insist then he, together with all of the admirals and commanders, would be obliged to leave their posts. TsentroBalt accused Razvozov of calling for sabotage, but decided, however, not to insist on the immediate implementation of the new demands, fearing it would be left without experienced specialists. The Petrograd Naval Collegium, however, did not agree with Razvozov, explaining that an experienced officer had participated in the preparation of the decree – to wit Captain 1st Rank Modest Ivanov. This unprincipled, extremely ambitious and envious officer, up to this time filling the position of Chief of the 2nd Brigade of Cruisers (by election of the crews in the time of Maksimov) had by his outrageous and blatant demagoguery reduced his brigade to complete ruin well before the Bolsheviks. He was held in the very worst repute by all commanders of the fleet, not excluding even Maksimov himself. Not long before he had demanded that Razvozov make him an admiral, which he was sharply refused. Immediately upon the Bolshevik coup, seizing the moment, he took himself off to Petrograd without Razvozov's permission and offered his services to the new authorities, recommending himself as a convinced Bolshevik. As became evident later, two main considerations motivated him: to achieve the rank of admiral and to spite Razvozov. The Bolsheviks understood even then that without a cadre of senior officers they could not get anywhere and therefore were very pleased at his appearance. And since he was not only a qualified officer but a Brigade commander, almost an admiral, but even so a Bolshevik who had suffered under the authorities, this gave him the highest significance that could be imagined. They made him a member of the Naval Collegium 'in right of the Minister for the Navy', that is, as a specialist on the Collegium composed of sailors. Then his first dream was fulfilled – he was made an admiral.

So when Razvozov first protested about the implementation of the new order and TsentroBalt complained about him, Ivanov began to put into action his second dream, that is, to set in motion the achievement of his revenge against Razvozov. Up to this time Razvozov had felt some ground beneath his feet as, first, all those subordinate to him had agreed with him (at least in word). At the same time, his popularity with the ships' crews, especially those of the Destroyer Division and the 1st Brigade of Cruisers, had become apparent and the Bolsheviks could not but take this into account. All this gave Razvozov the possibility of conversing with TsentroBalt in more straightforward language, continuing to insist on the impossibility of implementing their demands about carrying the decree into full effect. Finally, the Naval Collegium apparently decided that Razvozov's persistence was undermining the prestige of the authorities and sent the Minister himself, that is, Modest Ivanov, to Helsinki to settle the conflict – that is, to bring the decree into effect.

Arriving at Helsinki without any warning, he began by going straight to the ship where the commander had been his former subordinate and ordered the raising of his pennant as Naval Minister. When Razvozov was advised of this incident he announced that he recognised no such Naval Minister and considered the raising of the pennant on a ship subordinate to him in the roadstead, where he himself was the senior officer as the Fleet Commander, to be an infraction against all existing rules and a personal insult to him, Razvozov. This was, of course, communicated to Modest Ivanov. I do not know what Ivanov had proposed to do previously but after this he went to TsentroBalt on the former yacht *Shtandart* and demanded the calling of an extraordinary session with the summoning of Razvozov to face depositions in relation to a whole raft of accusations hanging over him.

When news of this reached the officers, a group of commanders from Razvozov's closest friends in the Destroyer Division, the ships of which were anchored around the *Krechet* where Razvozov lived, decided to make an attempt to resolve the conflict in some way or other. It was not difficult to foresee that the situation now created, in the context of the bitterness and absolutely inappropriate behaviour of Modest Ivanov, would threaten Razvozov at the very least with prison. One of this group, Captain 1st Rank Vilken,[1] took upon himself the thankless task of conducting discussions with Ivanov. The latter, as the coward he was, had already begun to fear that he might come completely unstuck along with Razvozov and therefore he very eagerly came forward and announced that he had nothing against going to Razvozov for preliminary discussions, but he was not sure that he (Razvozov) would extend him his hand. After this the group talked it over with Razvozov and it was decided to deal with it in this way: a signal would be sent to gather all flag officers on the *Krechet*, after which, in about half an hour, Modest Ivanov was to arrive. The flag officers were to show support for Razvozov. So this they did.

In the half hour after our arrival on the *Krechet*, before the arrival of Ivanov, a plan of action was worked out, namely: in order not to insult Ivanov, to try to demonstrate to him the complete inappropriateness of his behaviour, to insist that he apologise to Razvozov for the impropriety of his actions and to persuade him not to take measures in TsentroBalt against Razvozov. Finding himself in the company of his former colleagues and comrades (no 'comrades' in quotation marks were present at the meeting) who were quite adversely disposed towards him, Ivanov immediately gave way and adopted the tone of an aggrieved child. Without the slightest difficulty, he agreed in words to all the points of our demands but under one condition: that Razvozov and all of us gathered on the *Krechet* should recognise him as Naval Minister. Seeing no way out, we agreed, but in our turn demanded from him written acknowledgement that he considered his account with Razvozov settled and would do nothing to harm him. After long wrangling in the meanest tones, he, finally, agreed and signed the paper we had composed earlier. But – alas, we lost sight of the fact that such a paper had no significance whatsoever for such a scoundrel ...

At three o'clock that afternoon a session of the TsentroBalt was convened on the former Imperial yacht *Shtandart*. We admirals had also been invited to this meeting and for the sake of Razvozov we decided to go. For the first and last time since the revolution, with a heavy heart and a bitter feeling, I trod the deck of the yacht, where in my time I had spent more than three years as executive officer and with which for me were enshrined such shining memories of the Imperial Family now incarcerated in far-off Siberia ... Times had changed: the Imperial yacht, in its time the favourite accommodation of the Imperial Family, the sole place, it seems, where the Sovereign found complete rest from his excessive toil, had changed into a den of murderers and thieves, ruining and destroying all that bore any relationship whatsoever to monarchist foundations ... What a wicked irony of fate ...

About forty members of TsentroBalt were at the long table in the Imperial dining room – exclusively sailors, dressed however suited them, only not in uniform, with an undisciplined, unmilitary appearance. Along the side, by the window, several seats had been placed for the admirals. At the servery part of the dining room, where previously the hors d'oeuvres table had been, some sort of lectern for speakers had been erected.

After the opening of the session, the initial word was given to comrade Modest Ivanov. The latter, forgetting all about his promises, in a long and passionate, although incoherent, speech delivered a complete denunciation against Razvozov. But fortunately for Razvozov, this speech was so personal, so evil, disclosing all the pettiness of the small and foul character of Ivanov, that it made a negative impression even on the rabble in the auditorium. After Ivanov the floor was given to Razvozov, who, in a firmly thought-out, restrained speech, devoid of any sort of personal reflections, replied to each of the accusations from Ivanov. Then began quite blind, unsystematic debates and discussions, by the results of which it became sufficiently evident that the majority was opposed to appointment of a commission to review the decree about the organisation of authority. However, the most severe question raised by Ivanov, of Razvozov's non-recognition of the existence of Bolshevik authority, turned out completely favourably. Strangely enough, this was thanks to the curious announcement by one of the influential members of TsentroBalt that this was a matter of personal conscience and we could enter into this sphere, as now there was freedom of conscience.

Sensing that the ground was slipping from beneath his feet, Ivanov promptly changed his tone and, wishing to adapt to the general mood, began to eulogize Razvozov, which was absolutely revolting to hear. Since Razvozov had in his justificatory speech referred to us, the admirals, we then became drawn into the general discussion. I do not exactly remember the precise formulation of the questions that we were asked but I remember only my own reply: I announced I was solidly behind Razvozov and in the event of implementation of the new order and the departure from his post of the Fleet Commander, I also would be obliged to go. The other admirals pronounced something similar.

As a result of this quite stormy session, a resolution was passed affirming the desirability of Razvozov remaining at his post right until the final implementation of the new order. Razvozov's justifications were considered satisfactory. Sensing the complete collapse of his game, Ivanov, in order to rectify the impression somewhat, decided to make a final noble gesture. In his closing speech he congratulated Razvozov for the complete trust shown in him on the part of the comrades and then, quite unexpectedly, advised him of his promotion to vice admiral, as if in accordance with a direction already given by the Supreme Naval Collegium. However, on this point, evidently, Ivanov had exceeded his authority: the fact of the promotion was not only not confirmed but on the contrary, after several days a decree came out abolishing all ranks, including, obviously, that of admiral.

On this occasion the victory over Ivanov had been complete, but it gave little comfort to Razvozov and the rest of us. It was felt that he departed from us as an irreconcilable enemy and further persecution was to be expected from his side. Several days after his departure in fact an event took place that broke our unsteady stability and plunged the fleet into a condition of terminal chaos. This event almost coincided with the decree about the abolition of rank and occurred, if I am not mistaken, about 10 December. In Helsinki the trusty lackey of Lenin and Trotsky, Raskolnikov, appeared, who achieved that which Ivanov had been unable to do. He arrived without warning, gathered on the *Shtandart* that part of TsentroBalt prejudiced against Razvozov (about fifteen people) and without difficulty insisted on them passing a resolution for his immediate arrest in the light of his obvious counter-revolutionary activities. The main allegation against him was his opposition to implementing the new order. Not long after this session several of the sailors who had participated, armed from head to foot, were dispatched by automobile to Razvozov's apartment, where they advised him of his arrest and took him in the car to the town prison. Immediately after this, that same evening, Raskolnikov went back to Petrograd.

By night time the news of Razvozov's arrest had spread through the ships and reached those members of TsentroBalt who had not taken part in it. On the initiative of several keen defenders of Razvozov, an extraordinary plenary session of TsentroBalt was summoned at which a resolution was carried on the complete illegality of the actions of the minority who had arrested Razvozov, ordering his immediate release and the arrest for arbitrary actions of the main guilty party in the whole proceedings – Raskolnikov. The latter order obviously could not be carried out, since by this time Raskolnikov had already departed from Helsinki. On the morning following his arrest, Razvozov was released and led ceremonially to the *Krechet* where, by the way, his flag had still not been struck. However, this event, proving the complete precariousness of the position of even such a popular person as Razvozov, filled the cup of his patience to overflowing. He announced that in such conditions he could no longer remain in his position. No manner of entreaties affected him and he went ashore right then and there, for the time being passing command to the Chief of Staff, Prince Cherkasskii.

On the same morning a gathering of all flag officers was held on the ship of the senior of the admirals present, Bakhirev, who flew his flag on the *Chaika*. Present were: Veis[2] (Patrol Brigade), Patton (2nd Brigade of Battleships), Zarubaev (1st Brigade of Battleships), Dmitriev (2nd Brigade of Cruisers), Mikhail Andreevich Berens (Chief of Staff to Bakhirev) and myself. Bakhirev referred to the general decision taken almost a month before, to leave the service in the event of Razvozov leaving and the implementation of the Bolshevik arrangements. In his opinion, this moment had come since Razvozov had already left and with his departure, obviously, there was no longer any obstacle to the implementation of the new arrangements. Doubtless the Bolsheviks would without difficulty find an officer who would replace Razvozov and agree to all conditions. Bakhirev proposed to compose a reasoned protest, connecting it with the announcement of relinquishment of one's position.

However, this proposal was met with unexpected protests. Zarubaev, who up to now had a reputation as a completely proper person, astonished us all with the unexpected announcement that 'the Bolsheviks had in fact taken power into their hands and it was our job to be subordinate to them, not to debate matters'. I have possibly not given his exact words but the sense was such anyway. Other admirals, while not expressing sympathy for Zarubaev's pronouncement, protested against immediately leaving the service, since, in their opinion, it was still not clear how the matter would turn out.

In the light of such vacillation in opinions, based, without doubt, on wisdom being overcome thanks to selfish interests but obviously to the detriment of personal propriety and steadfastness of convictions – Bakhirev announced that he remained of his previous view and in no circumstances would he stay and serve the Bolsheviks, helping them to ruin the Motherland and the fleet. Berens and I shared Bakhirev's opinion and after some time Patton also joined us. The rest remained silent and left.

From this moment a sharp schism took place among the admirals that divided us into two irreconcilable camps. In the first camp – the confirmed and solid opponents of Bolshevism, who would undertake no compromise and who considered that to remain in service with the Bolsheviks **voluntarily** was inconsistent with their conscience, their honour and their understanding of their service duty and usefulness towards their country. To this group belonged: Razvozov, Bakhirev, Prince Cherkasskii, Patton, Stark, Mikhail Berens and I. To the other group, working for the Bolsheviks not from fear but from conscience, were Zarubaev, Ruzhek and Zelenoi.[3] Finally, adhering to this camp from weakness, fearing for their own skin, were St. Dimitriev,[4] Veis and Kitkin.

The schism in opinions among the admirals played a huge role in the struggle over the implementation of the Bolsheviks' arrangements. It deprived the officers of their main weapons – solidarity and unity. The Bolsheviks understood that without experienced and educated specialists they could not succeed and very much feared that the whole mass of officers would quit, leaving them no better off than they were at the start. This must explain their caution in implementing the new arrangements and their delicacy towards Razvozov, whose popularity they feared. With the departure of Razvozov and differences of opinion having become clear among the admirals (who up to this point had welded the authority of Razvozov together), the Bolsheviks felt their hands to be untied and with a calm heart they set about implementing the reform.

The general run of the officers, until now prepared to go with their admirals, having learnt of the schism, lost their trust in them and decided to go each his own way. On the initiative of several energetic young officers, a general gathering of all naval officers present in

Helsinki was organised at the Naval Club. About 200 officers attended this meeting and discussed exactly that question which had been raised at Bakhirev's meeting. Several fiery, frank speeches, delivered without censorship, electrified the auditorium and a unanimous resolution was carried on the voices – all present refused to serve with the Bolsheviks. Unfortunately the resolution was not **immediately** confirmed with signatures. However, notwithstanding the outward unity, it appeared that far from everyone sympathised with the resolution, giving way to it only from fear of being taken for a renegade. Several orators (let us assume they were hissed off the stage) even put forward speeches quite similar to Zarubaev's announcement (Captain 1st Rank Dudkin[5]). Over the course of several days when signatures were being collected, already very many declined to support the resolution, citing the absence of unity even among the admirals. In this way the matter was decisively lost.

As mentioned earlier, I had personally decided to leave the service anyway. The departure of Razvozov served as the trigger, all the more so because by the beginning of December, from the condition of our ships, it had become quite evident that any sort of further naval engagements whatsoever were impossible. Besides that, the Bolsheviks had at that time begun to howl about 'peace with no annexations or reparations' and, any day now, one could expect the shameful conclusion of a separate armistice with Germany.

Therefore I sent to the Fleet Commander (although he no longer existed) a submission with the following content: 'The reform being implemented at the current time in the fleet will, in my opinion, lead to its decisive doom. For this reason, not having the ability to prevent this, and not considering myself entitled to take part in work deleterious to the fleet, I submit my request to relinquish my position.' Similar submissions were sent simultaneously by Bakhirev, Berens, Shevelyov and several others. Shevelyov's submission was written in somewhat sharper terms, as a consequence of which he was arrested and charged with insulting the powers that be. After some days, however, they released him, in which the sailors of his division of destroyers were helpful.

Our submissions similarly at first evoked strong concern at TsentroBalt, where they were discussed. They accused us of sabotage and threatened to imprison us in a coal bunker, but then, learning that the crews of the units subordinate to us were well-disposed towards us, decided to leave us in peace, forwarding our submissions to Petrograd for review by the Supreme Naval Collegium. At this time the position of Manager of the War Section was already occupied by Ruzhek,[6] who, it seems, had proposed himself for it. Until this Ruzhek had occupied the position of Chief of the Brigade of Minelayers, and so was to be counted among those who had been oppressed by the authorities. From the beginning of the revolution he had all the time played up to the comrades who had elected him to the position. He had never distinguished himself for anything at all, apart from a fondness for alcohol.[7]

Having sent in our request for discharge, we continued in our positions, voluntarily remaining in the service so as not to give grounds for excesses likely to harm other officers. Besides, I was also bound by my promise given to Razvozov, as before his own departure he had secured my word that I would not abandon the Brigade without having taken it to Reval and settled it into its winter quarters.

While remaining in our positions, however, we had no relations whatsoever with Ruzhek, completely ignoring his appointment. For the first week he also issued no orders, nor did TsentroBalt.

Between 15 and 20 December I moved with the Brigade to Reval. In this I acted without any direction from Ruzhek, but on the basis of the instructions already given by Razvozov. The deterioration immediately showed itself: the ships did not keep station, spreading out over several miles, and the *Oleg* ran aground on the way out. The booms had not been opened in a timely fashion. At Reval order was somewhat better and after several hours all ships were moored within the harbour. On the same day I tried to visit all the commanding people ashore in order to assess the degree of order in the fortified area and the potential for defence in the event of an attack by the Germans. It appeared that the senior officer (to whom, incidentally, the fleet was not subordinated) – the Fortress Commandant – was ill and not receiving anyone. At that time the Commandant was the Army General Izmestev,[8] who had tried by any means to mollify both the Bolsheviks and the local Estonians, who were already beginning to play at self-determination. The Chief of Staff was the young Colonel of the General Staff, Kostandi,[9] at that time sitting in the guard house on some accusation or other. He had been arrested certainly not by the authorities but by committeemen from among the soldiers.

It turned out that I was the senior among the naval commanders. On the following day I summoned all the commanders of separate sections to meet in the accommodation of the Signals Intelligence Service to discuss the situation. There gathered the Commander of the Port, Colonel Iaron, the Chief of the Signals Intelligence Service Captain 1st Rank Novopashennii,[10] the Chief of the Fortified Naval Front Captain 1st Rank Zherve[11] and the senior of the division commanders representing the Chief of the Submarine Division.

A completely forlorn picture emerged. The Army troops and the fortress units were in a state of complete demoralisation. The naval batteries, according to Zherve, were in a better position but against the background of general deterioration this did not have much significance. In connection with the possibility of a German attack, the general mood among the troops and the civilians of non-German origin was panic-stricken, which, however, helped to maintain some semblance of order in the town. A plan of evacuation had been worked out. In the opinion of the more pessimistic and perhaps more sensible commander, Iaron, we could expect the Germans in about three weeks, even more likely within four weeks, and there could certainly be no opposition to them. According to the Chief of the Signals Intelligence Service, all of the above-mentioned facts had been known to fleet Staff. I could only regret that I had taken the Brigade to Reval, as it was evident that in a few weeks it would be necessary to begin the evacuation of the fortress region and the Brigade could not have assisted in the defence of the fortress under siege by troops even in normal times as the Gulf had already begun to freeze over and naval operations were becoming impossible.

Following this I convened a meeting of all my commanders and one representative from each of the ships' committees on the *Riurik*, to which I had transferred my flag in the first days of my arrival. Setting out the situation, I turned to the committeemen and asked them to exercise what influence they could on the crews not to desert and to preserve the ships in readiness for taking to sea, which would be required in the event of a German advance on Reval. Rather strangely, my request was fulfilled exactly and after a month (by then without me) the ships successfully returned first to Helsinki and then to Kronstadt, escaping the Germans. I attribute this not to my influence or the influence of other commanders but simply to the natural feelings of self-preservation of the comrades and their wish not to quit their free accommodation – the ships.

Considering my role in the Brigade finished in this way, the next day I gathered together only the commanders, informed them officially of my departure, set out the relevant reasons and with that explained my point of view to them about how, in my opinion, the commanders and officers ought to respond to my departure. I said that each commander and individual officer must act as he wished, certainly not considering my decision and my opinion binding on himself — that I in no way judged nor would judge those officers who remained in service with the Bolsheviks against their will, as I fully understood to what difficult material conditions they would consign their families in the event of a departure, and secondly, I generally recognised the difference between **my** situation and that of **other** officers. Because of my position, I would be directly subordinate to the comrades, with which I could not reconcile myself. Others, more junior officers, continued to remain subordinate to officers – to commanders, senior officers and so on. Certainly, this latter proposition suffered from a degree of equivocation, but I did not wish for any officer to follow me out of a slavish imitation of one's senior rather than from conviction, and therefore I tried to give them a greater avenue for compromise with their conscience.

Following that I informed them that in accordance with the circular issued not long ago by the Supreme Naval Collegium, up to 50 per cent of fleet personnel were to be sent on a three-week furlough. Therefore I suggested that those officers who, like me, did not wish to remain in service with the Bolsheviks, should make use of this leave now, which would give them the possibility of leaving Bolshevik service without any sort of risk of being accused of sabotage and so on. The commanders listened to me silently, making almost no statements or responses. Subsequently, when the Brigade had to leave for Kronstadt, two of the commanders – Captain 1st Rank Rudnev[12] of the *Riurik* and Captain 1st Rank Politovskii of the *Bogatyr* – remained ashore and became prisoners of the Germans. Not long after my announcement,

50 per cent of officers went on leave, of whom the greater part did not return to their ships. Of the commanders in the Brigade there remained the commander of the *Makarov*, Captain 1st Rank Spolatbog (subsequently Commander of the Brigade) and the Commander of the *Baian*, Captain 1st Rank Stark,[13] who died soon afterwards.

From this moment I ceased in fact to be Commander of the Brigade, went ashore and settled to await news of my discharge or leave, about which the new Chief of the Staff, Captain 1st Rank Shchastnyi, had promised to inform me soon. I settled in the town, in a German-furnished house, where rooms had been taken earlier by two of my commanders – Politovskii and Stark.

During this short period of my life ashore at Reval only once did I have occasion to take part in naval matters not relating to the Brigade. One morning the office manager of the Naval Club, which had been closed since the moment of the Bolshevik coup, came to me and informed me that the local Estonian anarchists had just inspected the club's accommodation and told the watchman (the former doorman) that they intended to take from it all the property they found in it. To the watchman's objection that the club belonged to the Navy Department and without the permission of the local port authorities and the Port Committee nothing could be given to anyone, the anarchists replied that they spat on this and that in any event they would take the club, even if by force. It must be said that not long before this the Naval Club at Helsinki had been occupied by anarchists, only there they had done it without any warning and not even TsentroBalt had been able to dislodge them. The watchman became agitated and rushed with his report to the Port Commander, who, having investigated the matter, sent the office manager to inform me about the occurrence.

At first I did not understand what this had to do with me, but then I worked out that as the most senior of the local naval commanders, according to the rules I was President of the Council of Elders of the Club. Together with Iaron we worked out the following plan of action: to gather an unscheduled session of the elders immediately and carry a resolution transferring the club and its property, which incidentally was quite valuable, to the protection of the local Port Committee, which in its turn ought to guarantee its inviolability and defend it from encroachment on the part of any sort of irresponsible hooligan political party. And so we did. The resolution was carried and we then negotiated with representatives of the Port Committee (sailors), who eagerly took upon themselves the security of the club, providing me with the appropriate documentation. The anarchists who came in a few days were met by armed sailors, which sensibly induced them to retreat. Ultimately I realised that such a way out, that is, the transfer of the club to the sailors (even though only for security), did not guarantee anything in such troubled times, but I decided that it would be better that the club be plundered by sailors themselves rather than by hooligans who had had nothing to do with it.

About 26 December I finally received a telegram from Shchastnyi to the effect that I was permitted to go on leave up to my discharge from service and on the next day, having farewelled the commanders (the crews little interested me since naval engagements were no longer expected), I left for Helsinki with all my things. Leaving the roadstead on the small ice-breaker that maintained passenger services between Reval and Helsinki, I feasted sad eyes for the last time on the ships of my Brigade, not so long ago so powerful and dread, but now bereft of any military significance and converted into free accommodation for the conscious comrades ... My flag continued to fly for some days still on the *Riurik* while TsentroBalt had not got around to ordering it struck and suggesting to Spolatbog that he raise his pennant as Commander of the Squadron.

Apropos of which, I might mention that not long before my departure from the Brigade I had some curious discussions with the *Baian* on the matter of the flag. I had approached the commander of the *Baian* and asked that the flag that had been raised on that cruiser on the day of my appointment as Chief of the Brigade be given to me. After some days Stark, somewhat embarrassed, informed me that the ship's committee, which in fact ran the ship, refused to give me the flag on the grounds that it was state property. I asked then that the committee be advised that I was ready to pay the cost of the flag as recorded in the inventory as I was very keen to have it as a memento of the ship. Then, finally, I received the flag with a note from the committee in which it was said that the committee was fulfilling my request as a sign of respect to me but that they asked that I should never and in no circumstances whatsoever refer to the fact that the flag had been received from the ship, so that no unpleasantness might redound on the committee. How funny – in a time of almost complete ruin, such assiduity in respect of government property and apprehension of any sort of responsibility! In all truth, *Baian* had always been a very proper ship.

I had to pass about another ten days in Helsinki waiting on the necessary documents and permission to go 'home'.

Helsinki at that time had significantly changed in appearance. From the beginning of the Bolshevik coup Finland had declared its independence and at the end of November or the beginning of December the local Bolsheviks – Finns – supported by our comrades, had driven out the Senate and established their own power. However, this power differed significantly from ours. The local Bolsheviks, composed in the main of workers from the multitudinous suburban factories, turned out to be both more organised and more cultured than ours and, what was most important, were confirmed nationalists generally, not at all inclined to serve the International. As a consequence, reforms were carried out quite carefully and model order was maintained in the town. Only representatives of the local bourgeoisie – the Swedes – were subjected to investigation and arrest. Relations towards us Russians were completely proper. Such order, however, existed only for a very short time: with the advance of German troops, the Whites took heart and with the occupation of the region they finally wrested power into their hands.

Finally, things were finished. All the necessary documentation had been received, although not without obstacles on the part of TsentroBalt, and on about 10 January, with parting good wishes from our friends who were remaining for the time being in Helsinki, my wife and I left for Petrograd. About 15 January I received notification of my discharge without right of pension. This order was formulated thus:

> discharged from service without right of pension: naval servicemen – former Vice Admiral Bakhirev, former Rear Admirals Razvozov, Prince Cherkasskii, Timirev, former Captain 1st Rank Shevelyov

and still more whose names I don't recall.

In such a manner my Baltic period of revolutionary suffering finished. Forced to abandon my native fleet, to which I had one way or another devoted twenty-five years of my life, I was in the position of a person forced to begin life anew – without ground beneath my feet, without means, without any hope of anything in the near future, with one thing only – a quite dubious revolutionary experience.

The End

S Timirev, Shanghai 1922

Appendix No. 1

IN JANUARY 1915, THE Fleet Commander received from the Higher Command the task of laying a minefield across the German cleared channel to the north of Danzig.

The following forces were assigned for this operation: the 1st Brigade of Cruisers consisting of the *Riurik*, flag Rear Admiral Bakhirev, the *Admiral Makarov,* the *Bogatyr* and the *Oleg* and a half-division Special Squadron consisting of the *Sibirskii Strelok,* the *General Kondratenko,* the *Okhotnik* and the *Pogranichnik*, under the command of the Flag Captain of the Operations Section of the Fleet Staff, Captain 1st Rank Kolchak. The half-division Special Squadron carried mines and the cruisers *Oleg* and *Bogatyr* also had 100 mines each. The minelayers went to the operation along the shoreline, skirting around the island of Dago, but the cruisers were out to sea, proceeding by night to the north towards Gotland to take a bearing. The cruiser *Admiral Makarov* was at the head of the line.

The cruisers travelled for the greater part through thick broken ice and were therefore unable to pay out logs or sounding leads. The small Goth Sandö islet and Gotland itself were periodically clouded by squalls with snowstorms.

The cruisers proceeded at 16 knots. At 4 in the morning it was passed down the line to reduce speed to 12 knots. At 3:30 wet snow began and a snowstorm blotted out the horizon. The lighthouse at the northern end of Gotland could not be seen and Goth Sandö also was invisible. In view of this it was suggested that the cruisers were further from the shore than had been supposed, although the *Admiral Makarov* had deviated slightly to starboard from the course.

At 4:02 the *Admiral Makarov* changed course 10 degrees to port and lying at 190 degrees observed the weak light of the lighthouse.

At 4:07 the Brigade Commander ordered a course alteration to 160. At this time the *Riurik* felt a light blow. Speed was reduced to 12 knots. At this time the lighthouse was seen on the course, shining a powerful light. Immediately the order was given 'hard aport'. At this time the second blow was felt. The engines were stopped. I measured the distance to the lighthouse by range-finder to be about 12 cables (2.2km). No reef or shallows were marked on the charts at this position.

The *Riurik* had run upon an uncharted bank, damaging almost the entire external hull, taking on 2,700 tons of water. The between-hull area was flooded, the lower coal bunkers, the third boiler room and other compartments. The armoured belt had been pierced. The cruiser began to sink lower in the water once she slipped from the bank into clear water. The *Riurik*'s displacement on her departure had been 17,300 tons, but after the accident it became 20,050 tons. Her draft on departure had been 27.8ft, but after the accident, 32ft.

At half-past six in the morning we set a course for the cleared channel at a carefully slow speed of 6 knots and proceeded to the north towards the Utö lighthouse.

Subsequently the Investigating Committee inquiring into the causes of the accident came to the following conclusions:

1. The Commission found no guilt on the part of the Squadron Command or the cruiser commanders.
2. The navigational conditions for the voyage had been exceptionally difficult.
3. The reason for the proximity of the squadron to Gotland could be accounted for by a chance current, which could not have been foreseen.
4. The investigating Commission considered that the armoured cruiser *Riurik* had run upon a bank not marked on the charts, where the depth was shown as 6 fathoms.
5. Furthermore the Commission found it necessary to note that over the whole period from the beginning to the end of the voyage it had not found any dereliction of duty on anyone's part.

Former Flag Navigator, 1st Brigade of Cruisers of the Baltic Sea
Captain 2nd Rank N Kryzhanovskii[1]

Obituary from *Chasovoi* [*The Sentinel*] No. 90 October 1932 p.17[1]

Life and death of a Russian officer

ON 31 MAY 1932 Rear Admiral Sergei Nikolaevich Timirev passed away in Shanghai. The death occurred in the 58th year of his life and in the presence of his closest friend and shipmate Captain 1st Rank Krasheninnikov.

The deceased had been an outstanding officer of our Fleet. He graduated from the Naval College in 1895 as a midshipman in the 8th Fleet Depot. He left on an overseas voyage on the cruiser *Rossiia.* Returning to St Petersburg he was assigned to the Naval Guards, registered on strength in 1900. After that he sailed on the Imperial yachts *Aleksandr* and *Poliarnaia Zvezda.*

After this he was appointed to the battleship *Imperator Aleksandr* then building. At this time the Russo-Japanese war broke out. S N Timirev and Lieutenants Lagoda and Trukhachev were sent from the Naval Guards to the theatre of war.

S N Timirev went to Port Arthur, where he took part in all the operations and engagements of the 1st Pacific Squadron. During the siege of Port Arthur, when the crews of the ships were sent ashore to the front to assist the fortress garrison, Timirev with the crew of the battleship *Pobeda* was stationed at the 'Eagle's Nest', where he took part in repulsing all enemy attacks on this fortification. During an attack on the Eagle's Nest S N Timirev, along with those of the defenders remaining alive, was blown up by a Japanese land mine. He survived, but was seriously wounded. At the surrender of the fortress he was still recovering in hospital and, like many others, refused to give his parole that he would take no further part in the war. So he was sent to Japan as a prisoner of war. He returned to Russia in the spring of 1906, to the

Naval Guards. For military distinction in actions against the enemy and for the valiant defence of the Eagle's Nest, Timirev was awarded the Order of St Vladimir 4th Class with oak leaves and ribbon and the Gilded St George sabre engraved 'For bravery'.

In 1907 he was appointed to the *Tsesarevich* and later, in 1909, to be executive officer on the Imperial yacht *Shtandart*.

In 1912 he was transferred to the 1st Baltic Fleet depot and appointed commander of the training ship *Vernyi*, then in the summer of 1916 commander of the armoured cruiser *Baian*, participating in all the operations and engagements that fell to the lot of that cruiser.

In 1917 S N Timirev distinguished himself in the defence of the Gulf of Riga. He led the Brigade of Cruisers, having aboard the head of the Brigade, Rear Admiral Bakhirev. For this battle and his outstanding handling of his ship Timirev was promoted to Rear Admiral and appointed Head of the Brigade of Cruisers.

This brilliant Brigade long withstood the demoralisation that began after the revolution. On 4 December 1917 the Fleet Commander Rear Admiral Razvozov was removed. The Collegium took over the direction of the Fleet. From this moment S N Timirev went on leave, clearly recognising that there was no longer any possibility of doing anything to save the Fleet and the honour of Russia. He went to work for the War Industrial Committee and was appointed its representative in the Far East.

S N arrived in Vladivostok on 3 May 1918 and in November 1918, by decree of the Supreme Ruler Admiral Kolchak, was appointed Commander of Naval Forces in the Far East (the Siberian and Amur Flotillas).

From the spring of 1920 he was in Shanghai, from where he sailed first as a mate and then as captain on merchant ships. The last ship S N commanded was the *Haishun*, of Farmer and Company. From this ship on 4 April he was admitted to hospital already quite ill.

He suffered terribly. He suffered all the more, being deprived of material resources by such a disease as throat cancer, which gradually wears down the sufferer and from which there is no escape. The suffering of the deceased was unbearable, but he bore it valiantly, silently; bore it as through all the years of exile he had borne the pain and suffering of the loss of his homeland and of the wife and son he had left there.

Great was the mercy of God towards the deceased. Before death his suffering left him and quietly he literally fell asleep. The crossing from life to death was not noticed by any of those standing vigil with him. As S N had been an officer of the Legion of Honour, a platoon of French infantry was sent to the church for his funeral service. The funeral service was held at the St Nicholas military church. All who could be free from service or work at this time attended the service. As an honour guard at the casket stood, in the 1st watch – Rear Admiral Fyodorovich, Captain 1st Rank Struve, Captain 1st Rank Azarev, Captain 1st Rank Krasheninnikov; in the 2nd watch – Captain 2nd Rank Baron Fitingof, Captain 2nd Rank Chetverikov, Lieutenant Commander Chetverikov and Lieutenant Markov. The Rear Admiral's flag was placed on a white staff at the head of the casket. The coffin was drowned in flowers and wreaths. Among them, those from the Navy Wardroom, from the Society of the Legion of Honour, and the former ranks of the Army and Fleet particularly stood out.

Through the parade of French soldiers the hearse slowly went along the street, preceded by a choir singing 'Holy God'. The command was given, the French honour guard gave the final military salute and the cortege slowly made its way to the Lu-Ka-Vei cemetery. Among those accompanying it I noticed two foreigners with Legion of Honour ribbons and an officer of the French colonial infantry. He engaged me in conversation and in some agitation asked me to pass on to all Russian officers that he and the French officers in civilian dress had come to the funeral service having found out about Admiral Timirev's death from the newspapers. According to him, if the funeral had been announced officially, all the French officers would have come to accompany the admiral on his last journey. 'For us, you, having experienced all the torments of the European War and the horrors of the Civil War,' he said to me, 'represent a graphic example of the pre-eminence of strength of spirit over contemporary materialism. There is greater grandeur in this modest burial of a Russian admiral here in a foreign land than in a grandiose funeral, while behind the coffin march both Russian troops and all the foreign consuls. I am glad that I have been able to walk with you behind the casket of your admiral and ask you to convey to the

Russian officers the expression of my deepest respect and admiration in the face of the Russian strength of spirit and Russian culture.'

The coffin was gently lowered into the grave. Midshipman Baron Medem, bearing ahead the Rear Admiral's flag, slowly lowered it before the grave. The final singing of 'Eternal Memory', handfuls of soil cast, dully knocking on the lid of the casket, the grave filled in. General Valter pronounced a fine short valedictory speech and the funeral was finished. The grave of Rear Admiral Timirev lies on the left side of the main walkway of the Lu-Ka-Vei cemetery in the same row as that of the recently deceased Commander of French troops in Shanghai, Colonel Marker.

B Aprelev

Notice of Timirev's death in *Morskoi Zhurnal* [*The Naval Journal*] 1932, No. 55(7) July 1932, p.13

Deaths

REAR ADMIRAL SERGEI NIKOLAEVICH Timirev died in Shanghai on 13 June at 5:30 in the morning following a two-month severe illness from cancer of the throat. The Far Eastern newspapers, particularly in Shanghai, noted with regret the death of 'one of the outstanding members of the naval part of the Russian colony in Shanghai' and published appropriate descriptions of the life of the deceased. We will address the significance of S N Timirev for the Russian Fleet in a future number of the journal.[1]

North China Daily News, Shanghai 1932

OBITUARY

Rear-Admiral S. N. Timirev

The death occurred early yesterday, after a long illness, of Rear-Admiral Sergius Nikolaevitch Timirev, of the former Imperial Russian Navy, at the age of 58 years.

The late Admiral Timirev, who was born in St. Petersburg in 1874, was a member of a well-connected family of Novgorod. He entered the Russian Naval School and was made a midshipman in 1895. In 1901 he was transferred from duties on war ships to the Naval Guard Detachment at St. Petersburg, and was made second in command of the Imperial yacht.

He took part in the Russo-Japanese war and was in Port Arthur during its siege by the Japanese. He was severely wounded, and was subsequently made prisoner when the Japanese captured the field hospital in which he lay.

In 1906 he was released from Japan, where he had been held, and on his return to Russia was decorated with the St. George's Sword and other decorations, and again posted to the Naval Guard Detachment, with which he remained until the outbreak of the Great War.

During the Great War he was with the Baltic Fleet, first of all commanding the cruiser Bayan and, in 1917 after his promotion to Rear-Admiral, commanding the 1st Cruiser Squadron. The revolution caused him to leave the navy and he came to the Far East where, in due course, the late Admiral Kolchak, head of the Siberian Government, appointed him to command the Russian naval forces in Far Eastern waters. These comprised the Siberian squadron and the Amur flotilla.

After the collapse of the Siberian Government, Admiral Timirev came to Shanghai, where he joined the merchant service as an officer of China coasters. The last ship of which he was the captain was the Haishing.

The funeral will take place to-day at Lokawei Cemetery, after a service at the Russian Military Church, Route de Say Zoong. The funeral procession will leave the Church at 3.40 p.m.

Obituary 14 June 1932.

FUNERAL

Rear-Admiral Timireff

The funeral service for the late Sergius Nicholas Timireff, former Rear-Admiral of the Imperial Russian Navy, was held yesterday afternoon in the Russian Military Church in Avenue Joffre, followed by interment in the Lokawei Cemetery. Russian [illegible]hodox rites were conducted by [illegible] Rev. Father Alexander Pinya[illegible].

The pall-bearers were Rear-Admiral M. Fedorovitch, Captain N. Struve, Captain N. Azarieff, Captain P. Krasheninikoff, Commander S. Chetverikoff, Commander S. Ilvov, Lieutenant-Commander L. Chetverikoff and Lieutenant A. Markoff.

Among those sending wreaths were:—Mr. and Mrs. B. V. Jemchoojin; Mrs. G. I. Rybaltovsky; Mr. B. N. Rybaltovsky; Russian Naval Officers Club; Societe de la Legion d'Honneur; Shanghai Ex-Officers' Club; P. D. and K. D. Egicoff; K. C. Chetvergoff; Union of Russian Maritime Officers: French Group of Naval Officers; Capt. P. Krashenikoff; Family Yaron; Union of Russian Army and Navy Associations; Council of United Russian Public Organizations; Maria P. Veraneous; and others.

Arrangements were carried out by the International Funeral Directors.

In addition to the account of deceased's career which appeared in the "North-China Daily News" yesterday, it is stated that the late Rear Admiral Timireff, whose last official position in the Imperial Russian Navy was Commander-in-Chief of the Russian Naval Forces in the Far East, is survived by his wife and 18-year-old son, both of whom are at present in Moscow. He was one of the most popular members of the Russian community, being honorary vice-president of the Russian Ex-Officers Club, founder and president of the Ex-Imperial Navy Officers Association, and vice-president of the Union of Russian Army and Navy Men. Among the decorations he held was the Victorian Order the decoration of Officer of the Legion of Honour, and the Sword of St. George, as well as many Russian decorations.

Funeral Notice 15 June 1932.

Translator's Commentary

About the published text and translation

THE TEXT TRANSLATED HERE IS that published in New York in 1961 by The American Society for the Study of Russian Naval History. This text was re-published twice in Russia in the 1990s as a reflection of strongly renewed interest in the memoir literature of Russians abroad. The foreword to the New York publication indicates that the original memoirs were written in 1922 shortly after Rear Admiral Timirev settled in Shanghai and were sent to a 'relative' either then or soon after his death in 1932.[1]

Beyond that, how the manuscript came to be in the possession of the publishers is not clear and I have not been able to trace the original manuscript. There is some indication in the text that it may have come through Timirev's friend V V Romanov, who lived in Paris through the 1920s and 1930s. It seems unlikely that Timirev would have sent it to his family connections in Russia, in view of the danger that it might have presented to them at the time, as well as to other people named in the text. By the time it was passed to the publishers in the USA in 1958 Timirev's son had been murdered in the purges of the 1930s and his former wife Anna had only just been rehabilitated as a political ex-convict of the gulag. It may have come to the USA via his wife's sister, Maria Safonoff, who had a successful career as a concert pianist in the USA for many decades after emigrating there in 1921 with the assistance of the philanthropist Charles R Crane.[2] Unfortunately the Hoover Institution in Stanford, California, which holds the archive of the publisher, the American Society for the Study of Russian Naval History, advises that it contains no reference to the memoirs.

For the remainder of the twentieth century the published memoirs served as an authoritative source for Western historians who were unable to access Russian naval archives for this period.[3] In the 1990s they became a part of the flood of re-publications in Russia of émigré literature that, previously well-known to Western scholars, have played a part in triggering a wealth of new interest among Russian academic researchers and history enthusiasts. The memoirs have continued to be used as a source by historians both in Russia and in the West. In addition, many of Timirev's assessments of senior officers of the Russian Navy and his descriptions of engagements have been confirmed by archival sources newly available to scholars following the dissolution of the Soviet Union.

The memoirs have been written in a very compact style of Russian, which is reflected in sentences of considerable length and complexity, with paragraphs sometimes extending over a page of print. While this style is quite acceptable in Russian, and probably reflects the official reporting style of a naval officer, an exactly matching translation in English would be excessively complex and even ungainly. Consequently, in the translation I have broken many of these parts of the text into successive sentences and paragraphs, in order to present an English text that is more idiomatic in terms of contemporary style. I have also made a more liberal use of synonyms in English for words for that Timirev is happy to use the one term repeatedly. Nevertheless, I have tried to adhere to his text as closely as possible, even where this leads to what may strike English readers as some circumlocution.

Timirev uses various phrases from the contemporary revolutionary press, such as that describing the new government as 'invested with the trust of the whole nation', usually indicating his sardonic or contemptuous intent by enclosing them in quotation marks. Phrases such as 'deepeners of the revolution' refer to revolutionary activists on the left who were committed to social as well as political change, in contrast to more conservative activists in the Provisional Government. In this translation quotation marks have only been used where the text is clearly attributable.

In transcribing names I have followed the modified Library of Congress (LoC) system to the best of my ability, except for well-known names such as Kerensky, Yudenich, or the cruiser *Aurora*.

I have rendered the family name Savonov as Safonoff, as that is the transcription used by Maria Safonoff throughout her life in the USA. The family name Timirev is pronounced 'Timiryov', the 'e' being sounded 'yo' as in the English word 'yonder'. The stress should fall on the last syllable. For guidance on pronouncing Russian personal names, see Morton Benson, *Dictionary of Russian Personal Names with a revised Guide on Stress and Morphology*, rev. ed. Cambridge UP, Cambridge, 1992.

In the notes I have given the full names and brief biographical details, including the highest rank achieved, of people identified in the text where I have been able to trace them. Readers unfamiliar with Russian customs may be puzzled by the seeming prolixity of the names. Russian names consist of the personal name given at christening (usually a saint's name), the patronymic (i.e., their father's given name) and their family name. So Sergei was named after St Sergius, his father was Nikolai (hence his patronymic Nikolaevich) and his family name was Timirev: Sergei Nikolaevich Timirev. Female names follow the same pattern, with adjustment for the feminine gender and slightly different rendering of the patronymic: Anna Vasilievna Timireva (née Savonova).

I have rendered the Estonian island of Muhu as Moön (as in Moön Sound) to indicate to the English reader that it has two syllables and bears no relation to the English word for the moon. I have not translated other place names, except for Helsinki, for which Timirev always used the Russian name Helsingfors.

A number of naval terms present particular issues. The Russian word *min* (мин) is used both for a floating or tethered mine and for a torpedo. Usually it is clear from the context which is the intended meaning, but sometimes it is not. Similarly, the term *minonosets* (миноносец) literally means 'mine (or torpedo) bearer' but usually the English equivalent would be 'destroyer' rather than 'minelayer' or 'torpedo boat'. However 'destroyer' can also be signified by the word *esminets* (эсминец), and as the Russian Navy used destroyers and cruisers as well as dedicated minelayers for laying minefields, there can occasionally be some doubt as to the precise term intended. I have generally been guided by the context for the most probable reading. I have translated the 'Communications Service' (Sluzhba Sviazi) as the 'Signals Intelligence Service', as that phrase more clearly reflects the functions of this part of the Baltic Fleet. The Russian word *otriad* (отряд), used in relation to divisions of the Baltic Fleet, is usually translated as 'detachment', but I have used 'squadron' as more fitting a naval context and also as these units were in no sense 'detached' from the fleet. Additionally, the Russian Navy used the term 'flag officer' to signify any officer on the staff of a superior officer, such as an admiral, as well as some officers performing functions for the fleet as a whole (e.g. Fleet Gunnery Officer). However I have been advised that in the British and US navies the term 'flag officer' now usually refers only to an officer entitled to his own flag – i.e., an officer of commodore rank or above (with the exception that each such officer would have his own 'Flag lieutenant' as an executive assistant). Consequently I have translated the Russian titles as 'Staff officer' (with the exception of Flag lieutenant), or Fleet officer, to avoid possible confusion about ranks.

I have transcribed rather than translated the names of ships, as that is how they are listed in most international naval publications. For example, *Baian* means 'troubadour' or 'bard', but it is usually listed as *Baian* (or *Bajan* or *Bayan*). Ships names are given in italics.

Dates in the text are in the Julian calendar, which was used in Russia until February 1918. The discrepancy between the Julian and the Gregorian calendars in the twentieth century was thirteen days, so to get the corresponding Gregorian date simply add thirteen to the date cited.

The 1961 publication contains line drawings and an appendix that were obviously added by the publishers and are not the work of Timirev. The drawings are reproductions from the journal of the Society, *Morskiia zapiski* (*The Naval Records*), and do not bear any specific relationship to Timirev's text, except of course that they are of naval subjects. They are not reproduced here.

Geographical aspects of the Baltic Sea affecting naval operations[4]

The Baltic Sea is characterised by geographical conditions that significantly affected naval operations of both combatant navies during the war. The sea extends from the north-east, where the gulfs of Finland and Bothnia join, to the south-west, where it gives access via several openings between Denmark and Sweden to the Kattegat and the Skagerrak and beyond to the North Sea. For most of the First World War, it was bordered by Germany and Denmark on the south, Sweden on the north and Russia (including territory now covered by

Estonia, Latvia and Finland) on the east and north-east. It is wholly north of the 50th parallel of latitude. In winter the eastern portions of the Sea, in particular the gulfs, freeze over completely, usually from November through March, but sometimes over longer periods. This virtually prevented effective winter navigation of any ships, except by the use of ice-breakers. These limitations also affected submarines, which at that time were not sufficiently strong nor durable enough to operate under the ice for any significant period.

The northern regions of the sea, particularly near the entrances to the gulfs of Bothnia and of Finland, are strewn with skerries – the rocky remains of glaciation from the last ice age – which are often partly or wholly submerged, presenting serious risks to navigation in all weathers. The Åland skerries between Finland and Sweden had been demilitarised by the Treaty of Paris (1856), which settled the Crimean War. Russian diplomatic concerns not to imperil Swedish neutrality during the First World War limited attempts to fortify the skerries for naval purposes, although some Russian signals intelligence listening posts were stationed there and Timirev claims that batteries had been positioned on the islands in 1915. Admiral von Essen had encouraged his commanders to become skilful navigators of the many channels and entrances between the skerries and the Baltic Sea by forbidding them to use local pilots, as well as through exercises. This gave the Russians some advantage here over the Germans, who were not able to develop such skills.[5]

The eastern parts of the sea, and in particular the gulfs of Finland and Riga, presented additional navigational hazards in the form of frequent shallows and reefs around the islands that limited navigation to vessels of shallow draft. In places the shallow waters also enabled aircraft, in favourable conditions, to observe submarines that had already submerged below periscope depth. Russian defensive preparations in Moön Sound had included the dredging of a channel to permit the passage of larger ships through the northern part of the Sound, but even after that was deepened during the war, the largest ships could still not pass through it. The manoeuvrability of ships of all classes was thus affected by the danger of running aground in many parts of the sea.

Ofitserstvo – the Russian Imperial Navy Officer Corps in the First World War

Formal structure of the Naval Officer Corps

The Russian Naval officer corps had two main divisions in its formal structure: 'combatant' officers and 'admiralty' officers. Combatant (*stroevye*) officers were those who had passed the Naval College final exams and the subsequent practical sea-going training which gained them the initial rank of midshipman. Until 1907, as combatant officers, they then had to maintain 'naval eligibility' (*morskoi tsenz*) – that is, they had to have served or be serving on a ship at sea for the period prescribed for their rank.[6]

The naval eligibility rule had been introduced in 1885 to ensure that naval officers maintained their practical experience of sea-going service, after it was discovered that many of the most senior officers of the Navy had never done more than their initial midshipman's cruise. Various periods at sea were specified for the different ranks and promotion from one rank to the next was linked to the period of sea-going service – that is, one had to have a specified amount of sea-going service to be eligible for promotion to the next rank. However, in practice promotion became a matter of simply passing the time in a sea-going appointment. Following the Russo-Japanese War the sea-going qualification was heavily criticised as having produced a time-serving attitude rather than technical competence and having diminished the fighting capacity of ships by frequent changes of command personnel. Consequently, as part of the reforms to the Navy triggered by the war experience, the sea-going qualification had been abolished in May 1907. Nevertheless, most of the officers named in these memoirs would have been affected by it through their careers prior to the war and attitudes produced by it persisted among the more senior officers.[7]

Officers who were not able to maintain their sea-going eligibility could continue in the service as 'admiralty' officers. Admiralty officers were usually those who served in administrative or supporting roles in the Navy, such as in bureaucratic positions, onshore establishments and coastal fortresses. These officers could progress in rank through their service, but the higher ranks differed from those of combatant officers. For example, the equivalent rank of rear admiral for admiralty officers was major general. The number of admiralty officers in the Navy substantially exceeded that of combatant officers, which was logically limited by the number of ships in the Navy and the cycling of officers through them to maintain their sea-going eligibility.

In addition to the formal division between combatant and admiralty officers, there were various other formal distinctions within and between those groups on the basis of specialities, such as gunnery specialists, aviators or submariners, shipwrights, and medical staff. Each of these distinctions was reflected in differences in salary and entitlements, as well as in uniform and insignia of rank. There was consequently also a pyramid of informal distinction that reflected the higher social and service standing of combatant officers over admiralty officers. As the war progressed, a further distinction arose between officers recalled from the reserve for the duration of the war and those already serving as regular officers.[8]

Ranks

Ranks in the Russian Imperial Navy were similar to those of other contemporary navies, except that they also reflected the formal distinctions outlined above and mapped to the fourteen formal ranks specified for civil society that had originally been established by Peter the Great in the eighteenth century in his Table of Ranks.

Table of Ranks:[9]

Class	*Civil grade*	*Military*	*Naval*
1	Chancellor	Field Marshal	General Admiral
2	Active Privy Councillor	General of Cavalry General of Infantry General of Artillery	Admiral
3	Privy Councillor	Lieutenant General	Vice Admiral
4	Active State Councillor Over-Procurator Herald-master	Major General	Rear Admiral
5	State Councillor		

Class	*Civil grade*	*Military*	*Naval*
6	Collegiate Counsellor Military Counsellor	Colonel	Captain 1st Rank
7	Court Counsellor	Lieutenant Colonel	Captain 2nd Rank
8	Collegiate Assessor	Captain	
9	Titular Counsellor	Staff Captain	Lieutenant
10	Collegiate Secretary	Lieutenant	Midshipman
11	Naval Secretary		
12	Regional Secretary	Second Lieutenant	
13	Provincial Secretary	Ensign	
14	Collegiate Registrar		

Admiralty officers held ranks that were specified as military ranks rather than naval ranks. This also provided an alternative pathway into the naval officer corps, as candidates who had not passed through the Naval College had a range of alternatives through which they could progress from admiralty ensign to lieutenant and then, on passing the appropriate examinations and meeting the sea-going eligibility, switch to the combatant officer hierarchy as midshipmen. However, this route into the ranks of combatant officers was very much the exception in practice.

Promotion within a cohort of officers was affected by their date of seniority – the date from which they were appointed to their initial rank. Officers were expected to have served a prescribed amount of time at a specific rank before being eligible for promotion to the next rank. For example, a combatant lieutenant was expected to serve in that rank for just over six years up to the beginning of the war, and just over five years during the war. Admiralty officers, promoted more slowly, served longer in each rank, which did not really change much during the war. Despite these provisions, an officer could be promoted to the next rank for distinguished service, particularly in action. However, progression in rank for most officers actually slowed down during the war, largely because, although ship losses occurred sporadically throughout the war, the personnel attrition rate for the Navy was never as catastrophic as for the Russian Army, where thousands regularly perished in battle.[10]

In addition to the expected period of service at a given rank, the Navy also imposed an age limit at particular ranks, but these were relaxed during the war and officers could always switch to admiralty status for particular postings. For the most senior ranks the age limits were generally not implemented, as full admirals were usually members of the Imperial family or holders of honorific postings, such as to the State Council.[11]

As in most navies, an officer could be appointed to act in a rank above his substantive rank for a time, sometimes over an extended period. An acting appointment would have an effect on his pay and allowances for the period of acting but not necessarily on his entitlements to further promotion.

None of the rules set out above concerning appointments and promotions of officers in the Navy affected the right of the Tsar as autocrat to make whatever appointments he deemed desirable. This discretion was demonstrated in 1916 by the appointment of A V Kolchak to command the Black Sea Fleet and his simultaneous promotion to vice admiral, regardless of his lack of seniority and the relatively short time he had served in the rank of rear admiral.

Russian Navy officer ranks 1914–18[12]

Combatant and Engineer Officers	*Admiralty and Naval Ministry Officers*
General Admiral	
Admiral	General
Vice Admiral	Lieutenant General
Rear Admiral	Major General
Captain 1st Rank	Colonel
Captain 2nd Rank	Lieutenant Colonel
Senior Lieutenant (Starshii Leitenant)	Captain
Lieutenant	Staff Captain
Midshipman	Lieutenant (Poruchik)
	Sub-lieutenant (Podporuchik)
	Ensign (Praporshchik)
	Petty Ensign (Zauriad-praporshchik)

Comparative ranks of the main navies 1914–18

The navies of the major combatant powers in the First World War had similar formal structures and processes for educating and promoting officers for their fleets. A common issue was the recognition of the enhanced role of engineer officers following the replacement of sail by steam in the final decades of the nineteenth century. By the time of the war, most navies had removed many of the distinctions between combatant officers and engineer officers in terms of promotions and appointments, although the uniform and insignia differences persisted in several of them. The lower ranks of officers in the various navies do not exactly match, mainly reflecting the length of time that the different navies devoted to developing their officers from the initial stage of cadet. Otherwise there was no significant difference between the navies, although the numbers of officers at each rank varied widely between them.

Russia	*Britain*	*France*	*Germany*
General-Admiral	Admiral of the Fleet	Amiral de France	Grosseadmiral
Admiral	Admiral	Amiral	Admiral
Vitse-Admiral	Vice Admiral	Vice-amiral	Vizeadmiral
Kontr-Admiral	Rear Admiral	Contre-Amiral	Konteradmiral
Capitan 1st Rank (pervogo ranga)	Captain	Capitaine de vaisseau	Kapitän zur See
Capitan 2nd Rank (vtorogo ranga)	Commander	Capitaine de fregate	Fregattenkapitän
Starshii Leitenant	Lieutenant Commander	Capitaine de corvette	Korvettenkapitän Kapitänleutnant
Leitenant	Lieutenant	Lieutenant de Vaisseau	Oberleutnant zur See
Michman	Sub-lieutenant/ Midshipman	Enseigne de Vaisseau	Leutnant zur See
In most of the navies naval cadets did not count as officers until they had passed their final exams and had met the sea-going eligibility requirements.			
Gardemarin	Naval Cadet	Aspirant de 1st ou 2nd classe	Fähnrich zur See

13

Social background

Despite the formal distinctions within the Russian Naval officers corps noted above, there was a remarkable uniformity in the social background of the corps. More than 90 per cent of officers were drawn from the upper echelons of society, and particularly from the nobility.[14]

From the mid-eighteenth century the population of Russia had been legally sub-divided into a number of estates, of which the most populous was that of the peasantry, followed by townsfolk, skilled workers and merchants, and the nobility. Each estate had different entitlements and responsibilities in law. The nobility (*dvorianstvo*) represented a small minority of the population but had specific responsibilities and privileges in the governing structures of the state at local, regional and national levels. The major liberal reforms of the mid-nineteenth century that saw the emancipation of the serfs and the institution of law courts and other measures, such as the abolition of corporal punishment for certain estates, did not alter the estate basis of government administration. The rights and duties of the various estates, although altered from time to time, persisted right through until the October revolution in 1917.[15]

The nobility was divided into hereditary and personal, but in practice over time personal nobility had tended to lead to hereditary nobility. While measures were taken in the late nineteenth and early twentieth centuries to make entry into the nobility more difficult, the particular privileges and advantages of this estate meant that it continued to be sought after. In addition, government service continued to be an established pathway to both personal and hereditary nobility.

Membership of the nobility did not necessarily equate with economic wealth, as members of the lower estates such as townspeople, professionals and even peasants could have substantial property and income exceeding that of many of the nobility. Peter the Great's attempt to enforce primogeniture in order to build up great estates and engender a class of nobles obliged to earn their living through commerce, industry and state service, did not survive his death. Nevertheless, the customary equal inheritance of estates meant that many became increasingly less economic and by the beginning of the twentieth century there were many of noble birth who could not hope to earn a living from their family's land. So entry into the Naval College secured for many aspirants, especially sons of former officers, quite significant material benefits, including the possibility of a post-service pension.

In addition to the free education received at the Naval College, a Baltic Fleet midshipman could receive an annual salary of 504 roubles plus a dining allowance of 183 roubles, with sea-going allowance of 60 roubles per month, which rose to 62 roubles when abroad. More senior officers could receive even more substantial income: a captain 1st rank received an annual salary of 6,000 roubles plus allowances. For an admiral the sea-going allowance rates were 150 roubles internal and 300 roubles per month abroad – more than the annual salary of many workers. Naval salaries and allowances appear to have been comparable to those of similar grades in the civil service, according to the Table of Ranks.[16] In comparison, an ordinary seaman was paid as little as 9 roubles a year plus keep,[17] while a labourer's wage was about a third of the least qualified naval officer's and the annual salary for a schoolteacher in St Petersburg in 1911 varied between 301 and 433 roubles, without any allowances for accommodation or other expenses. All the naval salaries and allowances were increased by 50 per cent on the outbreak of the war, but were then progressively eroded by inflation through the course of the conflict. However, as all salaries were similarly affected by wartime inflation, the comparative position of officers remained relatively stable.[18]

In addition to the immediate benefits of a comparatively generous salary, naval officers could look forward to a pension after twenty-five to thirty years of service, which would ensure them and their families some security in later years. At the end of the nineteenth century the base annual pension ranged from 290 roubles for a midshipman to 1,145 roubles for a vice admiral. While representing only a fraction of their service salary, the pensions were in practice also supplemented by additional allowances for length of service at sea, distinguished service, responsibility for the construction of major ships and for awards for gallantry. Moreover, the pension benefits devolved to widows and minor children on the death of the serviceman.[19] Pensions had been increased following the Russo-Japanese War and at all times the Tsar retained discretion to increase a pension at his will.

However, recent analysis has shown that, despite their generous salaries, barely 5 per cent of serving officers personally owned any real estate, so the post-service pension would have had major significance for most of them.[20] The abolition of these pension rights after the revolution was a major blow to the economic position of officers and helps explain why many continued to serve under the new form of government – officers who had initially trained in the Imperial Navy remained a significant proportion of the command structure of the Soviet Navy up to and through the Second World War.

Nevertheless, the main reason why the naval officer corps was drawn almost exclusively from the nobility was that to be eligible to enter the Naval College the candidate had to be born of that estate and had to be capable of gaining endorsement from an appropriate nobility corporation.[21] In addition, the children of officers who had served in the Navy had a legal entitlement to enter the College. Exceptions to these rules, such as self-funded entrants, were rare.

Education and training

Russian naval officers of this period shared not only a uniform social background but also a common educational and service experience. The St Petersburg Naval College,[22] founded by Peter the Great, had passed through various changes by the early twentieth century but it remained the principal educational and training establishment for officers of the Navy, whether they served in the Baltic or the Black Sea Fleets or in the Pacific. A comparable college had been established in Sevastopol in 1851 for the Black Sea Fleet, but it was severely constrained after the Crimean War and by the early twentieth century operated as an arm of the St Petersburg College.[23] The curriculum of the College had been significantly updated after the experiences of the Russo-Japanese War of 1904–05 and many of the instructors had themselves experienced active service during that war, so the professional education of Russian naval officers was at least as advanced as that of other European navies by 1914.

Cadets spent six years at the College, the final three of which were specifically devoted to naval technical instruction. On graduation, the cadet had to serve on an active ship of the fleet for a year, during which cruise he would receive further technical and practical training. At the end of this practicum, he would gain the rank of midshipman (michman) provided he passed the required technical examination.

Officers could also subsequently attend specialist schools and courses in various fields, such as gunnery, mines and torpedoes, and later aviation. More senior officers also attended the Nicholas Naval Academy, established by Alexander II in 1877, which focused on technical and strategic level studies.[24]

There were alternative pathways by which candidates could enter the Navy officer corps and these were increased during the war as the need for officers was increased by the commissioning of newly built ships. Graduates of the universities could enter through various short courses established by the Navy Ministry, as could those from technical high schools and other educational institutions. These changes did not, however, significantly affect the social composition of the corps, as the cost of having achieved that level of education beforehand was itself a guarantee that only the more privileged classes and estates could take advantage of that pathway.

In addition to this common educational and training background, most of the senior officers named by Timirev in his memoirs shared active service experience from the Russo-Japanese War. Officers with this background were particularly prominent in the Baltic Fleet at this time, but less so in the Black Sea Fleet. However, in general terms, only 25 per cent of naval officers at the time of the First World War had active service experience from the war with Japan, so it is clear that these officers had an influence exceeding their actual number in the Navy.[25]

International comparisons

Most of the characteristics of the Russian naval officer corps described above, in terms of formal structures, social background and training, were typical of the major navies in Europe at the time of the First World War.

For example, the Austro-Hungarian Imperial and Royal Navy distinguished between 'officers' and 'officials' on much the same basis as the Russians did between 'combatant' and 'admiralty officers'.[26] All of the navies had formal distinctions between executive officers and the more technical or 'engineer' officers. All of the navies provided for the further training of officers in specialties such as gunnery, signalling and torpedoes.

Similarly, the arrangements for the professional induction of Russian naval officers also compared quite well with contemporary provisions in the other European navies, each of which had a naval college system to prepare officers.

The navies were also similar in terms of the social background of their officer corps, with the exception of the Americans and the British Dominion navies. For example, the British Royal Navy only began to broaden the class basis of naval officer recruitment and training in 1913, after a long campaign by Admiral Fisher, who succeeded in having naval college fees reduced to £40 per year for a quarter of applicants, which would still have put this education beyond the reach of many middle-class and almost all working-class aspirants.[27] The 'Mate' scheme introduced at the same time to allow promotions from the lower deck was only a partial solution. These changes had no impact on the cadre of senior commanders in the Royal Navy for the course of the war.

The career progression of officers was also relatively similar across the navies. Promotion in order of seniority was common – in the Imperial and Royal Austro-Hungarian Navy, when Captain Horthy was promoted in 1918 to rear admiral and appointed to the fleet command in circumstances similar to those of the Russian Vice Admiral Kolchak, he protested that many officers senior to him would find his promotion and appointment objectionable.[28] The Russian naval attaché to the British fleet commented on officer culture in the Royal Navy:

> Our Captain was typical of his class, with all its characteristic peculiarities. He was a good officer and had spent the greater part of his life on board large ships. He took little interest in historical or scientific questions, but had an excellent knowledge of everything concerned with the practical side of his duties and of naval etiquette. Like most of the Captains, he always had a copy of the Navy List, which was published nearly every month, lying on his table, and in this he regularly struck out the names of his seniors as they were promoted or left the Service.[29]

In the practice of ensconcing their wives and/or mistresses in local accommodation when they could, the Russians can scarcely be distinguished from either their allies or their opponents. For example, in the British Navy the perceived impact of the fleshpots of Edinburgh on the operational efficiency of the British Battlecruiser Squadron stationed at the Firth of Forth attracted attention.[30] For officers of the Russian Baltic Fleet, such an impact on operational efficiency was perhaps less significant, mainly because, for at least four of the winter months, active operations in the Baltic were halted by the winter freeze in the Gulfs of Finland and Riga. However, no Russian officers are recorded as having so departed from professional standards as to emulate the admiral in command of French naval forces in the Mediterranean, who not only established his mistress at Malta but shared operational details with her, which she guilelessly communicated to correspondents who were under the surveillance of the security services.[31]

However, it is a matter of judgement whether any of these factors had an influence on the competence of the Russian officer corps as professional naval officers. Few people doubted their courage, but as was remarked in relation to the Navy's performance in the Russo-Japanese War, 'to be well prepared to die for one's country is not the same as being prepared well to fight for it'. Prior to the European war, both the British and German naval attachés had offered critical assessments of the culture and social derivation of Russian naval officers and the impact on their competence:

> While many of the officers were 'intelligent and keen', they were drawn from a class in which the sense of responsibility is a less noticeable feature than its love of pleasure, a class whose conception of integrity, in both private and official relations, possibly is not quite the same as generally accepted by Western nations. Young officers, accustomed nightly to sit in the cafes-chantant of Kronstadt and St Petersburg until the early hours of the morning, who – badly paid as they are – help to support the most numerous and most expensive demi-monde in the whole of Europe, can hardly be expected to give much time or trouble on the following day to the tamer business of instructing, or superintending the instruction of, recruits taken from an illiterate inland peasantry, or, indeed, to any other duty.[32]

The evidence indicates, however, that in the crucible of the war, Russian officers in general performed as well as those of any of the other major navies. All the combatant governments placed severe restrictions on the engagement of their major naval units, the battleships and battlecruisers, a defensive strategy that led to significant problems with morale and fighting capability in those units. The difficulties experienced by the Russians in this respect were also experienced by the German and Austro-Hungarian navies and commanded conscious attention on the part of the British.[33] The new technologies of mining, torpedoes and submarines confronted all of the navies with challenges that tested their capacities to respond. The Russians were skilful and aggressive users of mine warfare and many of their technical achievements, such as shipboard direction finding, were ahead of those of other navies, while others seem to have lagged.

In contrast to the frequently critical comments about the quality and character of officers in the Russian Army, Allied observers with the Russian Navy during the war found its officers professionally well trained and in many respects ahead of others in techniques and the application of technology. For example, the British Admiral Phillimore, attached to the Russian Navy in the early years of the war, was very impressed with the capacity of the Black Sea Fleet to manoeuvre even in fog by using wireless while the British Royal Navy was still debating its use.[34]

The most notable advantage the Russians had over all of the other combatant navies was having a significant cadre of officers in senior positions who had experienced active service during the Russo-Japanese War of 1904–05. No other navy in Europe had officers who had experienced major fleet engagements in their service careers.[35] Even the catastrophic naval defeats of that war, which induced serious reconsideration of materiel, strategy and tactics and also of the training of officers during the inter-war years, had produced among officers a much more aggressive cast of mind than had previously been exhibited in the Far East. One gets the impression from the memoir literature that most Russian naval officers who had had this experience not only had a keen awareness of how much action in war differed from planned peacetime manoeuvres, but also that they shared a common feeling that the Navy owed their country a moral debt for its less than successful performance in that war. However, as the risk-averse strategies of the Higher Command never permitted the Russian fleets to commit their major units to engage the enemy in strength, this advantage was of little significance in the course of the First World War.

On balance there does not appear to be any particular feature of the Russian naval officer corps that would have distinguished it from those in any of the other major navies at the time of the First World War.

Admiral Kolchak and the fate of the Timirev family

The reader of these memoirs is unlikely to conclude from them that there was anything other than a wholly professional connection between Rear Admiral Sergei Nikolaevich Timirev and Admiral Alexander Vasilievich Kolchak, who became the anti-Bolshevik 'Supreme Ruler' from late 1918 to early 1920. There is no mention here of the intimate relationship between Kolchak and Timirev's wife Anna Vasilievna Timireva, née Safonoff. This relationship, however, would have been well known, if not notorious, to most of the Russian readers of the memoirs in 1961, and certainly to most of those whom Timirev expected in 1922 to be the readers of his memoirs. It was well known to all of the memoirists of the Kolchak government, including all of the Allied representatives in Siberia who provided support to that government. It was also well known to all subsequent historical commentators through the Soviet period of Russian history. It is now more known to a wider audience owing to the 2008 Andrei Kravchuk film *Admiral* (and its spin-off TV series) which glamorised that relationship and the period of the civil war in Russia from a Russian nationalist viewpoint.

As a representation of the historical period in which it is set, the film can most charitably be said to treat the factual historical evidence with sublime indifference, not to say gay abandon, subordinating it to the dramatic demands of a largely fictional perspective on the main characters and their period. The list of departures by the film plot from the historical record is extensive,[36] but the characterisation relevant to readers of these memoirs is that of Sergei Timirev, the husband of Anna. In the film he is represented as a boring old fuddy-duddy, cowardly and disloyal to his friends (he is shown as fleeing his comrades as they are shot down by revolutionaries), and ultimately a willing collaborator of the Soviet regime.

The relevant facts are these:
Sergei and Anna Timirev arrived in Vladivostok in April or May 1918 after Sergei, discharged from the service without pension and having to support his family, had used his naval connections in Petrograd to secure a position as representative of the War Industries Committee in the Far East, with responsibility to oversee the liquidation of its assets there. Their son, then not yet four years old, was sent to his maternal grandmother in Kislovodsk in the Caucasus region – more of his fate later. The War Industries Committees were voluntary organisations established on their own initiative under the Tsarist regime to assist the government with the organisation of industry to supply the needs of the Army. Although treated with suspicion by Tsarist officialdom, they persisted in their efforts for the Army throughout the war. The Bolshevik government formally abolished the committees in July 1918, but they persisted in the regions of Russia not controlled by the Bolsheviks, including in the Far East, where they played a continuing role in the various forms of government that arose there.[37] Shortly after the Timirevs arrived in Vladivostok, in early July 1918 the short-lived Bolshevik control of the city had been overthrown by the Czech Legion and foreign intervention forces soon followed.[38] So there is no evidence that Sergei ever had to compromise his conscience and work for the Soviet government.

Sergei Timirev was seven months *younger* than Aleksandr Kolchak, who was of short stature and slight build, with aquiline features and a constitution weakened by his polar explorations and Port Arthur service, which continued to affect his health throughout the remainder of his life. The only extant portraits of Sergei Timirev show him in portly middle age, but his wife asserted in her memoirs that she had married him because 'he was a handsome war hero'.[39]

Much is made in the film of Kolchak's dramatic gesture of throwing his St George Sword of Honour into the sea in defiance of the demand to surrender it to the revolutionary sailors. This is indeed a famous incident, which is recounted in almost every account of Kolchak's life, usually without reference to the sailors later shamefacedly sending down divers to recover the sword and return it to the admiral. What is little recorded in this context is that great numbers of Russian officers had been awarded the gilded St George Sword of Honour, both during the Russo-Japanese War and the First World War – including Sergei Nikolaevich Timirev for his bravery in the defence of the Great Eagle's Nest at Port Arthur when he was blown up in a Japanese attack.[40] There is no evidence to suggest that he was a coward.

In contrast, Admiral Kolchak is shown in the film as a decisive and capable leader who had his nation's fundamental interests at heart. This was an opinion that does not seem to have been shared by almost all of the memoirists of the Kolchak government, both Russian and international. Even participants in the government, such as the one-time Commander-in-Chief, Lieutenant General Konstantin Viacheslavovich Sakharov, were bitterly critical of the competency of the government. In his memoirs published in 1923, Sakharov, in a telling reference to the Restoration Bourbons, described the Kolchak Government as having 'forgotten nothing and learnt nothing'. He went on to claim that that government:

> represented in its very essence the first appearance of fascism ... The White movement was not a fore-runner of fascism but the very manifestation of fascism. In fact if one clearly looks into the stimuli moving the Whites, there one finds all that creates fascism in other countries.[41]

A rabid anti-Semite who shared Kolchak's view that the revolution had resulted from an international Jewish and Masonic conspiracy,[42] Sakharov meant this assessment as an accolade. He became a leading proponent of Russian fascism through the inter-war period. Nevertheless, the accuracy of these judgements has been substantiated in every serious study of the Kolchak government since its collapse in early 1920.[43] The commander of US intervention forces in Siberia, General Graves, described the situation in Siberia as a disgrace to civilisation, a conclusion that any objective reader of the sources would be hard put to dispute.[44] In private correspondence with Anna, Kolchak himself expressed his admiration for the militarists then consolidating power in Japan and espoused the Social Darwinist view that war was a path to national regeneration.[45]

For more than two generations the standard interpretation of the Kolchak regime in Soviet Russia treated the assessment of his government as a political issue more than as one of historiography. When in the late 1960s the journalist and writer Georgii Vasilievich Yegorov, from the Altai region of Siberia, began research on Kolchak, including interviews with Anna Timireva for a novel about the Civil War, he found himself being interrogated by the KGB; he was expelled from the Communist Party and his son expelled from university.[46] A decade later when G Z Joffe's study, based on archives and émigré publications, was published in 1983, it contained the obligatory references to the writings of Lenin but nevertheless treated the subject as an historical issue rather than a live political one. A decade after that, after the dissolution of the Soviet Union, there was a flood of re-publications inside Russia of émigré memoirs and literature of the post-revolutionary period,[47] widely known in the West but previously suppressed and virtually unknown inside Russia. Among these re-publications was the work of S N Timirev – *Recollections of a Naval Officer* (AVIAR, Moscow, 1993).

The past thirty years has seen a resurgence of interest inside Russia in the Kolchak government, and in the romantic relationship between Kolchak and Anna Timireva. The cause of the Kolchak government has been particularly taken up by Orthodox nationalist elements in Russia, who have pressed for a 'rehabilitation' of Kolchak as a Russian patriot.[48] Sentimentalists both inside and outside Russia have seen in the passionate relationship between Anna and Kolchak a mitigation of the unspeakable excesses and gross incompetence for which his government was responsible, much as others remind us that Adolf Hitler, although responsible for the premature deaths and suffering of tens of millions of people, liked children and dogs.[49]

The memoirs of Anna Timireva, written in the 1960s, were originally published in Russian in the West in 1985/86.[50] They provide brief details about her marriage to Sergei, her relationship with Kolchak and her repeated imprisonments in the decades following his execution in February 1920 until her rehabilitation in 1960. These memoirs were re-published in Russia in 1996, along with a selection of her correspondence with Kolchak, her poetry and fiction writing.[51] In 2002 another selection of the correspondence between Anna and Kolchak was published by the Russian Federal Archive Agency.[52]

Anna was one of the five daughters of Vasilii Il'ich Safonoff (1852–1918), the concert pianist and director of the Conservatorium of Music in Moscow and conductor of the New York Philharmonic Orchestra. Descended from southern Cossacks, the family was by the beginning of the twentieth century in the upper levels of the Russian artistic intelligentsia and most of the children became either painters, illustrators or musicians. Anna had been educated in painting and languages at the Obolenskii gymnasium in Moscow. Although the Timirev family home was in the north of Russia near St Petersburg, and the Safonoffs' in Kislovodsk in the Caucasus in the south, they were in fact second cousins.

From these sources it is possible to sketch the fortunes of the Timirev family after Sergei's discharge without pension from the Navy in January 1918. By March he had secured the position with the War Industries Committee in Vladivostok, travelling there in April via the Trans-Siberian Railway with his wife and their friends, the Krashenninikovs, whom they had known in Helsinki. At Blagoveshchensk, Anna came across a naval acquaintance who told her that Kolchak was at Harbin. Kolchak had initiated an increasingly intimate correspondence with Anna after his appointment to command the Black Sea Fleet and despite the difficulties of the times they had maintained this contact during his later travels abroad.[53] Soon after arriving in the east she wrote to Kolchak on 20 April 1918 and arranged to visit him at Harbin in June.[54] On this visit she recognised the overwhelming nature of their passion and decided to remain with Kolchak. Returning to Vladivostok in July, she separated from Sergei despite his pleas, entrusting him to the care of the Krashenninkovs, who she knew 'would do whatever they could for him'. Following Kolchak to Japan and subsequently to Omsk in Siberia, where he later established the military dictatorship as Supreme Ruler in the coup d'etat of November 1918, she was to remain with him until his execution by socialist revolutionaries in Irkutsk on 7 February 1920. Although her early letters to Kolchak show an interest in pre-revolutionary politics, there is no evidence she had any influence at all on the policies or practices of the Kolchak military dictatorship.

While he managed to get himself promoted to full admiral on his accession to power, Kolchak never arranged to divorce his wife and regularise his relationship with Anna. He remained married to Sofia Fyodorovna Kolchak (1876–1956), who had escaped with their son from southern Russia to Paris, where she lived until her death.

On joining Kolchak in Japan, Anna Timireva had told him: 'I know that one must pay a price for everything. But let be it poverty, sickness, whatever, only not the loss of our complete intimacy of spirit – I agree to everything.' She wrote in her memoirs: 'Well it turned out to be a terrible price to pay, but I have never regretted that I had to pay it.' She was not, however, the only one to have to pay.

Anna, arrested with Kolchak at Irkutsk as the White army was fleeing in collapse to the east, was subsequently sentenced to work in a labour camp. Freed briefly in the amnesty of May 1921, she attempted to flee to the Far East, presumably to re-join Sergei in Shanghai. She was re-arrested and sentenced to imprisonment, only returning to Moscow in 1922, where in the same year she married railway engineer Vsevolod Konstantinovich Knipper (1888–1942). In 1923 she was joined by her son Vladimir after the death of his maternal grandmother, who had been raising him in Kislovodsk in the Caucasus since the Timirevs had gone to the Far East in April 1918. In 1925 she was sentenced to exile from Moscow for three years. In 1935, following the murder of Kirov in the preceding December, Anna was again sentenced to internal exile for three years. In 1938 at the end of this period of exile she was again arrested and sentenced to eight years imprisonment.

Sergei and Anna's son, Vladimir, was raised by her sister Yelena from the time of her first exile from Moscow in 1925 onwards. In March 1938, when he was not yet twenty-four years old, Vladimir was arrested by the NKVD. He had allegedly been denounced by his girlfriend's mother as the stepson of Kolchak, whom he can last have seen when he was less than three years old.[55] The 'incriminating evidence' found in Vladimir's accommodation when he was arrested was said to have included correspondence with his father, which must have been quite anodyne, given his father's awareness of the dangers and the fact that he had died six years earlier. Vladimir was shot on 28 May 1938 at the Butovo firing range outside Moscow and posthumously rehabilitated in 1957.[56]

At the end of her period of imprisonment in 1946, Anna was required to live away from Moscow, to which city she was not able to return until 1960 when she was formally 'rehabilitated'. She had married Knipper in 1922, but she assumed the name Timirev-Knipper through the years she tried to discover the fate of her son, who she had been told in 1957 had died of pneumonia in 1943. An habitual smoker, she suffered several heart attacks in the late 1960s and a fatal one in January 1975, dying in Moscow at the age of eighty-one.[57]

Sergei Timirev was appointed Commander of the White Naval Forces in the Far East by Kolchak in November 1918 and retained that office until February 1919, when he became the assistant Senior Naval Administration representative in the Far East (whatever that means). The reasons for these changes are not clear – Dotsenko implies that it was because he might not have been as bloodthirsty as his successor, Rear Admiral M I Fyodorovich.[58] He does not appear to have exercised any significant role in the Civil War in the Far East – only one of the memoirists, Dmitri Fedotoff-White, mentions him at all and that only in passing.[59]

The retreat of the Kolchak government eastwards from Omsk was not an organised retirement to secure positions – uprisings against it occurred spontaneously across Siberia and the Far East ahead of the retreating forces. On 4 January 1920 Kolchak had bequeathed his authority as Supreme Ruler to Denikin in the south of Russia and in the east to Ataman Semenov (of all people!). By 15 January he himself had been handed over to the socialist Political Centre in Irkutsk and was to be executed on 7 February.[60] By the end of January the representative of the Kolchak government in Vladivostok, the murderous General Rozanov, had been overthrown by the anti-Kolchak Provisional Government of the Maritime Zemstvo Board. Whatever role Sergei may have played in the White government up to this point was surely at an end. The US intervention forces departed from Vladivostok on 1 April and the Japanese took control of the city on 4 April 1920.[61]

Whatever the reason, Sergei appears to have left Vladivostok in early 1920 and was in Shanghai from the spring of that year. He found work in the cabotage shipping between Shanghai and Dairen. He was apparently able to send his wife some funds for the education of their son in following years – receipt of this money was one of the charges for which Anna was later exiled to the gulag.[62] According to her testimony to the NKVD in 1935, she maintained correspondence with him until about 1930.[63] He was a popular member of the Russian naval community in Shanghai and for a decade, as senior admiral, he was president of the local Russian Naval Wardroom, only relinquishing that position in 1931 owing to his seafaring commitments.[64] He died from throat cancer in June 1932 aged fifty-eight.

Notes

1961 Biography

1. The American Society for Russian Naval History published the memoirs in 1961 in New York. This 1961 publication is available online at http://rmzb.narod.ru/books/78Timirev.pdf
2. SNT was born 14 May 1875, the second son of Kapitan-Leutenant Nikolai Ivanovich Timirev, 1840–1879 – Wiki RU (I V Anichkov – Obzor pomeschikchikh usadeb Novgorodskopi gubernii, 1916).
3. In fact he graduated in 1895 and won the Admiral Nakhimov prize of 300 roubles.
4. The Imperial Naval Guards (1710–1918) formed an honour service to the Tsar in his yachts and ships. See N Iu Berezovskii et al, *Rossiiskii Imperatorskii flot, 1696–1917: voenno-istoricheskii spravochnik* (*The Russian Imperial Fleet 1696–1917 – 300 year jubilee handbook*), Russkii mir, Moscow, 1996, pp.79–83. This book is available online at https://archive.org/details/rossiiskiiimpera00bere
5. At the Battle of Tsushima Straits, 27–28 May 1905, a Russian Fleet under Admiral Z N Rozhestvenskii, having with great difficulty circumnavigated the globe with the aim of gaining naval superiority by joining the squadron besieged in Port Arthur, was almost completely destroyed by the Japanese Imperial Navy. This defeat after the earlier surrender of the fortress triggered negotiations to end the war.
6. Called 'Hill 203' (metres) in contemporary English language sources about the Port Arthur siege – the dominating hill overlooking Port Arthur and its harbour, key to the land defence of the fortress.
7. In fact SNT died on 13 June 1932 (31 May old style) in Shanghai from throat cancer: B Aprelev – 'Zhizn i smert russkago offitsera', *Chasovoi* (*The Sentinel*), No. 90 Paris, 15 October 1932, p.17. His death was noted in the Shanghai English newspaper *North China Daily News* in an obituary on 14 June 1932, p.12 – see p.156 below.

Part I

Chapter I

1. Nikolai Ottovich von Essen 1860–1915. Naval College 1880. Admiral. Rapidly promoted to captain 1st rank to command battleship Sevastopol at siege of Port Arthur, Russo-Japanese War 1904–05. Commander of the Baltic Fleet 1908–1915. V K Pilkin, *V beloi borb'e na severo- zapade. Dnevnik 1918–1920* (*With the White struggle in the North – Diary 1918–20*), Russkii Put', Moscow, 2005, p.615. N V Skritskii, *Admiraly rossii* (*Admirals of Russia*), Feniks, Rostov on Don, 2013, pp.227–237. As a descendant of the Livonian nobility, Essen was entitled to the German nobiliary particle 'von', but in contemporary Russian sources it was customary not to recognise this, probably as a part of the Russification policies of the government. See the entry for Essen in the Brockhaus-Efron Encyclopaedic Dictionary 1890–1907, available online at www.vehi.net/brokgauz/index.html.
2. Modern Paldiski in Estonia.
3. The capital city of Estonia, from 1918 called Tallin.
4. Stepan Osipovich Makarov 1848–1904. Naval College 1858.

Vice Admiral. Distinguished by his active and inspiring command of the Russian Squadron at Port Arthur. Perished with his ship Petropavlovsk when it hit a mine early in his campaign. N V Skritskii, *Admiraly rossii (Admirals of Russia)*, Feniks, Rostov on Don, 2013, pp.212–218.

5. 'The school of the destroyers' – while rear admiral in command of the Destroyer Division immediately after the Russo-Japanese War, von Essen had encouraged his commanders to become skilful navigators of the many channels and entrances between the skerries and the Baltic Sea by forbidding them to use local pilots, as well as through squadron exercises. After he became Fleet Commander in 1908 he extended these methods to the larger ships and the fleet as a whole. See N B Pavlovich, *Flot v Pervoi Mirovoi Voine* Vol. 1 (*The Fleet in the First World War*), Voenizdat, Moscow, 1964, pp.76–78.
6. Ludwig Berngardovich Kerber (aka Ludwig Fyodorovich Korvin) 1863–1919. Naval College 1884. Executive officer cruiser *Rossiia* at siege of Port Arthur, 1904. Vice Admiral. Commanded Baltic Fleet 1915. Died London 1919. S V Volkov, *Ofitsery flota i morskogo vedomstva: Opyt martirologa* (*Officers of the fleet and Naval Ministry: Attempt at a martyrology*), Russkii put, Moscow, 2004, p.238; Pilkin, op.cit., p.543.
7. Aleksandr Koronatovich Bakhirev 1868–1920. Naval College 1888. Commander of the minelayer *Smelyi* at siege of Port Arthur 1904. Vice admiral commanding Russian naval forces in the Gulf of Riga 1917. Pilkin, op.cit., p.500.
8. Vladimir Konstantinovich Pilkin 1869–1950. Naval College 1890. During siege of Port Arthur, distinguished himself at the Battle of the Yellow Sea, 28 July 1904, for actions that saved the cruiser *Tsesarevich*. Rear admiral, Commander of 1st Brigade of Cruisers Baltic Fleet 1916, discharged on health grounds October 1917. Commanded Yudenich naval forces 1918–19. Emigrated France, died Nice 1950. Pilkin, op.cit., pp.5–28.
9. Baron Vladimir Evgen'evich Grevenitz 1872–1916. Naval College 1892. Captain 1st rank. Served on cruiser *Rossiia*, Vladivostok squadron, in the Russo-Japanese War 1904–05. Commanded dreadnought *Poltava* 1914–16. Died from self-inflicted wounds 1916. www.navy.su/persons/04/grevenits.htm
10. Adrian Ivanovich Nepenin 1871–1917. Naval College 1892. Commanded minelayers *Rastoropnyi* and *Storozhevoi* at siege of Port Arthur 1904. St George Cross 1905. Rear admiral in charge of the Baltic Fleet Signals Intelligence Service. Vice admiral. Commander of the Baltic Fleet September 1916–March 1917. Murdered by revolutionary sailors Helsinki March 1917. Pilkin, op.cit., p.568, Volkov, op.cit., p.334.
11. Anatolii Ivanovich Bestuzhev-Riumin 1873–1917. Naval College 1893. Rear admiral 1916. Officer of the watch battleship *Sevastopol*, Russo-Japanese War, wounded battle of the Yellow Sea 1904. St George Gilded Sword of Honour 1905. Commanded Kola peninsula squadron 1916–17. Died of heart failure 1917. See N Iu Berezovskii et al, *Rossiiskii Imperatorskii flot 1696–1917 Voenno-istoricheskii spravochnik* (*The Russian Imperial Fleet 1696–1917 – 300 year jubilee handbook*), Russkii Mir, Moscow, 1996, p.51.
12. Dimitri Nikolaevich Verderevskii 1873–1947. Naval College 1893. Rear admiral. St George Gilded Sword of Honour. Gunnery specialist, Commander of the Baltic Fleet 1917. Naval Minister, Provisional Government August–November 1917. Emigrated Paris France. Pilkin op.cit. p.510, Volkov, op.cit. p.84.
13. Petr Lvovich Trukhachev 1867–1916. Naval College 1887. Vice admiral. Commanded destroyer *Besstrashnyi* at siege of Port Arthur and Battle of the Yellow Sea 1904. Awarded St George Cross for defence of the Gulf of Riga 1915. See www.navy.su/persons/20/truhachev.htm; *Zakat tsarskogo flota: Morskie ofitsery pervoi mirovoi voiny* (*Sunset of the Tsarist fleet – Naval officers of the*

First World War), Yauza, Moscow, 2018, p.228.

14. Aleksandr Vladimirovich Razvozov, 1879–1920. Naval College 1898. Senior torpedo officer, battleship *Retvizan* at siege of Port Arthur, 1904. Rear admiral commanding Baltic Fleet 1917–18. Arrested March 1918 and again November 1919, died in prison Petrograd 1920. Pilkin, op.cit., p.578–9. His daughter Ekaterina later married Rostislav Kolchak (1910–65), the son of A V Kolchak, in France: Volkov, op.cit., p.394.
15. Mikhail Andreevich Berens, 1879–1943. Naval College 1898. Commanded minelayer *Boikii* at siege of Port Arthur 1904. Served Naval General Staff. Commanded destroyer *Novik*. Commander of White Naval Forces in the Far East January–August 1920. Rear Admiral 1919, commanded Russian squadron Bizerta December 1920–24. Pilkin, op.cit., pp.502–3; Volkov, op.cit., p.47.
16. Pyotr Ilyich Krasheninnikov 1880–1952. Naval College 1900. Served with White forces in Siberia. President of Officers' Wardroom Shanghai 1936–48, later emigrated to Australia. Volkov, op.cit., p.250; www.navy.su/persons/12/krasheninnikov.htm
17. Claude Valentinovich Shevelyov, 1881–1971. Rear admiral and Assistant Minister of the Navy, Kolchak Government 1919. Emigrated 1920–1945 Yugoslavia; after 1945 San Francisco USA. Volkov, op.cit., p.527.
18. Prince Mikhail Borisovich Cherkasskii 1882–1918. Naval College 1901. Navigation officer, first-class cruiser *Diana* at siege of Port Arthur 1904. Rear admiral, Chief of the Naval Staff of the Baltic Fleet 1917. Served with White forces in the Ukraine 1918, captured December 1918, executed January 1919. Pilkin, op.cit., p.602; Volkov, op.cit., p.515.
19. Aleksei Mikhailovich Shchastnyi 1881–1918. Naval College 1901. Led the 'Ice voyage' of the Baltic Fleet from Helsinki to Kronstadt following the White victory in Finland 1918. Executed by the Bolsheviks 22 May 1918. Volkov, op.cit., p.542. Rehabilitated June 1995 under the Russian Federation law of 1991 providing for the rehabilitation of those politically repressed under the Soviet regime: https://rgavmf.ru/sites/default/files/lib/siry_schastniy.pdf
20. Boris Petrovich Dudorov, 1882–1965. Naval College 1902. Staff officer to the Director of Mine Defences at the siege of Port Arthur, 1904. Chief of Naval Aviation under Nepenin. Rear admiral, Russian Imperial Naval Agent, China/Japan, White forces to 1922. Emigrated Palo Alto, California, USA. Pilkin, op.cit. pp.529–30.
21. Then capital city of the Duchy of Finland and a major Russian naval base.
22. Aleksei Dimitrievich Sapsai 1860–1917. Naval College 1880. Vice admiral, Commander of the training division of the Baltic Fleet. Killed by sailors Kronstadt, March 1917. Volkov op.cit., p.421.
23. Ivan Konstantinovich Grigorovich 1853–1930. Naval College 1892. Port Commander during the siege of Port Arthur 1904. Admiral, Minister for the Navy 1911–17. Served on Naval War Historical Commission 1920. Emigrated 1922, France. Pilkin, op.cit., p.524; Volkov op.cit., p.131.
24. Konstantinovich Vasilievich Stetsenko 1862–1920? Naval College 1881. Flag Captain to the Admiral Commanding the Pacific Fleet, Vladivostok during the Russo-Japanese War 1904–05. Admiral, 1916, Head of the Naval General Staff. Imprisoned 1918, fate unknown. Pilkin, op.cit., p.590.
25. Located on Cape Stirsudden on the northern shore of the Gulf of Finland.
26. Such 'controlled' or 'observation' mines depended on an onshore observer distinguishing between an enemy and a friendly ship to activate them. They had the advantage that they posed no threat to one's own ships while the firing circuit was open. Russian naval mines used by the Baltic Fleet during the war were usually of the type detonated by the triggering of a chemical detonator following the rupture of their 'horns'

after contact with a ship or other obstacle – see the description of a near disaster when launching such a mine in H Graf, *The Russian Navy in War and Revolution from 1914 up to 1918*, London, 1923, originally published in Russian as *Na Novike*, Munich, 1922, English edition reprinted Hawaii University Press 2002, p.82.

27. 1 August 1914. The Julian calendar was used in Russia until February 1918. In the twentieth century this was thirteen days behind the Gregorian calendar.
28. Anatoly Fyodorovich Blinov 1885–1964. Lieutenant. Emigrated to New York USA. Volkov op.cit., p.51.
29. Dimitri Dimitrievich Nelidov 1881–1957. Naval College 1901. Captain 2nd rank. Served naval forces of Yudenich Army, evacuation of White forces from Crimea 1919–22. Emigrated New York, USA. Volkov, op.cit., p.333.
30. Vladimir Sergeevich Timirev was born on 4 October 1914. He was known in his family by the diminutive 'Odia' (Vladimir = Volodia = Odia). See p.174 below.
31. Aleksandr Konstantinovich Girs 1859–1917. Naval College 1879. Killed by revolutionary mob Petrograd, March 1917. Volkov, op.cit., p.117. For the designation of ranks in the Imperial Russian Navy, see p.162 below.
32. Georgii Nikolaevich Mazurov 1867–1918. Major General of the Fleet. Served Battle of the Yellow Sea 1904 in Russo-Japanese War 1904–05. Arrested and drowned with others on a barge sunk by Bolsheviks in the Gulf of Finland, August 1918. Volkov, op.cit., p.289.

Chapter II

1. Timirev's wife Anna described this encounter in her memoirs as the first time she saw Kolchak: 'When I accompanied (my husband Sergei) to the railway station a shortish broad-shouldered officer hurried past us. My husband said to me: "Do you know who that is? That's the polar explorer Kolchak. He has recently returned from a northern expedition." There remained to me only the impression of a hurried pace, an energetic stride.' T F Pavlova, F Perchenok & I K Safonoff, *Milaia obozhaemaia moia Anna Vasilievna* (*Dear adorable Anna Vasilievna*), Progress, Moscow, 1996, p.73. For the relationship between Anna and Kolchak see p.170 below.
2. Pavel Mikhailovich Plen 1875–1919. Naval College 1893. Captain 1st Rank. Served siege of Port Arthur, Russo-Japanese War 1904–05. St George Gilded Sword of Honour 1907. Commanded battleship *Slava*. White recruiting agent Petrograd 1917–18, drowned when barge holding arrested officers deliberately sunk near Kronstadt by Bolsheviks late summer 1918. Volkov, op.cit., p.369. www.navy.su/persons/17/plen.htm
3. Evgenii Vladislavovich Kliupfel 1860–1934. Naval College 1884. Rear admiral, Director of Lighthouses and Buoys, Caspian Sea. Served with Kolchak government in Civil War. Gilded Sword of Honour, Russo-Japanese War 1905. Emigrated USA. Volkov, op.cit. p.223; www.navy.su/persons/12/klypfel.htm
4. Ships of the British Royal Navy, designed as long-range cruisers for patrol throughout the empire.
5. This operation, in which Kolchak influenced Rear Admiral Kanin not to turn back after they encountered German warships, is recounted in the diary of Rear Admiral V K Pilkin (op. cit., pp.88–89) and in the memoirs of D N Fedotov-White – *Survival through War and Revolution in Russia*, Philadelphia, U Penn Press, 1939, pp.34–36. In Pilkin's account, while Kolchak persuaded Admiral Kanin to persist with the venture, Podgurskii, captain of the flagship, told his navigation officer: 'Take orders only from me. So long as I personally do not put the helm over, do not turn back.' Pilkin's informant was P N Bunin (1886–1958), the navigation officer. The story is retold in multiple sources as an example of Kolchak's determination and decisiveness and of Kanin's vacillation.
6. Nikolai Lotsianovich Podgurskii 1877–1918. Naval College 1897.

Rear admiral, Commander of the Submarine Division Baltic Sea 1916. Senior torpedo officer, first-class cruiser *Baian* at siege of Port Arthur 1904. Distinguished himself onshore during the siege by devising hand grenades and projectiles in the defence of 203 Metre Hill. St George Cross 1904, St George Gilded Sword of Honour 1905. Died in the Spanish flu pandemic, Reval, November 1918. Pilkin, op.cit., pp.576–77.

7. Dimitri Petrovich Rudenskii 1882–1952. Naval College 1902. Captain 1st rank. Served cruiser *Gromoboi* Russo-Japanese War 1904–05. Served in White forces in Arctic waters. Emigrated Paris, France. Volkov, op.cit., p.408.
8. Mikhail Aleksandrovich Petrov 1885–1938 Naval College 1905. Captain 2nd Rank Imperial Navy 1915, Captain 1st Rank Soviet Navy 1935. Taught at Naval Academy 1919–29. Professor 1929, author of many historical and technical naval studies through the 1920s. Arrested and shot 1938. Volkov, op.cit., p.364, www.navy.su/persons/17/petrov.htm
9. Vladimir Aleksandrovich Svinin 1881–1915. Naval College 1901. Captain 1st rank. Served Porth Arthur and Battle of the Yellow Sea Russo-Japanese War 1904–05. Killed in action on battleship *Slava* 1915. www.navy.su/persons/19/svinin.htm
10. Baron Rudolf Romanovich Mirbach 1882–1965. Naval College 1902. Captain 2nd Rank. Served Port Arthur and Battle of the Yellow Sea 1904–05. Discharged April 1918. Emigrated to Berlin, Germany. Volkov, op.cit., p.313.
11. Aleksandr Nikolaevich Spolatbog 1880–1937. Naval College 1901. Captain 1st Rank. Served on cruiser *Tsesarevich* at siege of Port Arthur 1904–05. Staff Captain Administrative Section Baltic Fleet 1916. Commander cruiser *Admiral Makarov* 1917–18. Continued to serve in Soviet Navy in Black Sea and Sea of Azov. Discharged 1926. https://rgavmf.ru/books/iz-fondov-rgavmf/emelin-ayu-osiroteli-my-pamyati-admirala-no-fon-essena
12. It appears that Spolatbog had not been shot at the time SNT was writing his memoirs in the 1920s. There is some evidence that after his retirement from the Navy, as late as 1929 he worked in a research organisation studying the lower Dnieper River, where major hydroelectric works were under way in the 1920s–30s. See www.navy.su/persons/19/spolatbog.htm. He appears have been executed in the repressions of 1937: https://rgavmf.ru/books/ız-fondov-rgavmf/emelin-ayu-osiroteli-my-pamyati-admirala-no-fon-essena
13. Ivan Ivanovich Rengarten 1880–1920. Naval College 1904. Captain 1st Rank. Served siege of Port Arthur Russo-Japanese War 1904–05. From March 1918 taught at the Naval Academy Petrograd. Served Naval Historical Commission. Died of typhus January 1920. Volkov, op.cit., p.399; https://rgavmf.ru/books/iz-fondov-rgavmf/emelin-ayu-osiroteli-my-pamyati-admirala-no-fon-essena .
14. Viktor Andreevich Vinter 1868–192?. Lieutenant General (Engineer). Naval Technical College 1888. Passed Nicholas Naval Academy (Engineering) 1894. Chief Engineer 1905 onwards. www.navy.su/persons/03/vinter.htm
15. Aleksandr Aleksandrovich Martianov 1881–? Naval College 1901. Served battleship *Sisoi Veliki* at Battle of Tsushima Straits 1905. Alexander Military-Legal Academy 1909. www.navy.su/persons/14/martyanov.htm
16. See p.162 below about civilian ranks in the Russian Empire.
17. Fedor Iulievich Dovkont 1884–1960. Naval College 1906. Captain 2nd Rank. Lieutenant general, Republic of Latvia, 1920–30s. Minister for Defence Latvia. Latvian ambassador to Argentina, where he remained after his country was overrun by the Soviet Union in 1939. Volkov, op.cit., p.150. www.navy.su/persons/05/dovkont.htm
18. Pyotr Ignatievich Tirbakh 1887–1953. Naval College 1910. Lieutenant Commander. Served White forces in Far East. 1919 Harbin, then harbour-master Fuchow, China. Emigrated

1948, Los Angeles California USA. Volkov op.cit., p.471.

19. Mikhail Mikhailovich Komelov 1890–? Naval College 1912. Lieutenant. Served Kolchak forces Siberia. Arrested with Kolchak Irkutsk 1919. Fate unknown. Volkov, op.cit., p.233.
20. Ironically, this defensive position in support of the Army is exactly what the situation came to be for the Russian Baltic Fleet.
21. Between modern Turku in Finland (until 1812 the capital of Finland) and the archipelago of Åland to the west.
22. The Central Position lay on a line from Nargen Island on the southern edge of the Gulf of Finland to Porkallaud in the Finnish coast. In Russian naval pre-war planning the forward defensive position of the Baltic Fleet gradually moved from the inner Gulf of Finland near the island of Gogland westwards to the Nargen/Porkallaud line. As more powerful ships came into commission during the war the Advanced Position based on the Baltic Islands and the Gulf of Riga was strengthened with shore batteries and minefields. See D W Mitchell, *A History of Russian and Soviet Sea Power*, Macmillan, New York, 1974, pp.267–290, and N B Pavlovich, *Flot v Pervoi Mirovoi Voine* Vol. 1 (*The Fleet in the First World War*), Voenizdat, Moscow, 1964, pp.64–71.
23. According to H Graf's eyewitness account, the destroyers had been ordered out to escort the returning cruisers and had just sighted them on the horizon when the *Pallada* exploded. H Graf, *The Russian Navy in War and Revolution from 1914 up to 1918*, London, 1923 (re-published by Hawaii University Press, 2002), pp.11–12. *Pallada* was sunk by the German U-boat *U26* – see D W Mitchell, op.cit., p.297, and the German Official History – R. Firle, *Der Krieg in der Ostsee Vol. I*, Berlin 1921, pp.197–202. The wreck of the *Pallada* was discovered off Hanko by Finnish divers in 2012 – see www.naval-encyclopedia.com/ww1/Russia/bayan-class-cruisers-1905
24. Andrei Semyonovich Maksimov 1866–1951. Naval College 1887. Commanded minelayer *Bezshumnyi* at siege of Port Arthur 1904. Vice admiral. Commander of the Baltic Fleet March–June 1917, from November 1917 Second Assistant Minister for the Navy. Discharged 1927. Died Moscow 1951. Pilkin op.cit., p.559.
25. Arkadii Konstantinovich Nebolsin 1865–1917. Naval College 1886. Rear admiral. Killed by revolutionary sailors Helsinki March 1917. Volkov op.cit., p.330.
26. Pyotr Nikolaevich Leskov 1864–1937. Naval College 1885. Rear admiral. Discharged 1918. Held a range of positions in Soviet Navy. Arrested and shot 1937. Rehabilitated 1989. www.navy.su/persons/13/pn_leskov.htm
27. Konstantin Alekseevich Kitkin 1873–1941. Naval College 1893. Captain 1st Rank. Emigrated to Paris, France. Volkov, op.cit., p.219.
28. Mitrofan Mitrofanovich Skalovskii 1886–1928. Naval College 1887. Major General of the Fleet 1916. www.navy.su/persons/19/skalovsky.htm
29. The harbour at Helsinki.
30. Lev Karlovich Teshe 1863–1917. Naval College 1884. Served siege of Port Arthur and Battle of Yellow Sea Russo-Japanese War 1904–05. Killed by revolutionary sailors Kronstadt March 1917. Volkov, op.cit., p.469.
31. Vladimir Vladimirovich Kovalevskii 1872–1950. Naval College 1892. Rear admiral. 1918–19, Director Naval Personnel, Kolchak Government. 1920–33 Philippines, then San Francisco, USA. Pilkin, op.cit., p.547.
32. Ivan Aleksandrovich Shtorre 1862–? Naval College 1882. Vice admiral 1915. Discharged on health grounds December 1915. Known to be living in Petrograd in 1917. www.navy.su/persons/26/shtorre.htm
33. Aleksei Alekseevich Shchetinin 1876–? Naval College 1895. Captain 1st Rank. Served defence of Port Arthur 1904–05. Commanded cruiser *Rossiia* 1915–17. Discharged November 1917. www.navy.su/persons/27/shetinin.htm
34. Vasilii Aleksandrovich Kanin 1862–1927. Naval College 1882. Admiral. Commander of the Baltic

Fleet 1915–16. Minister for the Navy in the 2nd Crimean Government 1918, Commander of the Black Sea Fleet 1919. Died Marseille 1927. Pilkin, op.cit., pp.540–541. Volkov op.cit., p.207.

35. The Baltic-German barons were the landed nobility of the Baltic littoral of the Russian empire (Latvia, Estonia, Lithuania) who had continued to exercise governmental authority as servants of the Russian crown. While seeking to preserve their privileges over the indigenous populations, they resisted the russification policies of the later nineteenth and early twentieth centuries. They were viewed as having an undue influence in the Navy command structure, but in fact only about 10 per cent of officers had Baltic German ethnic background – see Kirill Nazarenko, *Zakat tsarskogo flota*, op.cit., pp.156–174.
36. This phrase, usually attributed to Trotsky, refers generally to the more radical sailors of the Baltic Fleet and more specifically to the sailors at Kronstadt fortress. Trotsky's enthusiasm for their revolutionary commitment did not prevent him from killing thousands of them later in 1921 when suppressing the revolt against the Soviet government at Kronstadt. See Israel Getzer, *Kronstadt 1917-1921: The Fate of a Soviet Democracy*, Cambridge UP, New York, 1983.
37. Konstantin Dmitrievich Nilov 1856–1919. Admiral, Flag Captain to the Emperor. Naval College 1876. Arrested and died in prison 1919. Vokkov, op.cit., p.339.
38. Nikolai Pavlovich Sablin 1880–1937. Naval College 1898. Captain 1st rank. Served Battle of Tshushima Straits, 1905. Evacuated from Crimea to Constantinople 1921. Emigrated to Germany. Volkov, op.cit., p.415.
39. Vasilii Mikhailovich Altfater 1883–1919. Naval College 1902. Junior navigation officer on cruiser *Askold* at siege of Port Arthur 1904. Rear admiral. Served as Commander of Naval Forces RFSSR 1918–19. Pilkin, op.cit., p.499. Died Moscow 1919, reportedly of heart disease.
40. These conditions did not of course apply to enlisted sailors, who were subject to stringent limitations in relation to leave and recreation – see Norman E Saul, *Sailors in Revolt – The Russian Baltic Fleet in 1917*, University of Kansas Press, Lawrence, Kansas, 1978. The issue of morale and of productive relationships between officers and men was common to all the combatant fleets – see the comprehensive discussion in J Goldrick, *After Jutland: The Naval War in Northern European Waters, June 1916–November 1918*, Annapolis, Naval Institute Press, 2015, pp.18–30.
41. Manoeuvring bases behind the skerries to the west of Helsinki.
42. These locations are all near the approaches to the Gulf of Finland.
43. 'Stavka' was the archaic Russian word for marquee, tent, pavilion or other temporary accommodation. It probably derives from the verb stavit, meaning to place or to post, as in 'post a sentry'. In a military context it meant a sentry post or the location of the field or army commander's position. During the First World War it became a shorthand for the Supreme Headquarters of all Russian forces (all arms) wherever it was located. See Dahl, *Dictionary of the Living Russian Language*. Vol. IV, and http://enc.biblioclub.ru/Termin/1194630_STAVKA
44. Dimitrii Vsevolodovich Neniukov 1869–1929. Naval College 1889, Academy 1908. Vice admiral. Served Port Arthur 1904–05, wounded in action Battle of the Yellow Sea 1904. Head of the Naval office at Supreme Headquarters (Stavka). Served White forces as Commander of the Odessa naval port, and after August 1919 as Commander of the Black Sea Fleet. Evacuated to Yugoslavia. Volkov., op.cit., p.333. www.navy.su/persons/15/nenykov.htm
45. Nikolai Mitrofanovich Grigorov 1873–1944. Naval College 1892. Senior navigation officer on the 2nd class cruiser *Almaz* at the Battle of Tsushima Straits, 1905. Rear admiral. Emigrated Nice, France. Pilkin, op.cit., p.523; Volkov, op.cit., p.131.

46. Timirev appears to be saying that Grigorov was often surprised both by the unexpected results of his labours, and by having to take responsibility for initiatives which he had not planned.
47. Another victim of *U26* – D W Mitchell, op.cit., p.300.
48. Konstantin Viktorovich Prokhorov 1873–1915. Naval College 1894. Took command of cruiser *Aurora* after commander killed in Battle of Tsushima Straits 1905, Russo-Japanese War 1904–05. St George Gilded Sword of Honour 1915. www.navy.su/persons/17/prohorov.htm
49. Modern Ventspils in Latvia.
50. On the eastern shore of the island of Gotland.
51. The German official history, however, says the damage was not sufficient to put the *Roon* out of service: H Rollman, *Der Krieg in der Ostsee – Das Kriegsjahr 1915*, Mittler, Berlin, 1929, pp.173–198.

Chapter III

1. Modern Saaremaa and Muhu in Estonia.
2. According to www.navy.su/persons/19/sveshnikov.htm, the officer whose name was suppressed by Timirev was Vladimir Vladimirovich Shelting 1864–? Naval College 1883. The other officer remains unidentified..
3. The motivation and objectives of this German operation continue to mystify. The German Official History, published in 1929, indicates that the initiative came from Prince Henry, the Kaiser's brother, who held overall command of naval forces in the Baltic. In a conversation with the then Commander-in-Chief, General von Falkenhayn, he was advised that a 'demonstration' by the navy in the Gulf of Riga might be of some use to distract Russian forces from the projected attack on the southern front. The prince convinced the Kaiser to agree and Admiral von Pohl to lend a couple of more powerful ships from the High Seas Fleet to support the operation. But as was explained by Admiral Reinhard Scheer in his 1920 memoirs (*Germany's High Seas Fleet in the World War*, Cassell, London, 1920 – p.92) 'at that time the Army had no troops available to support the entrance of the fleet into the Gulf of Riga, and no importance was attached then to the possession of the town'. This raises more questions than it answers. If the fleet was unable to retain control of the Gulf without the army holding the southern shore, one wonders what the local naval commanders were given to understand their actual objective was. The German Secretary of State for the Navy, Admiral von Tirpitz, had strongly advised against the expedition but too late: 'When the State Secretary gave reasons on the afternoon of the 15th – "Without the participation of the army, we would have to leave the Gulf of Riga after a short time. This would be represented by Russia as a success." – the operations were already under way.' (Rollman, op.cit., p.256). The official history attributes the withdrawal to the 'exhaustion of the minesweeping divisions', while also making it clear that naval and military co-ordination had indeed failed completely (ibid., p.280). Professor Halpern's judgement is persuasive: 'One could seriously question whether the destruction of a pair of small gunboats and a few merchantmen in the gulf was worth the loss of two destroyers and a minesweeper and the even greater potential risks to capital ships involved, particularly if the Germans were not going to establish a permanent naval presence in the gulf.' (Paul Halpern, *A Naval History of World War I*, Naval Institute Press, Annapolis, 1994, p.199).
4. The German destroyers were *V99* and *V100*, units built using material originally intended for additional *Novik* class units for the Russian Navy, but at this stage only armed with 88mm guns, rather than *Novik*'s 102mm. *V99* ran into a minefield and triggered two mines. She was run ashore and became a total loss, with twenty-one dead and twenty-two wounded. See Friedrich Ruge, *SM*

Torpedo Boat B110, Warship Profile No. 27, Profile Publications, Windsor, 1972, p.54.

5. The details of this action from the point of view of the *Novik* are recounted in H Graf, *The Russian Navy in War and Revolution from 1914 up to 1918*, London 1923 (re-published by Hawaii University Press, 2002) pp.48–59. Graf had been the executive officer of the *Novik*. Graf identifies the gunnery officer as Lt Dmitri Ivanovich Fedotov. Fedotov (1889–?) continued to serve in the Soviet Navy and later worked on the Naval Historical Commission. Discharged 1925, fate unknown: www.navy.su/persons/22/fedotov.htm
6. The length of a cable varies depending on the standard applied in each navy but is generally one tenth of a nautical mile. The Russian naval cable was the same as for the British Royal Navy – 185.3m. See S E Zakharov et al, *Krasnoznamennyi Tikhookeanskii Flot* (*The Red Banner Pacific Ocean Fleet*), Voennizdat, Moscow, 1973, p.36n. So the Tserell battery range was 27.8km (approx. 12.6 miles).
7. Modern Sloka in Latvia.
8. Sergei Sergeevich Viazemskii 1869–1915. Naval College 1888. Rear admiral. Executive officer cruiser *Zhemchug* in Battle of Tsushima Straits 1905. Posthumous St George Sword of Honour 1915. www.navy.su/persons/03/vyazemsky.htm
9. Vladimir Aleksandrovich Svinin 1881–1915. Naval College 1901. Captain 1st rank. Gunnery specialist. Served battleship *Retvisan* Port Arthur, 1904–05. KIA 1915. www.navy.su/persons/19/svinin.htm
10. Nikolai Ivanovich Ignatiev 1880–1938. Naval College 1899. Captain 1st Rank. Battle of Tsushima Straits 1905. Gunnery and armour specialist. Served under Bolsheviks from 1921 at the Naval Academy; technical specialist, arrested by OGPU several times. Finally arrested 1937 and shot 1938. www.navy.su/persons/10/ni_ignatev.htm
11. Pavel Ottovich Shishko 1881–1967. Naval College 1901. Captain 1st Rank. Served Russo-Japanese War 1904–05, Battle of Tsushima Straits 1905. Commanded Reval Shock Battalion, Moön causeway 1917. Tank commander, Yudenich North Western Army 1919–20. Emigrated USA 1921, died Groton, Connecticut 1967. Volkov, op.cit., p.534.
12. Modern Cape Kolka in Latvia, at the southern entrance to the Gulf of Riga.
13. Rear Admiral Dudorov claims in his biography of Nepenin that this operation was the idea of the Tsar and its failure to materialise effectively became the cause of his losing faith in Kanin as Fleet Commander. This claim is based on the recollection of Captain 2nd Rank F Iu Dovkont, at the time serving in the Operational Section of Stavka. See *Morskiia zapiski* (*The Naval Records*), Vol. XIX No. 1/2–54 June 1961, pp.93–95.
14. Captain 1st Rank Rengarten noted in his diary: 'The disbandment of the squadron was recognition that it was unnecessary and of the fact that it had been created for personal reasons. But the tragedy was that in relation to Kerber his being chucked out of his job was an act of black ingratitude; in this matter there was too much of personal relations. Unfortunately, it must be recognised that Kerber himself was often too tactless and fatally could not speak Russian well – from which he became very unpopular'. Russian State Archive of the Naval Fleet – fond P-29, inventory 1, item 199, pp.275–276 (РГАВМФ. ф.Р-29, оп.1, д.199, л.275–276)) cited at https://rgavmf.ru/books/iz-fondov-rgavmf/emelin-ayu-osiroteli-my-pamyati-admirala-no-fon-essena
15. The St George Cross was the highest of Russian Imperial awards for bravery. Under the protocols for Imperial awards, senior members of each Order constituted the College (Duma), which decided future nominations to receive the award. That is, certified brave men could certify other men as brave. The Sovereign could, however, make the award independently as Autocrat (see above p.38). Non-College awards became more common among the White armies during the civil war

when previous protocols for awards for bravery broke down. See the entry for College of Chivalry (Duma kavalerskaia) in the Brockhaus-Efron Encyclopaedic Dictionary 1895–1907 available online at www.vehi.net/brokgauz/index.html. See also A Iu Emelin 'K istorii Georgievskoi dumy i dumy Georgievskogo oruzhiia flota Baltiiskogo moria 1914–1917 гг' (Towards a History of the Colleges of St George Cross and St George Sabre in the Baltic Sea Fleet 1914–1917), in *Elaginskie chteniia* (*Yelagin readings*), SPB 2016 Vol. VIII available online at https://rgavmf.ru/sites/default/files/lib/elaginskie_chteniya_8.pdf

In 1915 the College of St George on the Southern Army Front awarded the Cross of St George to the Tsar for his bravery under direct enemy fire when visiting troops at that front. The Tsar, who never promoted himself above the rank of colonel, nevertheless accepted this award. See V N Voeikov, *S tsarem I bez tsaria*, (*With and without the Tsar*), Zakharov, Moscow, 2016, pp.132–133 (first published Helsinki, 1936).

16. The eastern entrance from the Kattegat to the Baltic Sea between Denmark and Sweden. The British sent four smaller 'C' class submarines in 1916 via Archangel and the canal system between the White Sea and the Baltic.
17. Then Captain Francis Cromie RN, left as charge d'affaires at the British Embassy in Petrograd when the ambassador was withdrawn, was taken by surprise by Bolshevik intruders who were pursuing assassins of the head of the Petrograd Cheka, M Uritsky, on 31 August 1918. He was shot in the back while running down the front staircase of the embassy. An eyewitness account of his murder is given in M Britneva, *One Woman's Story*, Arthur Barker, London, 1934, pp.67–86. See also M Occleshaw, *Dances in Deep Shadows*, Carrol & Graf, New York, 2006, p.229.
18. 'from Ingrian–Finnish sailboats' – the Russian is 's chukonskikh laib'. Chukhonets is the Russian word for the Ingrian Finnish population of the region around St Petersburg. It was generally pejorative: its root (chukh) comes from the word for 'pig' (chukhna), of which a form is the abusive chukhnia (brainless simpleton) – see the entries in Dal's *Dictionary of the Living Russian Language* (V Dal' *Tolkoviy slovar' zhivago veilikorusskago iazyka*, SPB, 1882, re-published Moscow, 1982). Of Finnish ethnicity, the Ingrians had inhabited the region since before it became a part of the Russian Empire in the eighteenth century and had been subjected to the Imperial russification policies of the nineteenth century. Although initially recognised in the USSR as an ethnic nationality, their loyalty continued to be suspect and many were deported to the gulag in the 1920s and 1930s (see 'Ingrian' in Wikipedia; gulag memoir). Dahl's dictionary defines a laiba as a large Chukhon or Finnish sailboat with one or two masts, sometimes with a deck. Timirev is most likely implying both deception by the Germans and disloyalty by the Ingrians in his assertion that they were probably used for sowing mines. There is no evidence, however, that any German mines were laid in this unlikely and risky manner. V Dal' *Tolkoviy slovar' zhivago veilikorusskago iazyka*. (*A defining dictionary of the living Russian language*) Vol. IV SPB 1882 (re-published Moscow, 1982).
19. Pyotr Pavlovich Kitkin 1876–1954. Naval College 1896. Rear admiral Imperial Fleet 1917; Rear admiral Soviet Fleet 1944. Served defence of Port Arthur, Russo-Japanese War 1904–05. St George Gilded Sword of Honour 1916. Mines and torpedo technical specialist. www.navy.su/persons/12/kitkin.htm
20. Nikolai Gotlibovich Rein 1870–1917. Naval College 1890. Rear admiral (1916). Served on cruiser *Rossiia* Vladivostok Squadron, Russo-Japanese War 1904–05. Cross of St George 1904. Murdered by sailors Kronstadt March 1917. www.navy.su/persons/18/reyn.htm
21. Nikolai Vasilievich Krotkov 1875–193? Naval College 1894. Captain 1st rank. Executive officer,

battleship *Peresvet* at siege of Port Arthur 1904. Continued to serve in Navy under the Bolsheviks. Assistant with the Naval Historical Commission 1921–23. Discharged 1925. www.navy.su/persons/12/krotkov.htm

22. The largest island of the Åland archipelago, directly west of Helsinki. Not to be confused with Öland, south-east of Sweden and south-west of Gotland.
23. Otton Ottonovich Richter 1871–? Naval College 1891. Rear admiral 1915. Served Battle of Tsushima Straits 1905. Reserve list 1916. www.navy.su/persons/18/rihter.htm
24. Dago, modern Hiiuma in Estonia, is the northern-most island of the archipelago.
25. According to www.navy.su/persons/19/sveshnikov.htm, the officer not named by Timirev was Vladimir Vladimirovich Shelting 1864–? Naval College 1883.
26. Dmitrii Aleksandrovich Sveshnikov 1864–? Naval College 1884. Rear admiral 1916. Discharged 1917. Served on the Naval Commission of Inquiry into the loss of Moön Sound www.navy.su/persons/19/sveshnikov.htm
27. Vladimir Platzidovich Przhilenski 1869–? University of St Petersburg. Fleet cadet 1892. Served on cruiser *Bogatyr* Vladivostok Squadron during Russo-Japanese War 1904–05. www.navy.su/persons/17/przhilentskiy.htm
28. According to Occleshaw op.cit., pp.93–94, Ernst Konstantinovich Fetterlein offered his services to the British Navy in March 1918 and became a valuable addition to the famous Room 40 responsible for British naval signals intelligence for the remainder of the war. Fetterlein apparently lived for the rest of his life in Britain.
29. In the Russian Navy at this time crews joined their ships while they were fitting out in the shipyards and remained on them while they were being repaired – see N E Saul, *Sailors in Revolt – The Russian Baltic Fleet in 1917*, University of Kansas Press, Lawrence, Kansas, 1978, p.19.
30. Leonid Leontevich Ivanov 1875–after 1939? Naval College 1895. Rear admiral 1917. On cruiser *Diana* at siege of Port Arthur 1904–05. Twice commanded White naval forces in the northern ocean during Civil War 1918–20. Emigrated Rome. www.navy.su/persons/10/ll_ivanov.htm

Chapter IV

1. Captain 1st Rank Prince Cherkasskii agreed with this assessment of Kanin at the time: 'at the head of the Fleet stood an un-military person, an excellent family man, a good bridge player, knowledgeable about mine-sowing and possessed of many other good but non-military qualities.' Russian State Archive of the Naval Fleet – fond 418, inventory 1, item 5651, p.1 (РГАВМФ. ф.418, оп.1, д.5651, л.1) cited at https://rgavmf.ru/books/iz-fondov-rgavmf/emelin-ayu-osiroteli-my-pamyati-admirala-no-fon-essena
2. Aleksandr Mikhailovich Gerasimov 1861–1931. Naval College 1882. Senior officer on the battleship *Pobeda* at siege of Port Arthur 1904. Vice admiral. Director Naval Gunnery School and Commandant Peter the Great Fortress Reval and Governor General of Estonia and Livonia 1914–17. Commander of the White Navy Office Southern Russia 1918–20. Director Naval College Bizerta 1920–25. Died Tunisia 1931. Pilkin, op.cit., pp.519–20; Volkov, op.cit., p.112.
3. Altfater continued his career in the Soviet Navy and was the Russian Naval delegate at the Brest–Litovsk negotiations between the Germans and the Bolshevik government of Russia. Occleshaw implies he spied for the British (op.cit., p.79, 279), with whom he shared information about the negotiations, mainly concerning the proposed fate of the Russian fleets under the treaty. Possibly he was just indiscreet, as Timirev describes him. He died of heart failure in April 1919, although General Max Hoffman, a German delegate at the negotiations, alleges in his memoir *A War of Lost Opportunities*, originally published in 1924, that he was murdered. However, there is no reason to believe

that Hoffman was reliably informed about this.

4. The *Variag* was a famous ship in Russia, having been scuttled by its commander in Chemulpo (Inchon) harbour in Korea in January 1904 after a gallant but unequal fight with a Japanese battle squadron off Korea at the beginning of the Russo-Japanese war. The Japanese had subsequently raised and refitted it and former Russian cruisers from Port Arthur, including the *Baian*, for use as training ships, which made annual trips through Asia and the South Pacific, during which they completed detailed mapping of the waters through Southeast Asia, around the Pacific Islands, and the coasts of Australia and New Zealand.
5. The Russian original is in the second person singular, which is used stylistically as a sign either of personal closeness (as between family, friends or close colleagues) or of a highly condescending stance on the part of the speaker (such as master to servant). A literal translation would be: 'I do not understand what thou seekest? Surely thou hast received from thy 'adventure' all thou sought – have they not promoted thee to admiral?' English has lost this handy use of the second person singular. It remains in French, German, Russian and other languages.
6. The *Peresvet* had run aground and had to be repaired when the remainder of the squadron left Vladivostok. She was sunk probably by a German minefield laid by submarine *U73* near Port Said in January 1917 – see Paul G Halpern, *The Naval War in the Mediterranean, 1914–1918*, Allen & Unwin, London, 1987, p.325.
7. The cruise of this squadron from Vladivostok to Murmansk was described by B P Aprelev in his memoir *Na Variage* (*On the Variag*), Shanghai, 1934 (reprinted SPB 2013). The squadron took a very leisurely and circuitous route from Vladivostok, leaving on 18 June 1916 through the Indian Ocean, the Mediterranean and the North Atlantic to Liverpool then to Murmansk arriving in late October (five months). None of the ships saw action, and the *Variag*, sent to Britain for refit shortly afterwards, was after the revolution sold for scrap by the British to acquit Russian war debts but foundered on the western coast of Scotland, where a memorial was erected to it by Russian patriots in 2004. The whole venture must be judged to be one of the most profligate and irresponsible uses of both financial and human resources in the history of Russia in the war, of which unfortunately, there appear to have been many.
8. Boris Vladimirovich Muromstov 1886–1919. Naval College 1907. Captain 2nd rank. St George Sword of Honour, January 1917. Committed suicide Moscow 1919. www.navy.su/persons/14/muromtsev.htm
9. Aleksandr Parfenovich Kurosh 1862–1919. Naval College 1882. Vice admiral 1916. Arrested and dismissed from service 1917. Arrested by Bolsheviks 1918, shot 1919. www.navy.su/persons/12/kurosh.htm
10. Vladimir Stepanovich Vecheslav 1876–? Naval College 1894. St George Cross 4th Class 1916. Continued service in the Soviet Navy, Discharged 1922. www.navy.su/persons/03/vecheslav.htm
11. Nepenin secured this promotion despite never having commanded a first-class ship, which would otherwise have been expected. See V N Fotuniants, 'Morskaia krepost Imperatora Petra Velikogo v biografii A I Nepenin' (The naval fortress of Emperor Peter the Great in the biography of A I Nepenin), in *Elaginskie chteniia* (*Yelagin readings*), SPB 2016 Vol. VIII, available online at https://rgavmf.ru/sites/default/files/lib/elaginskie_chteniya_8.pdf
12. Andrei Avgustovich Ebergard 1856–1919. Naval College 1879. Admiral. Commanded battleship *Tsesarevich* at Port Arthur 1904. St George Gilded Sword of Honour 1905. Commander in Chief Black Sea Fleet 1911 to 1916. Appointed to the State Council 1916. Discharged 1917. Arrested by Cheka 1918. Died 1919 Petrograd. Volkov op.cit.,

pp.545–6; www.navy.su/persons/31/ebergard.htm

13. Aleksandr Dmitrievich Bubnov 1883–1963. Naval College 1903. Senior navigation officer, battleship *Orel* at the Battle of Tsushima Straits 1905. Rear admiral. Naval staff officer, Stavka. Chief of Staff of the White Fleet in the Black Sea 1919–20. Naval representative of Kolchak Government at the Versailles Peace Conference. Professor at the Naval Academy Yugoslavia 1923–30. Pilkin, op.cit., pp.505–6; Volkov, op.cit., p.65; www.navy.su/persons/02/ad_bubnov.htm
14. Bubnov claims in his memoirs that it was dissatisfaction with Ebergard's passivity towards the German forces in the Black Sea that led Admiral Rusin and Navy Minister Grigorovich to recommend his replacement to the Tsar – A D Bubnov, *V tsarskoi stavke; vospominaniia admirala Bubnova* (*At the Tsar's Supreme Headquarters – the memoirs of Admiral Bubnov*), Chekov, New York, 1955, pp.156–157.
15. Mikhail Aleksandrovich Kedrov 1878–1945. Naval College 1899. Flag officer to admirals commanding the Pacific Fleet, Makarov and later Whitgeft, at the siege of Port Arthur; seriously wounded in the Battle of the Yellow Sea 1904. Vice admiral. Assistant to Naval Minister Guchkov in Kerensky Government. White naval agent London 1917–20. Commanded White Russian naval squadron Bizerta 1921. Died Paris 1945. Pilkin, op.cit., pp.541–2. Volkov, op.cit., p.214.

Chapter V

1. Nikolai Dmitrievich Tyrkov 1871–1931. Naval College 1892. Captain 1st rank 1915. Commanded minelayer *Burnyi* Port Arthur 1904–05. Reserve list 1917. Recalled to Fleet 1920. Discharged 1921. Arrested, imprisoned and released 1921. Worked in Leningrad port and industry up to 1930. www.navy.su/persons/20/tyrkov.htm
2. Aleksandr Konstantinovich Veis 1870–1935? Naval College 1891. Rear admiral. Continued to serve in naval forces of RFSSR. Arrested 1931, 1933, 1935. Exiled to Orenburg 1935. Volkov, op.cit., p.83.
3. Boris Vasiievich Katkov 1882–1917. Naval College 1902. Captain 2nd rank 1915. Served Port Arthur, Russo-Japanese War 1904–05. Shot himself at home, in Petrograd April 1917. www.navy.su/persons/12/katkov.htm
4. Possibly Konstantin Sergeevich Ukhov 1889–1938? Naval College 1909. Lieutenant 1912. Continued service under the Bolsheviks. Assistant manager of the Hydrographic Department of the Soviet Fleet 1930–32. Instructor in sea-going astronomy to 1938. www.navy.su/persons/21/uhov.htm
5. A peninsula on the Finnish coast south-west of Helsinki.
6. Pyotr Petrovich Vladislavlev 1872–1917. Naval College 1895. Senior officer of the Watch, first-class cruiser *Gromoboi* at Vladivostok, Russo-Japanese War 1904–05. Rear admiral, Commander submarine forces Baltic Fleet April 1917. Died by accident or murder 5 October 1917. Pilkin, op.cit., p.514; Volkov, op.cit., p.91.
7. Sergei Valerianovich Zarubaev 1877–1921. Naval College 1896. Senior gunnery officer, cruiser *Variag*, at the Battle of Chemulpo, Korea 1904. Rear admiral. Senior Naval Officer Kronstadt 1918. Director of Training Baltic Fleet 1919–21. Arrested and shot August 1921. Pilkin, op.cit., pp.535–6.
8. The northern promontory of the island of Dago where a signals intelligence station was located.
9. Modern Daugavgrīva in Latvia.
10. Vasilii Vasilievich Selitrennikov 1882–1938. Naval College 1901. Continued to serve in Naval Academy of USSR. Arrested 1931, probably shot 1938. Volkov, op.cit., p.427.
11. Vladimir Vladimirovich Kovalevskii 1872–1950. Naval College 1892. Rear admiral. Discharged 1918. Served Kolchak forces Siberia 1919–20. Emigrated USA. www.navy.su/persons/12/vv_kovalevsky.htm
12. Modest Ivanovich Ivanov 1875–1942. Naval College 1894 (in 36th place). Navigation officer gunboat *Otvazhnyi* Port Arthur, Russo-Japanese War

1904–05. Actively participated in TsentroBalt (Central Committee of the Baltic Fleet) during the revolution. Promoted rear admiral and appointed Assistant Minister for the Navy (and later Minister) in November 1917. From 1918 continued service in the Soviet fleet, as well as the Cheka and OGPU. After 1925 worked in the Soviet commercial fleet. Died during the siege of Leningrad 1942.

13. The State Council of the Russian Empire, established in 1810 by Emperor Alexander I, had been reformed in 1906 to be the upper house of the new Russian parliament after the 1905 revolution. Half its members were appointed by the Tsar, usually from the nobility, officials and distinguished army and naval officers, and half elected for a period of nine years from a restricted franchise. One-third of elected members retired every three years, being replaced by election. Members had to be over forty years old, have at least secondary education or equivalent, and not be foreign subjects. As the appointed members attending the Council could not exceed the number of elected members, appointed members took their place on rotation over three years, so the position was not necessarily onerous. See Mark Lvovich Levenson, *Gosudarstvennyi Sovet* (*The State Council*), Petrograd 1915; N P Eroshkin, *Istoriia gosudarstvennykh uchrezhdenii dorevoliutsionnou rossii* (*History of the government establishments of pre-revolutionary Russia*), Vysshaia shkola, Moscow, 1983.
14. Dudorov claims that not only Altfater, but also the junior officers Cherkasskii, Rengarten and Dovkont were involved in trying to influence Stavka to ensure that Kanin was replaced by Nepenin after Kolchak had been appointed to the Black Sea command. See *Morskiia zapiski* (*The Naval Records*), Vol. XIX No. 1/2 – 54 June 1961, pp.96–98.
15. Timirev's wife Anna wrote to Kolchak on 31 October 1916: 'Your colleague – Adrian Ivanovich – is storming around as previously and inspiring wild panic in all around, the circle of whom has been significantly depleted – some leaving of their own accord, others sent away by him, still others sitting on suitcases ready to disappear any minute over the horizon. Evidently Adrian Ivanovich is even more terrifying than you, my dear Aleksandr Vasilievich – who'd have thought it?' T F Pavlova et al. *Milaia khimera v admiralskoi forme – pisma A V Timirevou A V Kochaku 1916–1917 gg* (*Dear chimera in admiral's uniform – the letters of A V Timireva to A V Kolchak 1916–1917*), 2nd corrected edition, D Bulanin, St Petersburg, 2017, p.78.

Chapter VI

1. Alexei Alexeevich Birilyov 1844–1916. Admiral. Naval College 1864. Briefly commanded Pacific Fleet June 1905. First Russian Naval Minister 1905–07. Played central role in re-establishment of the Navy after Russo-Japanese War. www.navy.su/persons/02/birilev.htm
2. The letter addresses Timirev in the second person singular – ie., using the intimate 'ty' as between friends, rather than the formal 'vy'.
3. Rear Admiral Dudorov in his very sympathetic biography of Nepenin argues that Nepenin's disciplinary excesses had been exaggerated and that Timirev misinterpreted the genuine character of Nepenin's apology. See *Morskiia zapiski* (*The Naval Records*), Vol. XIX No. 1/2–54 June 1961, pp.111–113. However, Dudorov also recounts several instances of Nepenin's tactless communication style: 'far from being subservient, in matters affecting the service he allowed himself to enter into altercations (with superiors) in quite a sharp way'. When Vice Admiral Gerasimov asked for him to be transferred to his command, the Navy Minister, Admiral Grigorovich warned him he could be a difficult subordinate: 'He's even bawled me out you know!' *Morskiia zapiski* (*The Naval Records*), Vol. XIV No. 4–43 December 1956, pp.14–15. At a dinner for the Tsar's nephew Rear Admiral Grand Duke Kirill Vladimirovich, the

Grand Duke responded to a remark of the presiding admiral by saying: 'I think that's stupid thinking.' Nepenin broke the embarrassing silence that followed by saying: 'Yes that's what I have been saying!'

4. Aleksandr Mikhailovich Pyshnov 1873–? Naval College 1894. Captain 1st rank. Transferred to Naval Ministry Reserve May 1917. Continued to serve in central administration of the Soviet Navy after the Civil War. Fate unknown. www.navy.su/persons/17/pyshnov.htm
5. An island in the inner Gulf of Finland, west of Kronstadt.
6. Robert Nikolaevich Viren 1856–1917. Naval College 1877. Admiral and Governor of Kronstadt Fortress. Captain of cruiser *Baian* at Port Arthur and later rear admiral commanding Pacific Squadron, Russo-Japanese War 1904–05. St George Cross and St George Gilded Sword of Honour for defence of the fortress. Murdered by revolutionary sailors 1 March 1917. Volkov, op.cit., p.89.
7. The *Baian*, confined to the harbour by damage from a mine, had been sunk by artillery fire at Port Arthur after the Japanese capture of Hill 203. Raised by the Japanese after the war, she was refitted and used for a decade as the training ship Aso in the Imperial Japanese Navy, regularly cruising the Indian and Pacific Oceans and visiting every major port in Australia. The same design was used for the *Admiral Makarov* (1908), another *Baian* that Timirev commanded, and the *Pallada* (1911), which all saw action in the Baltic. See Mitchell, op.cit., pp.229–231, www.naval-encyclopedia.com/ww1/Russia/bayan-class-cruisers-1905 and www.navy.su/1850-1917/cruisers/bayan/index.htm
8. Great Eagle's Nest was a critical fortified position in the hills above Port Arthur.
9. Russian officers who would not give their parole to take no further part in the war after the fall of Port Arthur were held in Japan as prisoners of war until after the settlement of the Treaty of Portsmouth that ended the war.
10. Vladimir Simonovich Sarnavskii 1855–1916. Naval College 1876. Admiral 1915. Commanded cruiser *Pallada* at Port Arthur 1904–05. Awarded Gilded Sword of Honour for courage at Port Arthur 1907. Commander of the Port of Sevastopol 1913. Died Voronezh 1916. www.navy.su/persons/19/sarnavsky.htm
11. Aleksandr Sergeevich Polushkin 1877–1962. Naval College 1896. Served cruiser *Izumrud* at Battle of Tsushima Straits 1905, Russo-Japanese War 1904–05. Head of the Hydrographic Office, Kolchak Government 1919. 1920 Yugoslavia, 1923 New York USA. Volkov, op.cit., p.377. www.navy.su/persons/17/polushkin.htm
12. Sergei Dimtrievich Koptev 1880–1920? Naval College 1898. Captain 1st Rank. Torpedo Officer, destroyer *Groznyi* at Batttle of Tsushima Straits 1905, Russo-Japanese War 1904–05. St George Cross 1907. Died December 1919 or early 1920. Volkov, op.cit., p.237, www.navy.su/persons/12/koptev.htm

Chapter VII

1. Timirev's wife Anna did take a lively interest in the cultural and political life of the capital. In a letter to Kolchak on 21 December 1916 she had greeted the news of the murder of Rasputin with delight: 'This murder evoked in me the greatest feeling of satisfaction and a sort of malicious joy, and I don't imagine that I was alone in this.' Like most of her generation, she was to have reason to regret deeply the adoption of murder as an instrument of politics. *Miliia khimera v admiralskoi forme*, op.cit., p.116
2. Anna described this visit in a letter to Kolchak on 22 February 1917: 'We spent 5 days at the village. They fed us until we were bursting such that for a whole day I could scarcely breathe from being gorged, a truly quite ghastly condition. But all the same it wasn't so bad – astonishing quietness and snow – singularly beautiful: all through the winter they had not had a single thaw. In all I

had never yet seen such purity and whiteness. There was frost morning and evening of 20–25°, but the sun was already warming, icicles on the roofs and trees and the pussy-willow beginning to bud. We went for sleigh rides, simply strolled through the snow, sat in the lounge-room and chatted with my mother-in-law about any and everything, or I read *Don Quixote* – and all around the farmstead such isolation, snow and silence that occasionally it was even hard to remind oneself that beyond the limits of all this a rowdy and complicated life was going on: *Dear chimera in admiral's uniform*, op.cit., pp.162–163.

3. Vladimir Vadimovich Romanov 1876–1962. Naval College 1895. Captain 2nd Rank. Served Battle of Tsushima Straits, 1905, Russo-Japanese War. Recalled to service from reserve 1914, served Naval General Staff to 1918. White forces Northern Front 1919. Emigrated France, died Paris 1962. Volkov, op.cit., p.405.
4. Anna was writing to Kolchak from an address in the 7th Rozhdestvenskii borough in the curve of the River Neva to the east of Nevskii Prospect, where the population was mainly government employees or skilled craftsmen, with fewer than 10 per cent factory workers or labourers – see James H Bater, *St Petersburg Industrialization and Change*, McGill Queen's University Press, Montreal, 1976, pp.198–199.
5. Aleksandr Ivanovich Iaron 1874–1935. Military Engineering Academy 1899. Engineer Colonel. Commander of the Vladivostok Port 1919. Shanghai China 1922–35. Volkov, op.cit., pp.557–8. www.navy.su/persons/33/yaron.htm

Part II

Chapter I

1. Georgii Ottovich Gadd 1873–1952. Naval College 1894. Commanded the minelayers *Silnyi* and *Boikii* at the siege of Port Arthur 1904. Served with Mannerheim forces Finland 1918–19. Rear admiral, representative of Grand Duke Kirill Vladimirovich Romanov (claimant to the Russian throne) in Denmark 1930s. Pilkin, op.cit., pp.517–18. Volkov, op.cit., p.104. G K Graf, *Na sluzhbe imperatorskomu domu rossii 1917–1941 vospominaniia* (*In the service of the Russian imperial house 1917–1941 Memoirs*), Blits, St Petersburg, 2004, p.639.
2. Modern Katajanokka, a seaside suburb of Helsinki.
3. The wharves either side of the Katajanokka peninsula in Helsinki harbour.
4. In his memoirs Admiral Bubnov agrees with Timirev's assessment of Maksimov, referring to his speaking Russian with a heavy Finnish accent and being distinguished by complete lack of principles and huge pride out of all proportion to his basic lack of capability. Bubnov attributed his election as Fleet Commander to the German secret service. A D Bubnov, *V tsarskoi stavke; vospominaniia admirala Bubnova* (*At the Tsar's supreme headquarters, the memoirs of Admiral Bubnov*), Chekhov, New York, 1955, pp.334–335.
5. However, Tirbakh, who found Nepenin's body and prepared it for burial, says it showed only two bullet and three bayonet wounds. See Dudorov, *Morskiia zapiski* (*The Naval Records*), Vol. XX No. 1/2–56 April 1962, pp.55–58.

Chapter II

1. However, Timirev's wife Anna wrote to Kolchak on 12 May 1917: 'Life here goes on as usual. On the cruisers they shot two young officers – one on Sergei Nikolaevich's *Baian*. It seems this is becoming the fashion in the fleet.' T F Pavlova et al., *Dear chimera in admiral's uniform*, op.cit., p.223.
2. Fyodor Isaakovich Batkin (1892–1923) was the leader of a delegation of sailors from the Black Sea who toured Moscow, Petrograd and the Baltic advocating continuation of the war to victory over Germany in opposition to Bolshevik arguments for a separate peace. Allegedly a member of the Socialist Revolutionary Party, he had been a student in Liège before the war, fought in the Belgian army as a volunteer, after the February

Revolution returned to fight in the infantry in Russia and was awarded the St George Cross for bravery. Kolchak supposedly enlisted him in the Navy to lead the delegation. Later he served with the Volunteer Army of Denikin in the civil war in southern Russia but in emigration in Turkey was enlisted by the Cheka. Returning to the Crimea in 1923, he was arrested and shot by the local secret police.

Chapter III

1. Pyotr Petrovich Vladislavlev 1876–1917. Naval College 1895. Rear admiral 1917. Served Vladivostok Squadron Russo-Japanese War 1904–05. Cross of St George 1904. St George Sword of Honour 1916. Accidentally drowned or murdered October 1917. www.navy.su/persons/03/vladislavtsev.htm
2. After the revolution, many ships with imperial names were renamed to more appropriately republican ones, so in this case from '*Crown Prince*' to '*Citizen*'.
3. Vladimir Grigorevich Antonov 1876–1954. St Petersburg University 1899; Midshipman by examination 1901. Captain 1st Rank. Served Battle of Tsushima Straits 1905, Russo-Japanese War. Served Anglo-Russian forces Archangel 1919–20. Emigrated Belgium, died Brussels 1954. Volkov, op.cit., p.23. www.navy.su/persons/01/antonov.htm
4. The Russian SRs – Socialist Revolutionaries – were agrarian socialists who opposed both tsarism and the other socialist parties based on the industrial workers of the cities. See Oliver Radkey, *The Agrarian Foes of Bolshevism; promise and default of the Russian socialist revolutionaries, February to October 1917*, Columbia U.P., New York, 1958 and Manfred Hildermeier, *The Russian Socialist Revolutionary Party before the First World War*, St Martin's Press, New York, 2000.
5. Infantry General Lavr Georgievich Kornilov (1870–1918; St George Cross 1915), previously Commander of the Southern Front, had been appointed Supreme Commander by the Kerensky government in July 1917. Believing he had the support of Kerensky to re-establish order in the Army, including the death penalty, in late August Kornilov moved troops loyal to him from the south towards Petrograd with the aim of replacing the garrison there and dispersing the Soviet. Accused by Kerensky of counter-revolution, he was dismissed from his post and arrested, his forces dissuaded from supporting him by activists from Petrograd and the Baltic Fleet. Whether Kornilov intended to overthrow the government has remained controversial ever since, as has the apparent duplicity of Kerensky. For a summary of the evidence and discussion see Joergen L Munck, *The Kornilov Revolt: A Critical Examination of Sources and Research*, Aarhus, Aarhus University Press, 1987. Although remarkably uneventful, this 'affair' was subsequently seen as presaging the civil war that was to ravage Russia for several years. Freed from prison in the confusion following the Bolshevik seizure of power, Kornilov fled to the Don region in the south, where he raised the Volunteer Army, which became the core of the White anti-Bolshevik forces in the south. He was killed in the assault on Ekaterinodar in April 1918. In 2004 there was a museum exhibition on him in Ekaterinodar and in 2013 a monument erected to him at Krasnodar.
6. These murders are described detail and the victims named in Graf, *The Russian Navy in War and Revolution*, op.cit., pp.165–168.
7. Georgii (Iurii) Karlovich Stark 1878–1950. Naval College 1898. Senior Torpedo Officer, 1st class cruiser *Aurora* at Battle of Tsushima Straits, 1905. Rear admiral, Commander of the Destroyer Division of the Baltic Fleet 1917–18. Commanded Volga-Kama Flotilla of the Kolchak forces and later the Siberian Flotilla. Commanded the evacuation of White forces from Vladivostok to the Philippines 1922–23. Shanghai 1930s, then taxi-driver France. Died Paris

1950. Pilkin, op.cit., p.589; Volkov, op.cit., p.453.

Chapter IV

1. The account given here by Timirev from memory is largely confirmed by the later official histories and by two recent studies based on access to the naval archives: Michael B Barrett, *Operation Albion: The German conquest of the Baltic Islands*, Bloomington: University of Indiana Press, 2008. Gary Staff, *Battle for the Baltic Islands 1817 – Triumph of the German Navy*. Pen & Sword, Barnsley, 2008. See also Goldrick, *After Jutland*, op.cit., p.187ff.
2. Morits Georgievich Kniupfer 1882–1952. Naval College 1902. Captain 1st rank. Executive officer 1st class cruiser *Dmitrii Donskoi*, wounded in head and shoulder at Battle of Tsushima Straits 1905. Guards Depot. Taken prisoner by Germans, Svorbe Peninsular 1917. Chief of Staff of the Northern Corps, liaison with British forces 1919. Emigrated England. Died London 1952. Pilkin, op.cit., pp.546–47; Volkov, op.cit., p.224.
3. Dimitri Pavlovich Eiler 1883–1943. Naval College 1903. Captain 2nd rank. Served cruiser *Variag* at Battle of Chemulpo 1904, Russo-Japanese War 1904–05. St George Cross 1904. White forces southern Russia, evacuated to Bizerta, Tunisia 1919–23. Emigrated France, died Paris 1943. Volkov, op.cit., p.546.
4. Three of the British 'C' class submarines were available, of which two carried out attacks on German ships. See Goldrick, *After Jutland*, op.cit., pp.192–193.
5. The flag letter 'buki' was the standard signal in the Russian Imperial Navy to raise anchor and move into position.
6. Day-shapes were three-dimensional spherical, triangular or square shapes that, raised singly or in combination, signal various movements or conditions of the ship, such as 'Stopped'.
7. Timirev seems to have been unaware that the refit of the *Slava*'s guns the previous winter had extended her range so that she outranged the enemy dreadnoughts and had scored hits. However, her newly-fitted forward turret failed during the action and she ended with only her after turret in action. See Goldrick, *After Jutland*, op.cit., pp.194–196. See also Georgiĭ M Nekrasov, *Expendable Glory: A Russian Battleship in the Baltic, 1915–1917*. East European Monographs 636. Boulder, Colorado, 2004.
8. This count appears to have been based on the mistaken appreciation of the lookout that there were three dreadnoughts. Only two German dreadnoughts were present – *König* and *Kronprinz*. Each carried ten guns of 30.5cm calibre, so the total was twenty. See Goldrick, *After Jutland* op.cit., pp.193–195. The *Baian*'s useless midship 8in gun had been fitted in the previous winter without any protective shielding for its crew. The Russians generally overestimated the strength of the German forces opposing them. The Government urgently requested a diversionary sortie by the British Royal Navy, believing that the entire German fleet was in the Baltic. In this failure of intelligence appreciation one can see the most immediate effect of the murder of Admiral Nepenin, who would surely not have made such a mistake. See A J Marder, *From the Dreadnought to Scapa Flow, Vol. IV 1917 The Year of Crisis*, Oxford University Press, London, 1969, pp.241–24, and G K von Schoultz, *With the British Battle Fleet: War Recollections of a Russian Naval Officer*, Hutchinson, London, 1922, pp.307–309.
9. The narrow channel between the island of Vormsi and the mainland north of Haapsalu in Estonia.
10. Timirev has simplified the decision-making in the retreat from Moön Sound. Bakhirev had intended to continue to engage the Germans in Kassar Basin, but the abandonment of Dago Island made the 'advanced position' untenable. Admiral Razvozov, the Fleet Commander, had intelligence that the Germans were moving in force north of Dago to cut off the retreat of the Russian

ships from Moön Sound and he proposed to bring the whole fleet out to cover the retreat. However, he was overruled by the Government, which did not want to risk the loss of the fleet, so he only got as far as Lapvik. The Germans had also called off the pursuit as they had achieved their objectives and did not want further risk. Post-war Russian naval appreciations of the battle criticised the Fleet Commander for being prepared to risk the fleet to save the damaged ships but not prepared to risk it to forestall the invasion itself. This is a reasonable criticism but overlooks the fact that naval intelligence had suggested that the Russians might meet the entire German fleet, which could have had only one outcome. There is also considerable doubt whether an aggressive sortie at the beginning of the battle or before the landing could have in any case been carried into effect, given the attitudes of the crews of the big ships as described by Timirev. See Goldrick, *After Jutland*, op.cit., pp.198–203. See also A M Kosinskii, *Moonzund 1917 - Poslednee srazhenie russkogo flota* (*Moön Sound - last battle of the Russian Fleet*), St Petersburg, 1928, (reprinted Eksmo, Moscow, 2009), pp.240–251.

Chapter V

1. Sergei Andreevich Kukel 1871–192? Naval College 1902. Captain 1st rank. 2nd Assistant Navy Minister 1917. Naval Historical Commission 1918. Naval administration review 1919. Continued to serve Soviet Fleet, discharged 1922. www.navy.su/persons/12/kukel.htm
2. Aleksei Pavlovich Kapnist 1871–1918. Naval College 1891. Rear admiral 1917. Served Naval General Staff 1914–17. Assistant Navy Minister 1917. Executed by Cheka of the Northern Caucasus 1918. www.navy.su/persons/12/kapnist.htm
3. Mikhail Iosifovich Dunin-Barkovskii 1878–1927. Naval College 1898. Captain 1st rank. Served Naval General Staff from 1906 to 1919. Arrested 1920. Emigrated Italy, died Rome. H K Graf, *Na sluzhbe Imperatorskomu Domu Rossii 1917-1941 Vospominaniia* (*In service to the Imperial Household of Russia, 1917-41. Memoirs*), Blitz, St Petersburg 2004, p.644.
4. This Russian custom, a sign of approbation, was bestowed on the American Admiral Glennon during his visit to the Tserell batteries in 1917: see D N Fedotoff White, *Survival Through War and Revolution in Russia*, U of Pennsylvania Press, Philadelphia, 1939, pp.160–161. One of the YMCA representatives in Siberia also received the honour: Edward Thornton Heald, *Witness to Revolution: Letters from Russia, 1916–1919*, Kent State UP, Kent Ohio., p.306.
5. Sergei Sigismundovich Politovskii 1880–1936. Naval College 1900. Captain 1st rank. On cruiser *Oleg* at Battle of Tsushima Straits, 1905, Russo-Japanese War. Served Yudenich North Western forces 1919–20. Emigrated Estonia, died Tallinn 1936. Volkov, op.cit., p.376.
6. The metric system was legislated in Russia in 1899, but old measures continued in common use. The desiatina was equivalent to 2.7 acres or just over 1 hectare. So 50 desiatinas = 135 acres (c.54 hectares). This was about three to five times the average peasant holding in the Bochevo region of Novgorod guberniia where the Timirev estate was located. See K B Nazarenko, *Zakat* ... op.cit, p. 147; see also Geroid T Robinson, *Rural Russia under the Old Regime*, Macmillan, NY, 1932, pp.235–237, et seq.; Jerome Blum, *The End of the Old Order in Rural Europe*, Princeton University Press, Princeton, NJ, 1978, pp.435–438.
7. Yevgenii Andreevich Berens 1876–1928. Naval College 1895. Captain 1st rank 1916. Navigating officer of the *Variag* in the Battle of Chemulpo Bay Korea 1904, Russo-Japanese War. Remained in service with Soviet Navy, appointed C-in-C Soviet Navy 1919–20 following the death of Altfater. Held several senior Soviet Navy and diplomatic positions. Died Moscow 1928. J Smele, *Historical*

Dictionary of the Russian Civil Wars, 1916–1926, Rowman & Littlefield, London, 2015, p.191.

8. The 'changing signposts' movement (smena vekh) in Russian émigré circles advocated acceptance of the 'reality' of Communist Party power in Russia and a nationalist spirit of dedication to the development of Russian society and culture. Those of its followers who returned to Soviet Russia were of course disappointed in the reality they found. See: Robert C Williams, *Culture in Exile: Russian emigres in Germany 1881–1941*, Cornell, Ithaca NY, 1972, and Hilde Hardman, *Coming to Terms with the Soviet Regime: the 'Changing signposts' movement among Russian emigres in the early 1920s*, Northern Illinois U P, Dekalb, 1994.

Chapter VI

1. Pavel Viktorovich Vilken 1879–1939. Naval College 1899. Served Battle of the Yellow Sea 1905, Russo-Japanese War. St George Gilded Sword of Honour 1905. Commander of the battleship *Sevastopol*. Served Yudenich North-western forces, commanded squadron of torpedo boats. Emigrated Finland, died Viborg or Helsinki 1939. Volkov, op.cit., p.87; www.navy.su/persons/03/vilken.htm
2. Aleksandr Konstantinovich Veis 1870–? Naval College 1891. Rear admiral 1916. St George Gilded Sword of Honour 1916. Chief of Staff Baltic Fleet 1919. Continued in service with Bolsheviks through the early 1920s as commander of hydrographic ships. www.navy.su/persons/03/veys.htm
3. Aleksandr Pavlovich Zelenoi 1872–1922. Naval College 1892. Rear admiral 1917. Senior Naval Officer Finnish waters 1918. Senior Commander Soviet Naval forces Baltic Sea 1919–20. Soviet Naval representative Finland 1920. www.navy.su/persons/09/ap_zelenoy.htm
4. Stepan Nikolaevich Dmitriev 1878–1921. Naval College 1897. Rear admiral 1917. Served defence of Port Arthur, Russo-Japanese War 1904–05. Commander Brigade of Battleships 1920. Participated in Kronstadt uprising 1921. Arrested by Cheka and shot. www.navy.su/persons/05/sn_dmitriev.htm
5. Vasilii Fyodorovich Dudkin 1881–? Naval College 1903. Captain 2nd rank. Served battleship *Pobeda* at siege of Port Arthur 1904–05. Submariner. Discharged 1918. Served Red forces Sea of Azov 1920, Baltic Sea 1921. Discharged 1924. Fate unknown. www.navy.su/persons/05/vf_dudkin.htm
6. Aleksandr Antonovich Ruzhek 1877–1930. Naval College 1897. Rear admiral. St George Gilded Sword of Honour 1914. Held various commands in the Russian river fleets during the Civil War and later in the Black Sea, including with the OGPU border forces. Discharged 1926, died Tomsk 1930. www.navy.su/persons/18/ruzhek.htm
7. Timirev is selective in his condemnation of hard drinking: Admiral Trukhachev, whom he praises, was recalled by others as a competent officer but notorious drunkard; see www.navy.su/persons/20/truhachev.htm. Captain N Kryzhanovskii claimed that Bakhirev, Nepenin, Plen, Kolchak and many other senior officers regularly participated in drinking bouts, Plen being distinguished because he drank heavily when anchored but never while at sea. The only woman admitted to these sessions was Trukhachev's wife, who could presumably hold her own with the other drinkers. Kryzhanovskii attributed the hard-drinking culture of the officers to traditions from the time of sail and from 'the absence of a sex life'. The latter subject is rarely discussed in Russian sources. See N Kryzhanovskii, 'Admiral Mikhail Koronatovich Bakhirev i ego sovremenniki' (Admiral Michael Koronatovich Bakhirev and his contemporaries), *Morskie Zapski* (*The Naval Records*) Vol. XXI(1)(58), New York, 1963, pp.57–70. Kryzhanovskii does not mention Timirev at all in this article.
8. Pyotr Ivanovich Izmestev 1873–1925. Major General. Served in Manchuria,

Russo-Japanese War 1904–05. Served Red Army 1918–21. Arrested by Cheka 1921. https://ru.wikipedia.org/wiki/Изместьев,_Пётр_Иванович.

9. Leonid Vasilievich Kostandi 1883–1921. Colonel. Commanded White forces Murmansk 1919–20. Captured by Red Army after Allied withdrawal 1920. Imprisoned 1920–21. Shot 1921. Rehabilitated by Russian Federation 2001. https://ru.wikipedia.org/wiki/Костанди,_Леонид_Васильевич
10. Pyotr Alekseevich Novopashennii 1881–1950. Naval College 1902. Captain 1st Rank. Participated in hydrographical expedition Northern Frozen Ocean 1913–15. Served in the naval administration of the Yudenich North Western forces 1919. Until 1945 in Berlin, captured by Soviet forces in Turingia and repatriated to USSR, died in gulag 1950. Volkov, op.cit., p.342.
11. Boris Borisovich Zherve 1878–1934. Naval College 1898. Served Port Arthur Russo-Japanese War 1904–05. Author and editor of many studies on naval technical and strategic issues. Remained in USSR. Director of the Naval Academy 1928–31. Arrested then released 1931; thereafter a teacher. Died 1934. Volkov, op.cit., pp.167–8, www.navy.su/persons/08/zherve.htm
12. Vladimir Ivanovich Rudnev 1882–1966. Naval College 1900. Captain 1st rank. Cruiser *Baiian* and Hill 203 at siege of Port Arthur 1904–05. St George Sword of Honour 1914. Served Northern White forces – Chief of Staff, Northern Frozen Ocean flotilla, later Karsk Sea forces 1918. Emigrated Estonia and Nice, France. Died Paris. Volkov, op.cit. p.408.
13. Aleksandr Oskarovich Stark, 1878–1922. Naval College 1897. Captain 1st rank 1916. Served cruiser *Dmitri Donskoi* at Battle of Tsushima Straits 1905. St George Gilded Sword of Honour 1907. Discharged April 1918. Died Helsinki 1922. www.navy.su/persons/19/ao_stark.htm

Appendix No. 1

1. This rather self-serving appendix was almost certainly added to the memoirs by the publisher rather than Timirev, as its author had drafted the map accompanying the New York edition of the memoirs: Nikolai Nikolaevich Kryzhanovskii 1886–1964 Naval College 1905. Captain 2nd rank. Served White forces, southern Russia to 1920. Emigrated USA. Translator at Columbia University. Died New York 1964. www.navy.su/persons/12/kryzhanovsky.htm

Obituary from *Chasovoi* [*The Sentinel*] No. 90 October 1932 p.17

1. Available online at https://archive.org/stream/chasovoiserialla4793orie#page/n1371/mode/2up

Notice of Timirev's death in *Morskoi Zhurnal* (*The Naval Journal*) 1932, No. 55(7) July 1932, p.13

1. I have not been able to trace that this promised article was ever published in this journal.

Translator's Commentary

1. Timirev wrote other memoirs at this time of his life, about his Port Arthur experiences and his four years on the Imperial yacht *Shtandart*. Only a fragment of the latter has been published ('Shkhernoe plavanie' (Sailing the skerries) – Voennaia byl', Paris, 1966; available online at http://lepassemilitaire.ru/shxernoe-plavanie-1907-g-s-n-timirev (Accessed 21 December 2019). The provenance of this fragment is unclear and these manuscripts now appear to have been lost.
2. See Norman E Saul, *The Life and Times of Charles R. Crane 1858–1939*, Rowman and Littlefield, Washington DC, 2012. Crane also sent funds to assist Anna in the 1920s: Pavlova, op.cit., pp.340–341.
3. See for example Evan Maudsley, *The Russian Revolution and the Baltic Fleet*, Macmillan, London, 1978; Norman E Saul, *Sailors in Revolt: The Russian Baltic Fleet in 1917*, Regents Press Kansas, Lawrence, 1978.
4. See the discussion of geographical constraints on naval operations in northern European waters in J

Goldrick, *Before Jutland – The Naval War in Northern European Waters, August 1914–February 1915*. Naval Institute Press, Annapolis, 2015, pp.42–44.

5. For a lively description of a Russian destroyer conveying the American Admiral Glennon from Reval to Helsinki through the skerries at full speed see D Fedotoff-White op.cit., pp.161–162. For Essen's order about navigating the skerries, see N B Pavlovich, *Flot v Pervoi Mirovoi Voine* Vol. 1 (*The Fleet in the First World War*), Voenizdat, Moscow, 1964, pp.76–78. In his memoir of his time on the Imperial yacht *Shtandart* Timirev describes how the yacht, with the Imperial family aboard, ran aground on uncharted rocks while navigating a supposedly clear channel in the skerries. See 'Shkhernoe plavanie' (Sailing the skerries) – Voennaia byl', Paris, 1966; available online at http://lepassemilitaire.ru/shxernoe-plavanie-1907-g-s-n-timirev (Accessed 21 December 2019).
6. See the article on 'morskoi tsenz' in the Brockhaus-Efron Encyclopaedic Dictionary 1890–1907, available online at www.vehi.net/brokgauz/index.html. For its abolition see Berezovskii et al. op.cit., p.163.
7. See J N Westwood, *Witnesses of Tsushima*, Sophia University Press, Tokyo, 1970, pp.5–7, and the article by V Iu Gribovskii, 'Lichnyi sostav Rossiiskogo flota v russkoo-iaponskskoi voine 1904–1905 gg' (Personnel composition of the Russian Fleet in the Russo-Japanese war 1904–1905), in *Sindrom Tsushimy* (*The Tsushima Syndrome*), Tsitadel, St Petersburg, 1997, available online at http://tsushima.su/RU/libru/i/Page_7/page_18/page_19/page_26/page_26_004/. Note that the same problem was recognised in the British Royal Navy – see A J Marder, *From the Dreadnought to Scapa Flow*, Vol. I, Oxford University Press, London, 1961, p.7.
8. A number of recent Russian studies of the Imperial Navy based on archival sources, previously unavailable to Western scholars, explain these various distinctions within the Navy and their variations over the period leading up to the war and the revolution. See in particular: Kirill Nazarenko, *Baltiiskii flot v revoliutsii 1917–1918 gg* (*The Baltic Fleet in the Revolution 1917–1918*), Iauza, Moscow, 2017, esp. pp.11–130; K Nazarenko, *Zakat Tsarskogo flota – morskie ofitsery pervoi mirovoi voiny* (*Sunset of the Tsarist Fleet – naval officers of the First World War*), Iauza, Moscow, 2018 and the other works cited therein. These studies largely confirm the earlier studies of the naval officer corps by Norman E Saul, *Sailors in Revolt – the Russian Baltic Fleet 1917*, University of Kansas Press, Lawrence Kansas, 1978, and Evan Mawdsley, *The Russian Revolution and the Baltic Fleet*, Macmillan, London, 1978. For a review of Russian naval historiography from the 1920s to the end of the twentieth century, see the historiographical essay in D Iu Kozlov, *Narushenie moskikh kommunikatsii po opytu deistvii Rossiiskogo flota v pervoi mirovoi voiny (1914–1917)* (*Interdiction of sea communications according to the experience of the Russian fleet in the First World War 1914–1917*), Nauka, Moscow, 2012,
9. See the entry for the Table of Ranks 24 January 1722 in the Brockhaus-Efron Encyclopaedic Dictionary 1890–1907 at www.vehi.net/brokgauz/index.html
10. See Nazarenko, *Zakat tsarskogo flota*, op.cit., pp.206–212.
11. Nazarenko, *Zakat tsarskogo flota*, op.cit., pp.190–200.
12. See Nazarenko, *Baltiiskii flot*, op.cit., pp.350–351.
13. Nazarenko, *Baltiiskii flot*, op.cit., pp.349–358.
14. Nazarenko, *Zakat Tsarskogo flota*, op.cit., pp.145–166. Note that some English language sources use the term 'gentry' rather than 'nobility' for this estate. Only males could serve in the Imperial Navy, whatever their rank or estate. During the war the Russian Red Cross organised the services of many women as nursing sisters for the armed forces, including in naval hospitals. Also many officers' wives worked as official censors of the

correspondence of serving sailors, but no women were ever a part of the formal Navy structure. After the revolution a short-lived women's naval unit was established in July 1917 but it was not deployed with the fleet – see www.calvertjournal.com/features/show/8302/revisiting-revolution-sea-change-female-sailors-gender-1917. Foreign subjects could serve in any of the armed forces with the permission of the Tsar. Few appear to have done so in the Navy.

15. See the entries for soslovie and dvorianstvo in Brockhaus-Efron Encyclopaedic Dictionary 1890–1907, available online at www.vehi.net/brokgauz/index.html. See also G L Yaney, *The Systematization of Russian Government 1711–1905*, University of Illinois Press, Urbana 1973, pp.338–345.
16. P A Zaionchkovskii, *Pravitelstvennyi apparat samoderzhavnoi Rossii v XIXv.* (*The state apparatus of autocratic Russia in the nineteenth century*), Mysl, Moscow,1978, pp.87–90.
17. Saul, *Sailors in Revolt*, op.cit., p.17; Nazarenko, *Baltiiskii flot*, op.cit., p.138.
18. Nazarenko, *Zakat tsarskogo flota*, op.cit., pp.140–144; and *Baltiiskii flot v revoliutsii*, op.cit., pp.92–116. Nazarenko claims inflation ran at more than 400 per cent over the course of the war.
19. See the entry for Naval Pensions (Pensii po morskomu vedomstvu) in the Brockhaus-Efron Encyclopaedic Dictionary at www.vehi.net/brokgauz/index.html. Pension rights could be diminished or lost for conviction of a crime during service.
20. A V Napalkov cited in Nazarenko, *Zakat tsarskogo flota*, op.cit., pp.144–145.
21. NN Kritskii claims that from 1894 to 1915 entry to the Naval College was restricted to sons of officers and hereditary nobles, only opening to personal nobles in 1915. See his 2002 master degree dissertation at www.dissercat.com/content/podgotovka-komandnykh-kadrov-voenno-morskogo-flota-na-dalnem-vostoke-rossii-vtoraya-polovina
22. The name of the college was changed from Morskoi korpus to Morskoi uchilishe and back to Morskoi korpus at different times in the late nineteenth and early twentieth centuries. I have translated the name as Naval College consistently, regardless of its name at a particular time.
23. Berezovskii et al. op.cit., pp.225–226.
24. Berezovskii et al, op.cit., p.169.
25. Nazarenko, *Zakat tsarskogo flota*, op.cit., and *Baltiiskii flot*, op.cit., has extensive data about the system of naval education and training and the estate composition of the officer corps on the eve of and during the war.
26. A E Sokol, *The Imperial and Royal Austro-Hungarian Navy*, U.S. Naval Institute, Annapolis, 1968, pp.78–79.
27. See Marder, op.cit., Vol 1 pp.31–32. Fees were only abolished at the Royal Naval College at Dartmouth in 1947. Education at the Russian Naval College had always been free and remained so up to the revolution, although this had no obvious impact on the social origins of cadets. Note that in the British Dominion navies, although their governments committed to a career open to talents rather than class, during the First World War the senior commands were all on secondment or transfer from the Royal Navy, so at this time the difference was of no significance.
28. M Horthy, *Memoires de l'amiral Horthy*, Hachette, Paris, 1954, p.81.
29. G K von Schoultz, *With the British Battle Fleet: War Recollections of a Russian Naval Officer*, Hutchinson, London, 1922, p.105.
30. See the discussion about the Firth of Forth in Andrew Gordon, *The Rules of the Game – Jutland and British Naval Command* 2nd ed, Penguin, 2005, pp.30–33.
31. See Paul G Halpern, *The Naval War the Mediterranean 1914–18*, Allen & Unwin, London, 1987, pp.174–175. For British peccadillos, see Gordon, op.cit., p.32.
32. Cited in Paul G Halpern, *The Mediterranean Naval Situation 1908–1914*, Harvard UP, Cambridge Mass., 1971, pp.301–302. As we have seen, Russian officers were not

poorly paid in comparison with other Russians.

33. See Goldrick, *After Jutland*, op.cit., pp.18–30 and Schoultz, op.cit. passim. For the morale problems in the Austro-Hungarian navy, complicated by the ethnic diversity of the empire, see Horthy, op.cit., p.80.
34. See the comments of Admiral Phillimore cited in N S Harrin, 'Pokhod s angliiskim admiralom' (Admiral Phillimore's (RN) visit to the Black Sea Fleet 1916), *Morskie zapiski* (*The Naval Records*), XXI (58), 1963, pp.99–106. For the Royal Navy's debates see the entries for W/T in Andrew Gordon, *The Rules of the Game*, op.cit..
35. Senior officers in the US Navy had battle experience from the Spanish American War of 1898, but none of this involved major fleet engagements and the US Navy in any case only became significant in the First World War after the Russians had effectively collapsed. The Japanese Navy had, of course, shared the battle experience of the Russians, but apart from a destroyer squadron in the Mediterranean,their forces were never deployed to Europe.
36. See the review of the film at http://polundra13.livejournal.com/56947.html Accessed 15 February 2019.
37. On the role of the War Industries Committees during the war see Lewis Siegelbaum, *The Politics of Industrial Mobilization in Russia 1914–1917*, MacMillan, London, 1983, pp.213–14. On their continuation in Siberia after 1917, see G Z Ioffe, Kolchakovskaia avantiura i ee krakh (The Kolchak venture and its collapse), Mysl, Moscow, 1983, p.229.
38. See Eleanor Pray, *Letters from Vladivostok 1894–1930*, University of Washington Press, Seattle, 2013, pp.173–175; Edward Thornton Heald, *Witness to Revolution: Letters from Russia, 1916–1919*, Kent State UP, Kent, Ohio, USA, 1972 includes a description of the Czech seizure of Vladivostok and the intervention in 1918: p. 214ff.
39. To judge if his son Vladimir was handsome, see the photos reproduced at http://rys-strategia.ru/publ/1-1-0-4005 Accessed 22/03/2019.
40. An incomplete list of forty-eight officers from the Russo-Japanese War and seventy-one from the First World War is given in the publication of the Prague Russian Naval Wardroom, *Morskoi Zhurnal* No. 12 December 1928, pp.264–5, which is available at the Internet Archive: https://archive.org/details/morskoizhurnalse008800/page/n263 Accessed 22/03/2019. Timirev is listed as 'D N Timirev', as this journal referred to Timirev throughout the time he was President of the Wardroom at Shanghai. Navy personnel who served in the Russo-Japanese War also received a range of campaign medals – see Berezovskii et al, op.cit., p.175.
41. *Belaia sibir vnutrenniaia voĭna 1918–1920 gg* (*White Siberia – the internal war 1918–1920*), Munich, 1923, p.314 (this citation is to the 1923 edition – p.372 in the version re-published in Russia in 2018). Sakharov died during an unsuccessful ulcer operation in 1941. For Russian fascism among the émigrés see John J Stephan, *The Russian Fascists:Tragedy and Farce in Exile, 1925–1945*, Hamilton, London, 1978.
42. For Kolchak's views see G K Guins, *Sibir, soiuzniki i Kolchak – povrotnyi moment russkoi istorii 1918–1920* (*Siberia, the Allies and Kolchak – the turning point of Russian history 1918–1920*), Peking, 1921, reprinted Moscow 2013, pp.464–465.
43. There is a vast memoir and secondary literature on the course, character and incompetence of the Kolchak Government. See the sources listed in the most comprehensive contemporary English language study by Jonathan Smele, *Civil War in Siberia: the Anti-Bolshevik government of Admiral Kolchak 1918–1920*, Cambridge University Press, New York, 1997. See also Norman E Saul, *War and Revolution: the United States and Russia, 1914–1921*, University Press of Kansas, Lawrence, 2001.
44. William Sidney Graves, *America's Siberian adventure 1918–20*,

New York, 1931. These views were endorsed by other observers, such as the representative of the International Red Cross in Siberia, George Montandon (*Deux ans chez Koltchak et chez les Bolchéviques pour la Croix-rouge de Genève 1919–1921*, Alcan, Paris, 1923), as well as by officers of the British Mission to Kolchak such as Francis McCullagh, *A Prisoner of the Reds: the story of a British officer captured in Siberia*, Murray, London, 1921, pp.323–327, who observed that Kolchak's cohabitation with Anna Timireva while still married to his first wife set an example of personal immorality that his subordinates were more than happy to emulate and which reflected the general character of his government: 'They (the Whites) are a class which has forgotten nothing and learnt nothing and is in every way unfit to rule.'

45. T F Pavlova, F Perchenok & I K Safonofff, *Milaia obozhaemaia moia Anna Vasilievna* (*Dear adorable Anna Vasilievna*), Progress, Moscow, 1996, pp.259–277.
46. *Kolchak Aleksandr Vasilievich – poslednie dni zhizni* (*Kolchak Alexander Vasilievich – the last days of life*), Altaiskoe knizhnoe iz-dvo. Barnaul, 1991.
47. As Kozlov notes op.cit., p.19: 'The change in the ideological paradigm (in the past two decades) has led to the appearance and circulation of countless panegyrics on the admirals and officers who took part in the White movement. In this the description of their activities as a rule consists of partisan literary hyperbole, often exceeding in their clumsiness passages of Soviet propaganda.'
48. See in particular V Zh Tsvetkov, *Admiral Kolchak – prestuplenie i nakazanie verkhovnogog pravitelia Rossiia* (*Admiral Kolchak – the crime and punishment of the Supreme Ruler of Russia*), Iauza, Moscow, 2018. The pro-rehabilitation arguments put forward here, based on the proposition that all acts of the Kolchak Government had been authorised by the legally constituted government of the day, would exonerate Adolf Hitler of any responsibility for the Holocaust, as the laws permitting such developments had been passed through the Reichstag!
49. N A Hafter, who briefly met Kolchak as a young teenager, noted that: 'He genuinely loved children. His friends realised how difficult it was for him to be separated from his only son Rostislav who was then living with his mother away in Paris. He was my age.' *Admiral Kolchak – Supreme Ruler & Commander-in-Chief of White Forces*, University of Melbourne, Parkville, 1998, p.4.
50. *New Review* June 1985, New York, pp.196–237; re-produced in *Minuvshee – istoricheskii almanakh* (*The past – an historical almanac*), 1, Atheneum, Paris 1986;
51. T F Pavlova, F Perchenok & I K Safonoff, *Milaia obozhaemaia moia Anna Vasilievn* (*Dear adorable Anna Vasilievna*), Progress, Moscow, 1996.
52. *Milaia khimera v admiralskoi forme – pisma A V Timirevou A V Kochaku 1916–1917 gg* (*Dear chimera in admiral's uniform – the letters of A V Timireva to A V Kolchak 1916–1917*), 2nd corrected edition, St Petersburg 2017.
53. In her memoirs Anna claims they had expressed their passion to each other before his departure for the Black Sea command, however the actual letters from that time make it clear that Kolchak initiated the correspondence from Sevastopol and Anna was at that time naïve about its significance.
54. Most sources say the Timirevs arrived in Vladivostok in May 1918, but Kolchak's reply to Anna from Harbin says she had written to him on 20 April. See Pavlova & Safonoff, op.cit., p.286.
55. According to Anna Timireva, the mother of Natalia Alekseevna Kravchenko, who worked for the NKVD, informed against Vladimir within days of his betrothal to her daughter. Anna herself was again arrested a few days after her son. Natalia, an artist and illustrator, died 18 November 2017 at the age of 101 apparently having accepted the view that her mother's action

had saved her life. See https://stroganov.livejournal.com/225676.html and http://pstgu.ru/news/life/2012/03/11/36027/ Accessed 27 June 2019.

56. See the reminiscences of his cousin and godson Ilya Kirillovich Safonoff /Smorodskii (1937–2004) at http://rys-strategia.ru/publ/1-1-0-4005 (Accessed 22 March 2019) and Pavlova, Perchenok & Safonoff op.cit., pp.443–445. Ilya's parents had starved to death in the siege of Leningrad and from late 1942 he was raised (and in 1950 adopted) by Anna's younger sister Yelena in Moscow, where he learnt about Vladimir from her and later met Anna. There are many tributes to Vladimir's talents as a budding watercolour artist and toy designer on the Russian internet.
57. Anna's later life is described in Pavlova, Perchenok & Safonoff, op.cit., pp.383–508.
58. Paul Dotsenko, *The Struggle for a Democracy in Siberia, 1917–1920: eyewitness account of a contemporary*, Hoover Press, Stanford, 1983, p.89. See also N G Fomin 'Katkii otchet o deiatelnosti ofitserov flota uchastvovavshikh v anti-bolshevistskom dvizhenie na Volge, Kame i Sibiri v period 1918–19gg.' (Brief report of the activities of officers of the fleet participating in the anti-Bolshevik movement on the Volga, the Kama and in Siberia in the period 1918–1919) in *Morskiia zapiski* (*The Naval Records*), Vol. XVI No.2–47 July 1968, p.45.
59. D N Fedotoff White, *Survival through war and revolution in Russia*, U of Pennsylvania Press, Philadelphia, 1939, p. 206: 'At the naval headquarters (in Vladivostok), after a perfunctory conversation with the Senior Naval Officer, Rear Admiral Timirev, I went over for a long talk with Vuich, a Naval Guardsman in charge of the Operations Division of the naval forces of the Whites in the Pacific.'
60. Ioffe, op.cit., pp.257–261.
61. Jonathan D Smele, *The Russian Civil Wars 1916–1926*, Hurst, London, 2015, pp.220–225. See also Canfield F Smith, *Vladivostok under Red and White rule: revolution and counterrevolution in the Russian Far East, 1920–1922*, University of Washington Press, Seattle, 1975.
62. Pavlova et al op.cit., pp.340–341.
63. ibid., p.348.
64. *Morskoi zhurnal*, No. 43–44 July–August 1931, p.164. Timirev's postal address when he was at sea was care of the Krashenninikovs – see *Morskoi zhurnal*, No. 10, October 1928, p.22/214.

Select Bibliography

There are many books in English that further explain the context of these memoirs. There are, of course, many other sources in Russian and other languages that are relevant – interested readers will find most listed in the bibliographies of the works cited below.

For a general summary of the revolution see:

Rabinowitch, Alexander, *The Bolsheviks in Power*. Bloomington: Indiana University Press, 2007.

Wade, Rex, *The Russian Revolution*, 1917. Cambridge and New York: Cambridge University Press, 3rd edition, 2000.

The Russo-Japanese War 1904–05 and the Siege of Port Arthur

Diedrich, Edward C, *The Last Iliad: The Siege of Port Arthur in the Russo-Japanese War 1904–1905*. Ann Arbor: Univ. Microfilms, 1982, New York U, 1978.

Hamilton, Sir Ian, *A Staff Officer's Scrap-Book During the Russo-Japanese War*. London: E Arnold, 1905. (Report of a British general who was an observer with the Japanese and whose warnings about the demonstrated effects of modern technology on infantry fighting were ignored by his colleagues.)

Martin, Christopher, *The Russo-Japanese War*. London; New York: Abelard-Schuman, 1967.

Nojine, E K, *The Truth About Port Arthur*. London: Murray, 1908. (A contemporary Russian account highly critical of the Russian conduct of the war.)

Sergeev, Evgeny, *Russian Military Intelligence in the War with Japan, 1904–05: Secret Operations on Land and at Sea*. Routledge Studies in the History of Russia and Eastern Europe Series 7. New York: Routledge, 2007.

Walder, David, *The Short Victorious War – The Russo-Japanese Conflict 1904–5*. London, Hutchinson, 1973.

Warner, Denis Ashton, and Warner, Peggy, *The Tide at Sunrise: A History of the Russo-Japanese War, 1904–1905*. London: Angus and Robertson, 1975.

Westwood, J N, *Russia against Japan 1904–05: A New Look at the Russo-Japanese War*. Basingstoke: Macmillan, 1986.

———, *Witnesses of Tsushima*. Tokyo, Sophia University Press, 1970.

The naval war in the Baltic 1914–18

Barrett, Michael B, *Operation Albion: The German conquest of the Baltic Islands*. Bloomington: University of Indiana Press, 2008. (A recent study of the Moön Sound operations based on archival sources as well as memoirs and secondary literature.)

Graf, H, *The Russian Navy in War and Revolution: From 1914 up to 1918*. Munich: R Oldenbourg, 1923; re-published University of the Pacific Press, Honolulu, Hawaii, 2015. (Memoirs of a Russian destroyer officer who later became the chancellery secretary in France to Grand Duke Kirill Vladimirovich Romanov, the pretender to the Russian throne. Like Kolchak, Graf believed the revolution was the work of Jewish conspirators.)

Greger, Rene, and Anthony J Watts, *The Russian Fleet, 1914–1917*. London: Allan, 1972. (A good chronology of the main naval operations in the Baltic and the Black Sea, as well as other theatres of war. Many photographs.)

Goldrick, James, *Before Jutland: The Naval War in Northern European Waters, August 1914–February 1915*. Annapolis: Naval Institute Press, 2015.

———, *After Jutland: The Naval War in Northern European Waters, June 1916–November 1918*. Annapolis: Naval Institute Press, 2018. (These two works by a former rear admiral of the Royal Australian Navy provide a succinct, authoritative and accessible account of the main naval operations in the Northern seas during the First World War. Both contain extensive bibliographies.)

Halpern, Paul G, *A Naval History of World War I*. Annapolis: Naval Institute Press, 1994. (An excellent overview of the naval war in all theatres.)

Lincol, Bruce, *Passage Through Armageddon, 1914–1918*. New York: Oxford University Press, 1986. (An onverview of the war as a whole.)

Longley, David, 'The February Revolution in the Baltic Fleet at Helsinki 'Vosstanie' or 'Bunt?' *Canadian Slavonic Papers/Revue Canadienne Des Slavistes* 20, No. 1 (1 March 1978): 1–22.

Marshall, Alexander, John W Steinberg, and Steven Sabol, *The Global Impacts of Russia's Great War and Revolution Book 1: The Arc of Revolution, 1917–24*. Bloomington, Indiana: Slavica, 2019.

Mawdsley, Evan, *The Russian Revolution and the Baltic Fleet. War and Politics February 1917–April 1918*. London: MacMillan, 1978.

Mitchell, Donald W, *A History of Russian and Soviet Sea Power*. Macmillan, New York, 1974. (A comprehensive but now very dated general history of the Russian Imperial and Soviet Navies.)

Nekrasov, Georgiĭ M, *Expendable Glory: A Russian Battleship in the Baltic, 1915–1917*. East European Monographs 636. Boulder, Colorado, 2004. (This is an account of the battleship *Slava* by a former commander in the Royal Australian Navy, based on published sources and personal recollections of Russian veterans known to the author.)

Pavlovich, N B (Rear Admiral Prof Nikolai Bronislavovich), ed., *The Fleet in the First World War – Flot v Pervoi Mirovoi Voine*. New Delhi: Published for the Smithsonian Institution and the National Science Foundation, Washington, DC, by Amerind Publishing Company, 1979. (This is the two-volume Soviet official history of the naval war, published in Russian in 1964. Volume 1, based on archival sources, covers Russian naval operations; Volume 2, based largely on secondary sources, covers those of other nations. Rear Admiral (1944) Pavlovich had completed the Naval College accelerated course in May 1917 and served in the de-mining operations in the Gulf of Finland after the war. He saw active service in the Finnish War in 1939 and in the Second World War but spent most of his career through the 1920s, 1930s, and 1940s in naval educational roles, retiring as a professor of the College. Unfortunately this English translation of this otherwise substantial work is less than satisfactory.)

Saul, Norman, *Sailors in Revolt: The Russian Baltic Fleet in 1917*. Lawrence: Regents Press of Kansas, 1978.

Staff, Gary, *Battle for the Baltic Islands 1917 – Triumph of the German Navy*. Barnsley: Pen & Sword, 2008. (A detailed study of the German joint operations to capture the islands of Oesel, Dago and Moön with many maps and photographs.)

Watts, Anthony J, *The Imperial Russian Navy*. London: New York: Arms and Armour; Distributed in the USA by Sterling Pub. Co, 1990. (Contains many photos of Russian ships.)

———. *Russian Naval Construction, 1905–45*. Studies in Soviet History and Society (London, England). Basingstoke: Macmillan in association with Centre for Russian and East European Studies, University of Birmingham, 1994.

Weeks, Charles J, Jr. *An American Naval Diplomat in Revolutionary Russia: The Life and Times of Admiral Newton A. McCully*. Annapolis: Naval Institute Press, 1992.

For a somewhat idiosyncratic introduction to Russian naval operations in the Black Sea, see:

Nekrasov G M, *North of Gallipoli, the Black Sea Fleet at War 1914–1917*. Boulder: East European Monographs; New York: Distributed by Columbia University Press, 1992.

The Kolchak military dictatorship 1918–20

Currently the most authoritative and comprehensive works in English on this subject are those by Dr Jonathan Smele of the University of London, listed below.

Bisher, Jamie, *White Terror: Cossack Warlords of the Trans-Siberian*. London; New York: Routledge, 2005.

Dotsenko, Paul, *The Struggle for a Democracy in Siberia, 1917-1920: Eyewitness Account of a Contemporary*. Hoover Press Publication 277. Stanford: Hoover Institution Press, 1983. (Post-war recollections of a Socialist opponent of the Kolchak military dictatorship.)

Fedotoff White, D, *Survival Through War and Revolution in Russia*. Philadelphia: University of Pennsylvania Press, 1939. (Eloquent memoirs of a naval officer who served under Kolchak in the Baltic and in Siberia. This book is available online at https://babel.hathitrust.org/cgi/pt?id=mdp.39015019487449;view=1up;seq=9. Accessed 22 March 2019.)

Fleming, Peter, *The Fate of Admiral Kolchak*. London: Hart-Davis, 1963. (A now dated study of Kolchak as Supreme Ruler.)

Gatrell, Peter, *A Whole Empire Walking: Refugees in Russia During World War I*. Indiana-Michigan Series in Russian and East European Studies. Bloomington: Indiana University Press, 1999.

Graves, William Sidney, *America's Siberian Adventure, 1918-1920*. New York, 1931. (The memoirs of the general commanding the USA intervention forces in Siberia. This book is available online at https://babel.hathitrust.org/cgi/pt?id=mdp.39015054066959;view=1up;seq=11 Accessed 22 March 2019)

Heald, Edward Thornton, *Witness to Revolution: Letters from Russia, 1916-1919*. ed. James B Gidney. Kent, Ohio, USA: Kent State U.P, 1972. (Selected correspondence of the US YMCA representative in Siberia overseeing the repatriation of prisoners of war. This book is available online at the Internet Archive: https://archive.org/stream/witnesstorevolut00edwa#page/n5/mode/2up)

Petroff, Serge, *Remembering a Forgotten War: Civil War in Eastern European Russia and Siberia, 1918-1920*. East European Monographs, No. 560. Boulder: New York: East European Monographs ; distributed by Columbia University Press, 2000.

Pray, Eleanor, *Letters from Vladivostok 1894-1930*. ed. B Ingemanson, Seattle, London, University of Washington Press, 2013. (Extracts of the correspondence of an American woman living in Vladivostok before, during and after the revolution.)

Robinson, Paul, *The White Russian Army in Exile, 1920-1941*. Oxford Historical Monographs. Oxford: New York: Clarendon Press; Oxford University Press, 2002.

Smele, Jonathan D, *Civil War in Siberia: The Anti-Bolshevik Government of Admiral Kolchak, 1918-1920*. New York: Cambridge University Press, 1997.

———, *The Russian Civil Wars 1916-1926*. London: C Hurst & Co, 2015.

Smith, Canfield F, *Vladivostok under Red and White Rule: Revolution and Counterrevolution in the Russian Far East, 1920-1922*. Publications on Russia and Eastern Europe of the Institute for Comparative and Foreign Area Studies, No. 6. Seattle: University of Washington Press, 1975.

Stephan, John J, *The Russian Far East: A History*. Stanford: Stanford University Press, 1994.

———. *The Russian Fascists: Tragedy and Farce in Exile, 1925-1945*. London: H Hamilton, 1978.

Émigrés in Siberia and Shanghai

The Russian post-revolutionary émigré literature is vast, but only a small part of it relates to experiences in Siberia and the Far East. Two that do are:

Nash, Gary, *The Tarasov Saga: From Russia through China to Australia*. Dural, NSW: Rosenberg Publishing, 2004. (An account of a Siberian family forced to flee via Shanghai, where they were some of the 'Russian girls' who served in the famous Kiessling & Bader bakery in the 1930s. Their journey from Siberia through Shanghai, then via the Philippines to Australia, provides proof that in the midst of a total failure of human character, some individuals were able to maintain the spark of compassionate charity.)

Yakobson, Helen, *Crossing Borders, from Revolutionary Russia to China to America*. New Jersey: Hermitage, 1994 (Memoirs of a later generation of émigrés from Siberia).

For the role of Russian émigré community in Shanghai see:

Abend, Hallett, *My years in China, 1926-1941* London: John Lane, the Bodley Head, 1944. (The memoirs of the New York Times correspondent in China, based largely in Shanghai.)

Davidson-Houston, J V, *Yellow Creek: The Story of Shanghai*. London: Putnam, 1962.

Index